MW01709229

Teaching SCIENCE

A **Handbook**
FOR PRIMARY & SECONDARY SCHOOL TEACHERS

Steve ALSOP and Keith HICKS

KOGAN PAGE

First Indian Edition 2003

Kogan Page India Private Limited
2/13 Ansari Road
New Delhi 110 002.

ISBN 81-7554-197-0

Published by Vinod Vasishtha for Kogan Page India Private Limited, 2/13, Ansari Road, New Delhi - 110 002, and printed at Raj Press, R-3, Inderpuri, New Delhi - 110 012

Contents

Series Editor's foreword

Science education is an area of great debate at both government and school level for many reasons: science is a core National Curriculum subject; developing, recruiting and retaining good science teachers is challenging; the National Curriculum in science is demanding, has depth, breadth and diversity; teaching and understanding the Curriculum requires a specialist knowledge of one area, plus a broader knowledge of all science subjects.

Teachers entering the world of science education need to appreciate the complexities of teaching science as well as understand that the pupils they teach will have a broad spectrum of ability and awareness of science-based issues. Developing successfully as a science teacher requires an acknowledgement and appreciation of these issues, in addition to the practical skills and personal direction that will assist in career development. This book aims to help teachers achieve all of these aims by giving authoritative guidance, backed up by practical tasks and theoretical perspectives. These will help readers to engage with ideas and concepts of science and science education across the curriculum and across the Key Stages.

Steve Alsop and Keith Hicks have assembled a rich guide and resource that clearly and accessibly reveals the broad academic, social, political and cultural contexts in which teaching and learning about science are addressed. The chapters draw widely from leading experts and tackle both the pragmatic and theoretical issues that underscore the delivery of the Science National Curriculum. The authors have a commitment to providing a high-quality learning experience and they reflect not only on the teaching of science, but also on learning outcomes in this subject.

The key elements of the book are its combination of generic and specific teaching ideas, its wide-ranging and expert perspectives, its regard for the future and its coverage of the requirements of being a science teacher today. These significant elements are presented to help experienced, newly qualified and trainee teachers alike. By addressing issues across phases, this book will be uniquely helpful for all teaching professionals.

Professor Gill Nicholls
King's College, University of London

Preface

Teaching Science is a practical source book for new science teachers to be used as a support and aid to classroom observations and experiences. The aim of the text is to help new science teachers become more aware of how they might teach more effectively. With this aim in mind, the text explores a series of contemporary themes in science education. However, this is not a book of top teaching tips: anybody who is looking for a recipe for good practice might be disappointed. The intent of the text is to provide readers with an informed framework to critically reflect upon their practice and set targets for professional growth.

Although *Teaching Science* derives from a substantial body of research and theory, we have deliberately kept the focus of discussion at the level of classroom practice. We felt this focus was appropriate for beginning practitioners. That said, we encourage those with the time and inclination to use the further readings highlighted at the end of each chapter to delve more deeply into the content explored.

Inevitably it has not been possible to cover all aspects of science education. We have selected and prioritized a series of themes that we consider important for new science teachers. That is not to say that other themes are not equally important but to highlight the selective nature of this text and the limitations of a book of this size.

Teaching Science is part of a series of learning to teach texts. It has been written and structured with the generic series text in mind (Nicholls, G (ed) *Learning to Teach: A handbook for primary and secondary school teachers*, London: Kogan Page, 1999). We recommend that you acquire and study this text because it both complements and extends our discussions and deliberations.

Acknowledgements

This book could not have been written without contributions from a number of people, and we are indebted to each of them for their support and encouragement. We would like to thank Marcus Barbor, Mike Watts, Robin Luth, Kendra McMahon, Dan Davies, Erminia Pedretti and Larry Bencze. We are also very grateful to our Kogan Page editor Jonathan Simpson and the series editor Gill Nicholls. We would also like to thank the reviewers for their helpful and thoughtful comments. We are grateful to the support provided by Elliott School, London and York University, Toronto. A very special thanks goes to Vanessa and Barry.

Finally, we would like to dedicate this text to the late Bronwyn Hicks-Bantock (an inspirational primary school teacher) and Dylan and Olivia Alsop.

Steve Alsop and Keith Hicks

List of contributors

Marcus Barbor is a senior lecturer in science education at the University of Surrey, Roehampton. He has authored a number of learning aids for biology at various levels, including a book and scale model of the human brain.

Larry Bencze is an assistant professor in science education at Ontario Institute for Studies in Education (OISE), University of Toronto. His research and development focus is on philosophical and educational issues relating to students' control of their own learning through student-directed, open-ended scientific investigations and invention projects.

Kendra McMahon and Dan Davies are both senior lecturers in primary science and technology at Bath Spa University College.

Robin Luth has worked in mainstream and special schools for nearly two decades. He is currently a special needs coordinator (SENCO) in a large inner-city comprehensive school. Robin's research and development interests include special educational needs and computer-aided learning (CAL).

Erminia Pedretti is an associate professor in science education at the Ontario Institute for Studies in Education (OISE), University of Toronto. She has a wide array of research and development interests, including science technology, society education and informal learning.

Part 1

Setting the Scene

1 Teaching science

Steve Alsop

I am happy to say that although initially I faced some bumps in the road I feel it was a very good learning experience. I have learned so much about children and science and I am excited about starting with my own class next year. (Angela, a trainee science school teacher)

Objectives

This introductory chapter provides opportunities to explore:

- your initial beliefs about science teaching;
- features of the *Teaching Science* text;
- models of teacher development.

Introduction

How teachers should be educated (or trained) is a sensitive issue that has received a lot of media attention lately. We believe that learning to teach is a multidisciplinary activity and the process of 'training' teachers is essentially an educational one. Throughout this text, the term 'training' is used in its broadest sense to mean 'education' because we view classroom teaching as a complex activity and consequently learning to teach is more than knowing science or acquiring a series of teaching top tips by following a recipe or rubric.

In this text we do not cover subject knowledge per se, although tangentially we do offer approaches and resources to explore subject content in follow-up activities. Here our aim is to facilitate the processes involved in learning to teach science; our focus is science education. We suggest that the content of the following 15 chapters point to key aspects of practice that complement a thorough understanding of your subject.

Like much contemporary work in education, this book is informed by constructivist theories of learning. It takes the view that knowledge is not passively acquired. Learning about science or furthermore learning how to teach science is essentially an active process. Adults, and children, reflect upon their experiences in all situations that they encounter to actively construct meaning and understanding. In learning to teach your experiences, views and beliefs must be drawn upon and expanded to form your opinions and guide your actions. We are not trying to 'tell you how to do it', but rather we hope to provide a series of chapters that help you to explore and contemplate issues that, we feel, are critical components of successful classroom practice. Reflective, creative and imaginative thinking drives our model of teacher training. To be a successful classroom science teacher, we believe you need to reflect upon your experiences, both inside and outside the classroom, and make decisions to shape your development and classroom practice. You need to be creative, imaginative and bold and dream up new ideas to overcome the hurdles that you will face. We encourage you to listen to children and model colleagues' practice with originality and innovation. This is demanding. So, to help you develop your practice, we have put together a series of chapters with the aim of assisting you to explore your thoughts and feelings about a range of contemporary themes in science education. We believe that good teaching can be developed and enhanced and that this is a continuous process. It does not stop after a pre-service course and it is not a simple binary case of either you can teach – or you cannot!

A TOP feature of the text

The text contains a series of reflective activities embedded into each chapter. There are three types of activities; Theory, Observation and Practice (TOP). Most chapters start by outlining relevant *education theory*. For example, recent research on children's learning in science is outlined in Chapter 4; Chapter 5 describes the UK statutory science curriculum; and recent studies of special educational needs in science classrooms are covered in Chapter 12. The theory provides the backbone to the text and this draws on recent research, our experiences of teaching and working with new classroom practitioners. In covering theory, our intention is to help you to develop a framework to reflect upon your teaching. Incidentally, we also encourage you to consider the framework that we advocate. Science education is a vast and complex area and any introductory text has to be selective. We have selected certain areas that we feel are important and have been useful in our teaching. What we offer is our interpretation of the field and this, of course, is open to criticism. The text is certainly not all-inclusive. For those who wish to take the issues further, each chapter includes some recommended additional reading.

Dispersed throughout the book are also series of *observation tasks* – these are are designed to help you explore the theory covered in light of your recent observational experiences. The purpose of the tasks is to help you reflect upon your observations as well as apply the educational theory outlined. Learning to teach is an active process and the tasks have been designed to help you to make connections between the content of the chapters and your school experiences. We hope you will theorize about your practice and put theory into practice. Above all we encourage you to talk about classroom experiences (successes and horrors!) with colleagues and friends – learning to teach is a social activity. It is essential, for instance, that you develop professional, open relationships with your colleagues because they should offer you the support and encouragement that you need to improve.

The text also contains *practice tasks*. For instance, a practice task in Chapter 4 encourages you to arrange a small group discussion with pupils to find out about their preferred learning style. In Chapter 7, you are encouraged to record and analyse your questioning techniques. Wherever possible, we encourage you to make time in your busy school schedule to complete these tasks. Try to incorporate the tasks directly into your school timetable – you might also use these as a basis for planning and discussion with your mentors.

So, in summary, three features permeate the text. When learning to teach, there is no doubt that the interaction and influences of theory, observation and practice are complex. One possible way to consider this interaction is represented in Figure 1.1. In this cyclic model each component interacts and leads to development. The extent to which learning to teach is as easily represented is, of course, open to challenge.

Throughout the text, we encourage you to actively focus on the three components represented (T, O and P). Our aim is to challenge and develop your knowledge, beliefs and values about science teaching, but above all we hope to develop your classroom teaching. Our intention is to offer a text, grounded in experiences and research, that impinges on practice: not a text that is solely an academic exercise. Above all we view learning to teach science as a process of empowerment; you need to feel a sense of ownership over your own learning rather than becoming increasingly dependent on colleagues (and books!) for advice and guidance. We would like you to become the teacher that you feel comfortable with. We would also like you to innovate and be creative, new teachers have much to offer the profession in the form of a 'fresh pair of eyes'.

From personal performance to pupil performance

So what is involved in learning to teach science? In the years to come you will no doubt face a series of challenges. Learning to teach is anything but an emotionally free experience. At times things will go well and you will feel energized and refreshed, at other times things will not go as planned and you may feel frustrated and anxious. As time progresses, the ups and downs will even out and experience will help you to come to terms with the unusual and unexpected.

The first point to stress is that you are not alone; learning how to teach more effectively is a shared goal for all those involved in education, and throughout the text we use a series of comments and quotations from experienced and new science teachers. However, of course,

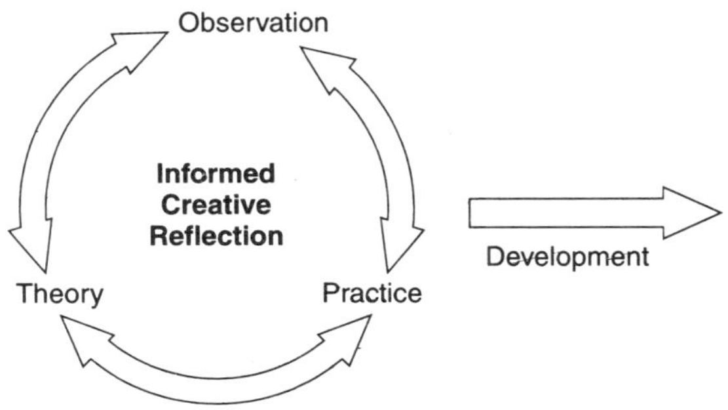

Figure 1.1 Theory–Observation–Practice–Development

different teachers have differing needs. When starting to teach the initial pre-occupation is often *personal performance*. New teachers are frequently concerned with thoughts like: How can I not appear nervous? How will I remember all the names? How will I deal with disruptive behaviour? Where should I stand? What are my rules? At this time new teachers are thinking their way into a social role (what it means to be a science teacher). Some new teachers struggle with the role, in particular with their image of what a science teacher should (or should not) be. Other teachers, who are perhaps more fortunate, identify with a particular teacher (often their mentor) who might have a style that they feel they can adapt and use. Others might try and imitate their mentor, almost like imprinting, and adopt a style that they never really feel happy or comfortable with. Needless to say this should be avoided – learning to teach is far more complicated than simply mimicking somebody else's style.

Adopting the role of a science teacher becomes internalized and automatic after a while. At this point the emphasis can shift to the *class performance*. The agenda now is not so much personal performance (teaching) but children's learning. New questions arise such as: Did the group grasp the concepts? Were enough questions asked? Were the pupils on task during the practical work? Did the class find the lesson interesting? Were they well behaved? Did they understand the concepts covered? These questions could form the basis of reflection both during and after a lesson. Frequently at this stage concerns about classroom management emerge as new teachers grapple with the demands of, for instance, managing a class discussion or a transition period such as packing away or getting out laboratory equipment.

Classrooms are comprised of individuals with particular needs (incidentally some of these needs are explored in more detail in Chapter 12). Often as new teachers gain experience they are able to concentrate more on individuals and to differentiate their classroom activities to meet these needs and so to analyse how their teaching impacts on *pupil performance*. At this point, the following questions surface: Did the lesson cater for all needs? Did I manage to spend time with those who needed me most? Was James able to cope with the linguistic demands of my worksheets? Was Latika sufficiently stretched by the content of the class?

When starting to teach, you might identify with these phases (see Figure 1.2). In so doing, you are analysing your practice. The phases offer you a means of setting targets: early on try

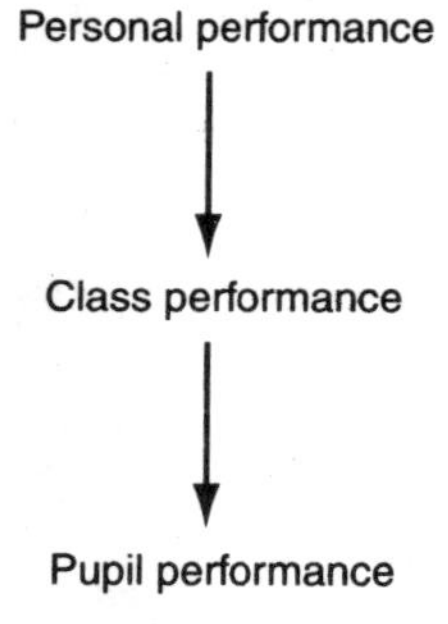

Figure 1.2 From personal performance to pupil performance

not to lose sight of learning and individual needs. Above all try to talk to and listen to children. In the end, teaching science requires you to reflect upon all these aspects of practice: developing personal performance, the performance of the group, and the performance of individuals is essential for successful practice.

So what determines your growth and development? In the end, quite simply, you do. With support and guidance from others you need to think about your practice and set a series of targets. You can actually start this before teaching your first lesson by exploring what you consider to be excellent practice. Later in this chapter, we include an activity to help you explore your beliefs, values and knowledge about what it means to be a science teacher. Other chapters contain tasks with a similar aim. Of course, teaching does not take place in a vacuum and the school setting or the school climate will mould and shape your practice and what can and cannot be achieved.

Models of teacher development

There are many models of teacher development and Schon's (1983) and Shulman's (1987) remain popular. Beverley Bell and John Gilbert's (1996) model has the advantage that it has a science focus. When learning to teach science, the researchers highlight the significance of social, personal and professional development. Their research offers a useful framework for some early reflections.

Teacher development has a social component, as Bell and Gilbert write:

> It involves the renegotiation and reconstruction of the rules and norms of what it means to be a teacher (of science, for example). Teachers need to be central contributors to this. It also involves the development of ways of working with others that enable the kinds of social interactions necessary for renegotiating and reconstructing of what it means to be a teacher of science.
>
> (Bell and Gilbert, 1996: 161)

You need to create spaces to listen and share experiences with colleagues (at school and on your training course). This can take a variety of forms, for instance face-to-face conversations, group discussions, email and telephone calls. Time needs to be made available for feedback and discussions about lessons, your professional growth and most importantly target setting. You should welcome observations, however formal, as a means to identify strengths and weaknesses. You should also take part in the wider social life of the school by attending staff meetings, in-service days, departmental meetings, parent evenings and social evenings. Learning to teach, as Bell and Gilbert (1996) indicate, is becoming part of, and contributing to, a social community.

Learning to teach also necessitates professional development. Professional development includes trying out new ideas, curricular resources and innovative approaches; rethinking your teaching style and assumptions; keeping up to date with curriculum innovations and education research and incorporating this into your practice. It also involves learning some science and keeping up to date with science. In England and Wales, the National Curriculum covers a number of degree specialisms; biology, chemistry, physics, earth science, astronomy and the history and philosophy of science. Few people have expertise in all these fields and so teaching science usually requires learning some science as well. New science teachers often comment how they are really coming to understand science concepts now they are teaching them. Professional development also requires exploring your ideology of teaching and learning as well as the ideology of the school curriculum. As Bell and Gilbert write:

> It involves not only the use of new teaching activities in the classroom but also the development of the beliefs and conceptions underlying the activities. The clarification of core values and commitments is important for the moral frameworks in education. It also involves learning science as well as science education.
>
> (Bell and Gilbert, 1996: 161)

Learning to teach science involves embracing change and exploring new possibilities. It also involves the ability to listen and respond to others, as well as being open about personal strengths and weaknesses, and being realistic about what can be achieved. Personal development incorporates the ability to take control of your own learning, the ability to set yourself a series of targets and in so doing manage and facilitate your own growth and development. It also includes managing emotions when things do not go as planned and those 'feelings associated with changing activities and beliefs about science education' (Bell and Gilbert, 1996: 15). It is not always easy to accept an aspect of practice as problematic, it is even more difficult to explore and challenge one's personal beliefs and commitments about education.

Observation Task Social, personal and professional development

As you observe science lessons and work with teachers try to identify with the social, personal and professional aspects of their practice. Try to arrange a time to sit down and talk, at length, to an experienced colleague and consider how they balance the various demands associated with teaching science. Use their comments as a means of isolating good practice and setting a series of personal, professional and social targets.

So what is learning to teach science really like?

When starting, new teachers are often anxious to find out what science teaching is like. They are quite understandably curious about the stresses and strains associated with the job and whether they have made an appropriate career move. Embarking on any new vocation can be nerve-racking. In teaching, new teachers are often concerned about their first lesson and whether they really can deal with 9C or 4A, on a Friday afternoon!

Practice Task Teach a lesson

Possibly the best way of finding out what science teaching is really like is by teaching a lesson (or part of a lesson). We recommend that you teach early on in your teacher training course. Try to keep the lesson simple and actively involve children in learning. Long lectures and expositions should be avoided, for instance. Get the children engaged in a task and spend time watching, listening and discussing their progress.

After the lesson is over, spend time reflecting on your performance. Are there things you would change? Why? How would you change things for next time?

Theory Task Some early reflections

Consider the following questions and if possible discuss them with your colleagues:

- What are your thoughts about learning to teach science?
- How do these compare with other trainees on your course?
- Do you have particular concerns and what are you looking forward to?
- What sort of environment do you need for support and growth?
- How can this environment be created?
- What are your early teaching targets and how are you hoping to achieve these?

Teaching science

This chapter has served as an introduction to the text. We have highlighted some of the features of the book and offered some initial comments about teacher development, in particular social, personal and professional development. Above all, what we hope has emerged is the importance of your opinions, beliefs and actions. Ultimately, the responsibility for becoming an effective teacher is yours. In the future, no doubt, you will be offered much advice and guidance; however, you are the person who must combine this into effective classroom practice.

This chapter concludes by introducing various parts of the text. Our intent is to provide an overview, a route-map, of the following 15 chapters.

The book's structure

Teaching Science is arranged in five parts. Part 1, 'Setting the Scene', has two chapters (including this chapter). Our focus here is on teacher training and development. More specifically, we concern ourselves with questions such as:

- What are key features in learning to teach science?
- What are the standards of practice for new teachers?
- How can you use these standards to develop your practice?

Part 2, 'Goals, Learning and the Curriculum', explores the science curriculum and learning. In this part, we discuss why we teach science in schools and the nature of school science. We also consider differences between teaching and learning, followed by an overview of contemporary thought about how children learn science. The section concludes by providing an overview of the National Curriculum for Science. In essence this part of the text is concerned with questions of the nature:

- Why do we teach science?
- What science should we teach?
- How do people learn science?
- What are we required to teach?

Part 3, 'Planning, Teaching and Assessing Science', has a practical emphasis. This part offers advice on lesson planning, teaching and learning activities and assessment. It comprises five chapters. Here, the focus is on exploring questions such as:

- What are the key aspects of successful short-term and long-term planning?
- What type of activities might you include in your lessons?
- How can you use information and communications technology successfully in science classrooms?
- What are the elements of successful assessment of learning?

Part 4, 'Issues in Science Education', focuses on science for all and the recent cross-curriculum themes of citizenship, literacy and numeracy. This part is driven by a series of questions including:

- How can we ensure equality of opportunity in science classrooms?
- What role does language and mathematics have in science education?
- What are the implications of citizenship for science education?

Finally, Part 5, 'Looking to the Future', contains just one chapter. The focus here is your future development and growth. This part covers questions such as:

- How do you apply for a teaching position?
- What happens in an induction year?
- Can you continue to develop professionally?

Using the book

Teaching Science is not meant to be read cover to cover in two or three sittings and we leave it up to the reader how to sequence the chapters. At different points during your practice you may identify with some chapters more than others. Some chapters are more practical than others. Ideally you will have read most of the chapters in the first four parts of the text before starting a prolonged period of teaching practice. The last section, Part 5, is something that you can read at a later stage. We forewarn readers in advance of the hazards associated with grabbing at any of the suggestions we make and inserting them thoughtlessly into a lesson. You need to think carefully and critically about the content of each chapter and how it might be reconstructed within your practice. Then, like all good science teachers, you need to evaluate its effectiveness.

Further reading

Bell, B and Gilbert, J (1996) *Teacher Development: A model from science education,* Falmer Books, London

During your training year(s), you will be working closely with school-based mentors. A series of excellent developmental and reflective activities for science teachers and mentors are contained in:

Monk, M and Dillon, J (1995) *Learning to Teach Science: Activities for student teachers and mentors,* Falmer Press, London

Shulman, L (1987) Knowledge and teaching: foundations of the new reform, *Harvard Educational Review,* **7**(1), pp 1–22

2 Developing science teaching standards

Keith Hicks and Steve Alsop

Although the standards are quite detailed, I found them useful in planing my practice. The key thing is getting to understand the jargon. This is important in the end because it is how you are assessed.

(Sonia, a secondary science teacher)

Objectives

This chapter is aimed at students on pre-service teacher education courses. The chapter facilitates critical reflection on the teaching standards as specified in the Department for Education and Employment Circular 4/98 (DfEE, 1998a). More specifically, the chapter explores in relation to this Circular:

- effective science teaching;
- how effective practice can be developed;
- links between the Circular and the following text;
- questions about assessing effective practice.

Introduction

As a new science teacher you will see a wide variety of lessons taught by a number of teachers. You will come to recognize some teachers as being outstanding practioners of their profession and hopefully you will want to emulate their success. But how will you come to recognize these people? What are the skills and features possessed by the best teachers and what makes their science teaching more effective than others? These are questions that we all have to come to grips with throughout our careers and like many obvious questions in education the answer is, of course, far from straightforward.

In the drive to raise standards in schools, over the last few decades of the twentieth century, successive governments have brought in a raft of reforms. The National Curriculum has probably been the most significant. Once a generic curriculum was firmly established in schools the government turned its attention to the training of teachers and the provision of 'high quality' teachers for schools. The results were a progressively tighter control of teacher training courses that culminated in the publication of the DfEE Circular 4/98. This in effect is a national curriculum for teacher training. The Circular sets out the criteria which all courses in initial teacher training must meet. In particular it specifies a national curriculum for initial teacher training courses in English, mathematics and science that must be taught to all trainees on all courses of primary initial teacher training (these are presented in Annexes C, D and E of the Circular). Also within Circular 4/98 is detailed a national curriculum for secondary English, mathematics and science which must be taught to all trainees on secondary courses specializing in those subjects (that for science teachers is presented in Annexe H). The Circular also lays down in Annexe A the standards for the award of qualified teacher status (QTS). These standards are a benchmark which prospective teachers are measured against. The standards, as you might imagine, are surrounded in controversy and debate. The extent to which a series of generic standards (in the form of a checklist) can be used to describe a good teacher is widely questioned. Is good teaching practice quantifiable in the same way as data is collected in school science experiments?

It is very difficult, as many authors have noted, to derive a definitive checklist of good practice. Nevertheless, the standards exist and offer a particular model of good practice. In the end, you will be judged against this model and consequently it is essential that you are familiar with the contents of the Circular. In many respects Circular 4/98 has much to offer; for instance, it makes explicit what in the past might have been implicit. The standards itemized are sensible and perceptive and offer much advice and guidance to the inexperienced science teacher. The extent to which they are exhaustive is, of course, questionable.

Observation Task Isolating 'good' practice

You should observe as many science lessons as possible. Using these observations choose a lesson you thought was particularly successful. Make a list of features in that lesson that led you to the opinion that it was a successful lesson – these may well include issues beyond the learning outcomes of the pupils. Having made this list, write a second list of the qualities of the teacher that contributed to that success. Reflect on those qualities and your own strengths and weaknesses, how you can develop as a teacher to take on some of those qualities. Obtain a copy of Circular 4/98 (available from www.dfee.gov.uk/circular/0498.htm) and look to see if the qualities that you have isolated are evident in this document.

Developing science teaching standards

As a new teacher you should expect to be constantly observed and evaluated to assess the extent to which you meet the standards specified. This process of observation and judgement of your professional performance is becoming increasingly common throughout the teaching profession. Some teachers may feel threatened by the process that now incorporates an element of assessment for pay review, but as a new entrant to the profession you should, perhaps, regard the process as a norm. With the development of this system of appraisal and performance management in schools there has been an attempt to provide 'checklists' to ensure a more objective assessment of performance. To teach the National Curriculum in science, newly qualified teachers (NQTs) are also expected to have a secure knowledge of the content of the information and communications technology (ICT) National Curriculum and the use of ICT in science teaching (outlined in Annexe B of Circular 4/98).

The following three sections outline the science specific queries:

- Section A: Pedagogical knowledge and understanding required by trainees to secure pupils' progress in science.
- Section B: Effective teaching and assessment methods.
- Section C: Trainees' knowledge and understanding of science.

The first thing to note is that Circular 4/98 is both detailed and prescriptive. Given that many initial teacher education courses last only the equivalent of an academic year, the contents of Annexe H largely dictate the entire content of those courses for secondary science teachers while Annexes C, D and E dominate the primary initial teacher training courses. On entering your first year of teaching (your induction year) as an NQT, you will have a career entry profile which will summarize your strengths and your priorities for development based on these three sections of the curriculum, with a view to your having an individualized programme to consolidate and develop these areas.

The following sections provide an overview of the content of Annexes E and H. The intention is to summarize the Circular and link the content to the following chapters of this text.

Section A: Pedagogical knowledge and understanding required by trainees to secure pupils' progress in science

In 'Section A', the standards specify the 'pedagogical knowledge' required for good science teaching. It is made explicit that you should understand the position of science in the curriculum and the reasons why it is taught to pupils in school. These issues are discussed in Chapter 3.

In defining the requirements for the progression of pupils' scientific understanding, the Circular advocates a pedagogical approach reflecting a constructivist view of learning. This view of learning is outlined in Chapter 4.

The standards also lay down a clear requirement for teachers in each of the Key Stages to understand progression through the Key Stages. You should be aware of the curriculum for the Key Stages that you are not intending to teach (see Chapter 5). It makes sense, for instance, for secondary science teachers to ensure that they are aware of the contents of the primary curriculum, particularly if they are going to be teaching pupils at Key Stage 3 science.

Section A is the longest part of the Circular and you should ensure that you take the opportunity to study it carefully. It is often difficult to assess all aspects of this section at the end of a relatively short period of teaching practice.

Section B: Effective teaching and assessment methods

While we all want to be effective teachers it would be a mistake, as we have previously noted, to believe that there is one method or style appropriate for all teachers, all pupils and all schools. Experienced teachers know that their method and style has to be adapted and changed to fit the local situation and external factors that may impinge on a lesson. None the less this section attempts to define a number of key 'generic' areas of teaching that should be demonstrated by all pre-service teachers if they are to be awarded QTS. Section B is divided into seven subsections relating to teaching activities and provides a useful framework for the discussion of teaching skills.

1) Effective questioning

Questioning is a central teaching strategy that has to be developed by new teachers. Knowing how and when to use open and closed questions and how to frame written questions to stretch and extend your pupils is a key skill in successful science teaching. In your observations of good science lessons you will have seen how questioning is used not simply to demonstrate a recall of scientific knowledge but to promote learning for understanding and to challenge students' alternative conceptual frameworks through discussion. Questioning also allows pupils to broaden their understandings of concepts by applying them to new and unfamiliar contexts. Further details about questions are to be found in Chapter 7 of this text.

2) Effective expositions

Knowing how to break down complex scientific concepts into easy to understand steps using concrete models and analogies to explain abstract ideas is something good science teachers are skilled at doing. Being able to carry out an effective demonstration to a whole class can often be a more effective method of introducing or reinforcing a new concept to a class than any amount of bookwork or even in some instances class practical work. Understanding how to present a good exposition to the class means being very clear about the aims of that exposition and appreciating the conceptual difficulties contained within it. In some ways we could say that this is what lies at the heart of good practice. See Chapters 6 and 7 for more details.

3) Use of experimental and practical work

The science curriculum comprises concepts and processes; and as a science teacher you need to plan activities that develop scientific concepts and practical skills. Facilitating progression in these skills is as important as progression in scientific concepts. A suitable knowledge of the health and safety aspects of work in a scientific laboratory is obviously essential. For further material on practical work and safety see Chapter 9.

4) Development of literacy

The introduction of the literacy hour into Key Stage 2 is now throwing the focus for this issue on to Key Stage 3. As a science teacher in any key stage you will have a responsibility towards ensuring your pupils' development of literacy skills through providing appropriate reading and writing exercises necessary to ensure that pupils also progress in their understanding of science. You will be expected to ensure that your pupils utilize a range of different written materials (including the Internet and CD-ROM) and learn how to extract and use relevant information from these sources effectively. In addition, you need to plan to ensure that pupils write effectively in science, adopting different styles of writing for different audiences. Literacy issues are explored in more detail in Chapters 7 and 13.

5) Development of numeracy and other mathematical skills

There is a requirement in the Circular for you to be aware of the expected level of mathematical knowledge demanded by the National Curriculum for students of the age you are teaching. You are expected to be able to encourage pupils to reinforce and apply mathematical knowledge in your science lessons. Annexe H of Circular 4/98 specifies a range of mathematical skills and processes that you are expected to be familiar with. These are also reflected in the numeracy test that you undergo as part of your end of pre-service course. You are also expected to understand the common difficulties which pupils may have with the mathematical skills used in science teaching and understand how to address these problems. For more details on numeracy see Chapter 13.

6) Teaching pupils to communicate their scientific understanding

As a science teacher you need to promote the skills associated with effective communication through accurate and concise written and oral presentations. This area includes the effective use of tables and graphs to communicate ideas and concepts studied in science lessons. Also see Chapter 13.

7) Exploring sensitive and controversial issues

This is clearly a skill possessed by effective science teachers who can promote a debate on sensitive issues such as genetic disease or evolution in such a way that pupils feel their views are respected while being effectively challenged. See Chapter 15 for more details.

As part of Section B, you need to plan for and demonstrate well-structured lessons and sequences of lessons that effectively ensure learning objectives are met. You will be expected to use a variety of teaching and learning techniques and methods with whole classes, groups and individuals to provide well-structured learning experiences. The issue of planning lessons and schemes of work are discussed more fully in Chapter 6. You should also know how to manage and select resources effectively for use in your lessons and to understand their usefulness in realizing teaching and learning objectives. This includes the use of ICT in your lessons, covered in Chapter 8.

Section C: Trainees' knowledge and understanding of science

Having sufficient subject knowledge is clearly fundamental to successful teaching in any Key Stage. As mentioned earlier this can be a challenge. As part of your pre-service course you will be expected to carry out a subject audit where you assess your subject knowledge against the demands of the National Curriculum and public examination syllabuses (where appropriate) and identify your strengths and areas that require development. During the course of your teacher education you will be expected to address these areas of knowledge to ensure your are conversant with the knowledge requirements for the sector in which you plan to teach.

Later in this chapter we provide a task and a further reading list to help you develop your subject expertise. This comes with a word of warning: successful teaching depends on more than a mere familiarity with key concepts. As a teacher it will be important that you understand the nuances, connections and applications of concepts across the subject so that you can deliver effective lessons and explanations to the pupils in your care.

One of the most common reasons for an individual to enter the teaching profession is because they have a love of their subject; while this is not the only requirement for being a successful practitioner, it is nonetheless an important one. You do need to feel enthused by your subject and be able to communicate that enthusiasm to what may well be groups of disaffected learners. Having said that, it is also important that you recognize that not all pupils will share the enthusiasms you have and you will have to learn ways of cajoling and encouraging those students to achieve understanding in areas of the curriculum for which they feel quite indifferent.

Keeping up to date

Science is an area of human knowledge that is constantly changing and moving forward. It has been estimated that the body of knowledge that we call science doubles every 10 years. In your career you may be looking at a period of over 30 years in the classroom so it is clearly important that you maintain an up-to-date knowledge of your subject. To do so you will need to plan a strategy that enables you to access information from a variety of sources that you should aim to use in your teaching. Indeed, as you progress through your career and reach the point where you apply to pass through the threshold and achieve the higher pay scales you will be expected to demonstrate and present evidence that you have kept up to date with scientific knowledge. Chapter 16 explores issues about continual professional development.

An additional area, which you will be expected to be familiar with, is that of the nature of science itself. This is a weakness in many new teachers who, having studied a subject at degree level, may never have studied anything on the philosophy of science. This is in itself a fascinating area of study that you may be inspired to follow through as you become more settled into your role as a teacher. Initially you will be required to recognize that scientific knowledge is either descriptive or based on agreed definitions and relationships. You also need to understand that the nature of scientific knowledge is never 100 per cent certain and must always be open to scrutiny and alternative explanation. Teaching the National Curriculum in science now has to incorporate the imparting of this view of science to pupils from very early stages. A significant part of Science Attainment Target 1 is to do with evaluating the reliability of evidence and suggesting alternative explanations for it.

Development of personal practice using teaching standards

The prescriptive nature of Circular 4/98 and the amount of material contained in the appendices may seem quite daunting at the start of your course. You may feel that what is required is some sort of super-teacher that is beyond the ability of most individuals! Do not despair. Whilst you are on your block teaching practices your mentors and tutors will complete a profile at various key points which will assess the extent to which you are meeting the demands of the requirements of the course. This profile will be completed in discussion with you and it gives you the opportunity to measure the development of your personal practice against this agreed national standard. We suggest a six-step process that you can use to develop your professional skills:

1. Familiarize yourself with the contents of Annexe A – the standards for the award of QTS.
2. Reflect and evaluate the extent to which you are meeting the standards in your practice.
3. Discuss your progress with your mentor and set short-term and long-term targets.
4. Devise a plan to meet those short- and long-term targets.
5. Put your planning into action.
6. Evaluate your progress.

The following theory task is designed to familiarize you with Circular 4/98 and enable you to use the Circular to set a series of personal targets.

Theory Task Developing ITT standards – a self-assessment task

Derived from the DfEE teaching standards, the following questions will help you complete a personal inventory of your progress. To complete the exercise you need to read each statement and decide if you:

Strongly Agree, Slightly Agree, Slightly Disagree or Strongly Disagree.

We recommend that you revisit these questions as your teaching progresses. For instance, try to complete this activity at the start of the course and then after a period of teaching practice. The task is designed to help you isolate some strengths and weaknesses with a view to setting a series of targets. It starts with questions about your subject knowledge.

Knowledge and understanding of science

1. I am aware of the strengths and weaknesses in my science subject knowledge.
2. I can build on my subject strengths in the classroom.
3. I can address my subject weaknesses.
4. I have ways of keeping up to date with my subject knowledge.
5. I have an understanding of the nature of scientific knowledge.

Pedagogical content knowledge

6. I can explain why is it important for pupils to learn science.
7. I appreciate how pupils learn science.
8. I know how to assess pupils' prior knowledge of scientific concepts and why this is important in my teaching.
9. I can take account of pupils' ideas of concepts (and science) in my teaching and planning.
10. I understand the concept of progression and continuity within and across Key Stages.
11. I use practical work to challenge pupils' concepts.
12. I am aware of the content of the National Curriculum (including Key Stages outside my age phase).
13. I can use models and illustrations to explain abstract concepts.
14. I can identify opportunities to teach scientific skills.
15. I am aware of the importance of language and mathematics in science.

Effective teaching and assessment methods

16. I can plan individual and sequences of lessons.
17. My planning is efficient and effective.
18. I use a range of resources (including ICT) to support pupils' learning.
19. I use open and closed questions in my teaching.
20. I am aware of what effecting questioning might entail.
21. I can plan and deliver effective expositions.
22. I am aware of and can use a wide variety of teaching methods.
23. I use practical work effectively.
24. I know how to develop language using a variety of source materials.
25. I am aware of the expected levels of numeracy.
26. I use and develop mathematical concepts in my science teaching.
27. I can handle sensitive and controversial issues in science.

28. I can carry out risk assessments where necessary.
29. I know why we assess.
30. I use a range of formative and summative assessment tools in my teaching.
31. I can evaluate the strengths and weaknesses of these tools.
32. I can relate my assessment to National Curriculum levels.
33. I can recognize and plan for pupils who have SEN and those who are gifted and talented.
34. I make effective use of base-line data in my planning and teaching.

Having completed the exercise you should look back at the judgements and use these to isolate some of your personal strengths and weaknesses. Once these are isolated you need to consider how you can develop your weaknesses and maintain your strengths.

Subject knowledge

As a teacher of science you will often have to teach outside of your subject area. As part of your professional development during your training year you will need to learn some science. The following task structures this process.

Theory Task Completing a science subject knowledge audit

For trainees on KS2/3 courses, using a copy of the National Curriculum KS2, KS3 and KS4 programmes of study, carry out an audit of your knowledge of the subject content of the curriculum. Make a list of the areas of knowledge from each of the four attainment targets where you feel insecure and where you feel you need to improve your knowledge.

For trainees on 11–16 courses, 11–18 courses and 14–19 courses, using a copy of the National Curriculum KS3 and KS4 programmes of study as well as the relevant A-level core, carry out an audit of your knowledge of the subject content of the curriculum. Make a list of the areas of knowledge from each of the four attainment targets and from the A-level core where you feel insecure and where you feel you need to improve your knowledge.

For trainees on 14–19 courses, carry out a subject audit of your knowledge and understanding of the science required to teach science post-16. In particular you should compare your knowledge to the requirements cited in the following paragraphs of Annexe H of Circular 4/98:

- Paragraph 13, pp 19–20, for biology.
- Paragraph 14, pp 20–21, for chemistry.
- Paragraph 15, pp 22–23, for physics.

Having completed your subject audit you need to plan a course of action to address the areas of weakness you have identified in your subject knowledge over the course of your pre-service course. By the time you complete your pre-service course you should be secure in your knowledge of science as laid down in the curriculum.

To help you to address areas in need of development we have recommended a number of texts in the Further Reading section at the end of this chapter.

Accurately assessing teaching

In an attempt to demonstrate that the requirements of Circular 4/98 have been met, institutes of higher education have scrambled to produce profiles often containing large tick lists for students and mentors to fill out to record the extent to which individuals meet the required standards. But to what extent can teaching be reduced to a series of ticks in boxes? Is successful practice simply made up of a series of standards? Can you be successful in the classroom and not achieve the standards? Possibly one of the most essential features of good teaching is that good teachers possess a vocation for the job and arguably no amount of tick boxes can assess that sense of vocation. Being a good teacher extends far beyond being a good *science* teacher, it includes being good with young people, being able to gain their respect and being able to change lives. What then is the place of the teaching standards laid out in Circular 4/98? Use them as a tool to identify and assess your own progress and as a means to highlight strengths and areas for development. Use them when you look at different aspects of the work of your peers and other teachers. But perhaps keep in mind that they are not the whole picture.

Further reading

Department for Education and Employment (DfEE) (1998) *Requirements for Courses of Initial Teacher Training*, Circular 4/98, DfEE, London

There are a number of texts that have been specifically written with the 'non subject specialist' primary science teacher in mind – excellent examples are:

Hollins, Whitby, Lander, Parsons and Williams (1998) *Progression in Primary Science*, David Fulton Press, London

Peacock, G (1998) *Science for Primary Teachers: An audit and self-study guide*, Letts, London

Other recommendations for the 'non specialist' secondary teacher include:

Foulds, K (1996) *GCSE Double Award Physics*, John Murray, London

Gater, S and Wood-Robinson, V (1996) *GCSE Double Award Biology*, John Murray, London

Wilford, L and Earl, B (1996) *GCSE Double Award Chemistry*, John Murray, London

Part 2

Goals, Learning and the Curriculum

3 The goals of science education

Steve Alsop and Keith Hicks

Science is valuable because it meshes with all our lives and allows us to channel and use our spontaneous curiosity. (Professor Susan Greenfield, cited in the Science National Curriculum)

Objectives

This chapter explores the aims and goals of science education. More specifically, the chapter discusses:

- the aims and goals of science education;
- the nature of science and school science.

Introduction

Why teach science? It is an obvious question and one you may be asked at an interview for a teaching appointment. Nevertheless, despite it being a common question it is not a question with a clear answer or one devoid of controversy and debate. For years, politicians have encouraged and legislated to make science a compulsory subject but there are very few reasons given as to why this should be the case other than some vague references to economic development and prosperity.

You need to consider why you teach science because it can influence how you teach. However, the reasons and justifications for teaching science have changed with remarkable fluidity over the years. Black (1993) pinpoints four possible reasons for this:

1. Changes in science, for instance the AIDS epidemic, issues surrounding genetics and increasing concern about the environment are three examples of relatively new priorities in science and science education.
2. Changes in our understanding of pedagogy and developments in ICT (particularly the Internet) are altering our view of what scientific knowledge is and how it should be accessed.

3. Changes by governments. The latest version of the Science National Curriculum effectively alters the (still unstated) aims of science education and it is most unlikely that the process of science curricular reform will halt with this most recent reincarnation of the curriculum.
4. Changes in our pupils and their needs, in particular changes brought about by influences outside of school such as family life, changes in patterns of parenting, the media and the stresses of life in the inner cities.

The school curriculum cannot remain fossilized in the light of external pressures. The introduction of the National Curriculum for Science, for instance, combined with the publication of league tables of SAT and GCSE results has arguably reduced the current debate about goals to one of achievement. Although we have a prescriptive curriculum, do we have clear educational goals? Very recently, science educators have suggested not. Millar and Osborne (1998), for example, when reviewing the curriculum note: 'The science curriculum lacks a well-articulated set of aims or an agreed model of the development of pupils' scientific capability over the 5–16 period and beyond.'

So what is the unique contribution a study of science makes to the education of the pupils in our schools? Why do we continue to teach this subject with its demands for specialist accommodation, expensive equipment and increasingly hard to come by specialist teachers?

The Initial Teacher Training (ITT) National Curriculum for Secondary Science (Department for Education and Employment (DfEE), 1998a) documents five reasons why it is important for *all* pupils to learn science:

1. Knowledge and understanding of science helps pupils make sense of natural phenomena.
2. Knowledge and understanding of science and of the ways scientists work can help pupils understand the basis for decisions in an increasingly technological world.
3. Through science pupils can develop investigative and practical skills which can help then to solve problems.
4. Science is interesting and intellectually stimulating.
5. Science is an important part of contemporary culture and is relevant to, and has implications for, people of all nations.

In the following sections we discuss these claims – we hope, as you progress through this book and your career, you will add to and expand on our deliberations. Needless to say, there are no uncontested answers to an issue as complex as this.

Theory Task Five reasons

What are your thoughts about these reasons? Do you feel that some are more important than others? Why? Now look at the curriculum, what reasons are evident in the curriculum? Does the curriculum focus on some reasons more than others? What should count as science education and why?

Reason one: Knowledge and understanding of science helps pupils make sense of natural phenomena

Science education helps pupils to look at the world in a different way. There is little doubt that knowledge of science provides a means for pupils to recognize and explore the complexity of natural phenomena. Objects fall because of gravity; the Earth revolves around the Sun (which is part of a spinning spiral galaxy); humans have evolved from apes; DNA carries the blueprint for life and the universe is made up of microscopic charged particles: these are scientific ideas that fundamentally change the way we think about ourselves and our world. There is an argument put forward that there is sufficient justification in knowing these ideas in themselves. In the past, scholars have claimed that knowing science is part of being 'learned'. That is, scientific knowledge has intrinsic merits. More recently, curriculum reformers have suggested that being 'learned' is not a sufficient curriculum aim or justification in itself. There needs to be more; it is not a simple case of knowledge for knowledge's sake. Although scientific literacy is not a new term, it has become a recent slogan in science education reform. In most definitions, being 'scientifically literate' embraces more than knowing – it also includes decision making and action. The suggestion here is that there is more to learning science than its intrinsic worth, we should learn science because we can use it in some way in our daily lives. The justification (or goal) for science education lies in its everyday applicability.

Reason two: Knowledge and understanding of science and of the ways scientists work can help pupils understand the basis for decisions in an increasingly technological world

There is an argument that in an increasingly technological world, people need knowledge of science as the basis for daily decision making. Everyday decisions might involve medical care (eg a decision over a new drug) or perhaps issues of food safety – deciding about whether to purchase organic produce or food with particular additives and preservatives. When buying a car, a decision might involve scrutinizing data from crash-tests to explore whether the figures cited are meaningful in everyday driving conditions. It might also involve researching the risks associated with living near, or under, a high-voltage electrical pylon. There is a broad acceptance that some knowledge of science is advantageous in these cases, but the interesting and widely debated question is what expertise is actually required of citizens, given that these are often subjects in which scientific experts disagree?

Theory Task Science and decision making

The Science National Curriculum has three components:

1. knowledge of scientific laws, theories and concepts;
2. skills and processes of scientific inquiry;
3. knowledge of what science is and how scientists interact with each other and society.

Using an example of everyday decision making, try to decide what expertise is needed in each of these components. For instance, what knowledge, skills, processes and knowledge of science are need to scrutinize crash-test data when buying a car?

It is often suggested that in our technological world, knowledge of science is required to operate hi-tech gadgets and artefacts that litter our everyday lives. However, Millar and Osborne (1998) suggest that this *utilitarian argument* is somewhat questionable. As graduates of science, are we actually better at operating things? One can operate a video-recorder, computer, motor car and TV with very little understanding of how they work. In this regard, technological advances seem to have reduced the need for understanding rather than increased it. As the authors note, there is more to science education than wiring a plug – particularly as most electrical appliances are now supplied with pre-wired and moulded plugs!

Many big issues facing society have a scientific and technological basis and increasingly citizens are expected to be able to understand, form opinions and make decisions on issues including, for instance, the genetic manipulation of crops, the advantages and disadvantages of nuclear power and causes of global warming. Issues of this type often feature in political debates, where citizens are required to make judgements of a *democratic* nature. There are also more local issues – the geographical 'neighbours' of science: residents living near a polluted stream, a proposed chemical factory or a new airport runway. In these settings there is also a sense of urgency about the need to understand some science (alongside perhaps other considerations of an economic, political and social nature).

In a democratic society scientists need to be held accountable and this also requires an informed citizenship. Much scientific research relies on large-scale funding and members of society have a vested interest in ensuring that research is being directed into areas of priority and need. Once more it is perhaps easier to identify the need rather than the expertise. What knowledge, for instance, is a necessary prerequisite for making an informed decision in the examples cited above? It is, we suggest, far from straightforward. We discuss how a science curriculum might explore decision making and citizenship in further detail in Chapters 14 and 15.

Reason three: Through science, pupils can develop investigative and practical skills, which can help them to solve problems

Science certainly provides an opportunity to demonstrate and develop a number of investigative skills and processes. The processes mentioned in the Science National Curriculum include observing, classifying, inferring, hypothesizing and evaluating. For instance, being able to classify is a process mentioned in each of the Key Stages starting with the simple classifications of plants and animals, to the classification of states of matter, through to the grouping and identification of different rocks and onto classifying the different bodies of the universe. Identifying variables and planning an investigation are also mentioned throughout the curriculum orders.

The extent to which these processes are subject specific is widely debated. Certainly, scientific investigations provide a means to solve problems, investigate and explore phenomena in science. They also stimulate enthusiasm and motivation and can provide a means of making abstract concepts more concrete. But do processes developed in science transfer to everyday situations? In other words, is it possible to teach processes as independent strategies that are universally applicable; can we teach pupils in science to be better observers, 'hypothezisers', predictors and 'classifyers' in every context? After completing a degree in science are we, for instance, simply better all round observers and predictors? Put this way, it does seem questionable. The idea that science teachers, for instance, train observation skills has long been in doubt. Studies of perception have clearly demonstrated that observation is fundamentally influenced by what the observer expects to see (their background knowledge). Magnetic fields with the help of iron filings become clearly visible when we know what to expect (lines issuing from the poles). In other words, background knowledge plays an essential role in seeing things in new ways. In terms of other processes, Millar (1989: 56) suggests they are also context dependent. What makes, for instance hypothesizing difficult is the 'complexity and sophistication of the data base and the conceptual ideas available'. A similar argument can be made for classification and inferring, Millar also suggests. To emphasize the importance of context perhaps we should refer to process skills in science which have the prefix 'scientific' – ie *scientific observation, scientific prediction, scientific hypothesis*, etc. What are your thoughts?

In addition to process skills, science also helps to develop a number of interpersonal social skills. Science classrooms should encourage teamwork, respect for others and promote equality of opportunity. Investigating and experimenting is a collaborative activity – the apocryphal image of the scientist working alone is a product of science fiction and needs challenging. Science education offers the opportunity to develop ideas of co-operation, respect for intellectual ideas, working to a common goal and exploring ideas. Employers often highlight the importance of these sorts of qualities, sometimes referred to as 'habits of mind'. Once again, the question here is the extent to which science offers something unique. If you explore and observe different subject lessons you are likely to see some teamwork in most subjects at some time during the week. As a science teacher you will need to develop the skills and techniques needed to promote teamwork, which should be part of your lesson planning and development. But is teamwork in science different in some way when compared with, for instance, teamwork in history or drama?

Observation Task Interpersonal skills – teamwork

The purpose of this observation is to see how teamwork is developed and organized in the science classroom. While a class practical lesson would be suitable for this observation do not ignore the fact that teamwork has some role to play in most lessons. If you get the opportunity it may be a useful activity to observe a non-science lesson to see how teamwork is developed in other subject areas.

Prior to the observation, familiarize yourself with the proposed lesson content either through discussion with the teacher or examination of the scheme of work or lesson plan. Discuss with the teacher what role you will play in the teamwork of this lesson. During the lesson observe social interactions within the groups.

Reflect on the following points:

1. How are the pupils arranged in the room? Does the arrangement of the pupils encourage or discourage teamwork? Does the teacher rearrange the pupils or the room at any stage to promote effective teamwork?
2. What is the nature of the tasks that involve teamwork? Eg written work, discussion, practical work, presentation?
3. How are the teams organized? Eg same sex, mixed ability, friendship groups, teacher directed?
4. Do the teams change during the lesson?
5. How is the lesson's work divided between the teams?
6. How does the teacher deal with those pupils who want to dominate or take a back seat in the team?

After the lesson you may take the opportunity to discuss with the teacher if developing the skills of teamwork was a key aim of the lesson. If it was, discuss how the teacher promoted that aim throughout the lesson and how the teacher evaluated his or her success in meeting that aim.

A good science lesson will always include discussion and debate of concepts, data, evidence and theory. The importance of pupils fully understanding the crucial difference between evidence and theory has been a source of much recent discussion (Duschl, 2000). Understanding concepts is also dependent upon pupils being able to restate concepts in their own language in order to explain phenomena in new contexts. Sadly much of the good work done by teachers in KS2 is overlooked when students enter KS3 where knowledge is presented as a series of sacred facts to be memorized and not questioned. Science lessons should be places of questioning and debate where students use their scientific knowledge to plan and explain patterns in data they have collected. This is reflected in Section 1 of the National Curriculum, which places a requirement on students to use their knowledge to design and carry out investigations. The development in pupils of the skills of discussion and debate is arguably dependent upon the teacher possessing adequate questioning skills and this is discussed more fully in Chapter 7.

Reason four: Science is interesting and intellectually stimulating

Ironically, interest and intellectual stimulation are often overlooked when discussing curriculum aims. Science can be (and often is) fun! It can provide a sense of wonder, marvel, awe, surprise, curiosity, confidence and pleasure. It can excite, stimulate and motivate. Watching the fascination on pupils' faces when a piece of sodium is added to water is perhaps sufficient reason, or justification, to complete this demonstration. Emotion has a central role to play in learning, as we go on to discuss in Chapter 4. It has important implications as Millar and Osborne point out:

> The science curriculum should sustain and develop the curiosity of young people about the natural world around them, and build up their confidence to inquire into its behaviour. It should seek to foster a sense of wonder, enthusiasm and interest in science so young people feel confident to engage with scientific and technical matters.
>
> (Millar and Osborne, 1998: 5)

The implication of this is that there needs to be a shift from emphasizing the value of scientific knowledge and claiming that it is going to be intrinsically useful to our pupils in their future life, to using it to excite an interest in the workings of the natural world and build confidence. For instance, a knowledge of the chemical equations for photosynthesis is unlikely ever to be of much use in our pupils' future lives, yet this tends to be prioritized over the knowledge of the importance of photosynthesis in maintaining the balance of gases in our atmosphere. Many of the themes that excite people such as the nature of life, relationships between living things, the nature of matter and the origin of the Universe are important areas of scientific study, yet does school science really address and capitalize on the interest people have in these issues? It is a challenge to us as science teachers to present science in a way that promotes an interest in the natural world as opposed to presenting a large collection of abstract, difficult to understand concepts that have to be written down and committed to memory.

Without doubt, science is intellectually stimulating. Here we might usefully distinguish between an education-*in*-science and education-*through*-science. Perhaps what we are suggesting is that science provides an ideal context for intellectual development. This is certainly the argument made by the CASE (Cognitive Acceleration through Science Education) team and we discuss their work in more detail in Chapter 4.

Reason five: Science is an important part of contemporary culture and is relevant to, and has implications for, people of all nations

When we talk about human culture there is a tendency to classify it in terms of great works of art or architecture but some of our truly great achievements have been in the field of science. Through science we have come to understand much about the Universe around us and to assess our place in that Universe. Science has been able to explain the Universe in a way described by laws and empirical relationships that have become embedded into our culture and are reflected in art and literature. With scientific ideas being so central to our culture it is important for young people to be able to understand the 'big ideas' so that they can grasp and engage with their cultural heritage. Millar and Osborne point out that a key role of the science teacher is to:

> Help young people acquire a broad, general understanding of the important ideas and explanatory frameworks of science, and of the procedures of scientific inquiry, which have had a major impact on our material environment and on our culture in general.
>
> (Millar and Osborne, 1998: 8)

Practical Task Pupils' views on the aims of science

In this chapter we have explored some of the arguments concerning the aims of science education. But what do pupils think the aims of science education are? To explore this question, we suggest you try out the following activity with a group of students:

1. Ask a small group of pupils to write down what they think the aims of science education are.
2. Ask each of the pupils to read out one of their aims and write it up on a flipchart or piece of sugar paper for all to see. Go round the group to see if you can come up with an agreed list.
3. Discuss with the pupils the extent to which they feel these aims are met through their science lessons.

The nature of science and the nature of school science

There is a key argument that school science should provide a means whereby students become aware of the nature of science such that as future citizens they are aware of the power and limitations of scientific knowledge claims. An awareness of the capacity and potential of science as well as its fallibility is important in making decisions of a personal and democratic nature, particularly given that in the public eye science seems to hold a mantle of authority – a provider of reliable, pure and certain knowledge. After all who actually questions their doctor or rejects medical advice? Advertising giants use a questionable image of science to suppress doubts in phrases like 'scientifically tested' or 'scientifically proven'. 'Here comes the science,' announces Jennifer Aniston in a contemporary shampoo advertisement. The misrepresentation of a scientist as a wise white male involved in the meticulous and logical pursuit of certainty is also widely recognized and commonly depicted in younger pupils' drawings. Some writers refer to the over-selling and valuing of science as 'scientism'. Others claim that science has no more claim to authority and certainty than a useful myth or story. In our post-modern society, some post-modern authors maintain, the ideology of science is bankrupt, on the point of breaking down.

What is the actual nature of science and scientific knowledge? Does science have its limitations or can it give ultimate answers? Is science progressing inexorably towards the truth? Or is science more like a modern myth? What image of science do we (and should we) present in the classroom?

These questions as you might imagine are complex and widely discussed. Unfortunately, there is insufficient space in a text of this nature to explore the diverse and multifarious field of science studies. However, we strongly urge you to read about the nature of science because it features in the Science National Curriculum (in Section 1) and also, it has been suggested, because how you think about these issues influences how you teach. We have included a number of texts at the end of the chapter, to help you to explore these issues further.

It is also important to remember that children also have ideas and beliefs about science. Circular 4/98 for new teachers (DfEE, 1998a: 9) lists some common misconceptions of pupils about the nature of science (and scientists) that all new teachers should be aware of. These are summarized in Table 3.1.

Table 3.1 Common misconceptions of pupils about the nature of science

Pupils' misconception	*Widely accepted viewpoint*
Thinking that scientific theories are incontestable and true for all time	Although some pieces of knowledge are more secure that others, all scientific knowledge is open to challenge and revision
Thinking that all scientific knowledge is generated by experiment and data collection	In fact many ideas are new and creative explanations of observed phenomena, eg the theory of evolution and plate tectonics
Thinking scientists make judgements in isolation	In practice many decisions involve ethical, social and economic factors, eg whether to use animals for experiments, whether to develop weapons technology
Thinking that science offers solutions to problems	Not realizing that while the application of science may offer the solution to some problems it may be the cause of others

As a teacher of science, the curriculum requires you to find out about, explore and extend children's ideas, images and beliefs about science. Arguably, before you can do this you need to have considered your nature of science and the nature of science implied by, and stated within, the curriculum. When viewed in this way, teaching about the nature of science involves bringing together and discussing a series of opinions and beliefs about 'your nature of science', 'pupils' nature of science' and the 'nature of science implied by the curriculum'. Like many aspects of classroom practice, when you start to scratch beneath the surface things become more complex. Teaching science is far more complicated than simply recounting a series of theories, laws and formulae!

Further reading

Black, P (1993) The purposes of science education, in *Challenges and Opportunities for Science Education*, ed E Whitelegg, J Thomas and S Tresman, Paul Chapman Publishing Ltd, London

Department for Education and Employment (DfEE) (1998) *Requirements for Courses of Initial Teacher Training*, Circular 4/98, DfEE, London

Millar, R and Osborne, J (eds) (1998) *Beyond 2000: Science education for the future*, King's College School of Education, London

Roberts, D (1988) What counts as science education, in *Development and Dilemmas in Science Education*, ed P Fensham, Falmer Press, London

Selected readings on the nature of science:

Barnes, B (1985) *About Science*, Blackwell, New York

Chalmers, A (1999) *What is This Thing Called Science?*, 3rd edn, Open University Press, Buckingham

Collins, H and Pinch, T (1993) *The Golem: What everyone should know about science*, Cambridge University Press, Cambridge

Couvalis, G (1997) *The Philosophy of Science: Science and objectivity*, Sage, London

Gould, S J (1989) *Wonderful Life: The burgess shale and the nature of history*, Hutchinson, London

Latour, B (1987) *Science in Action*, Harvard University Press, Cambridge, MA

Levinson, R and Thomas, J (1997) *Science Today: Problem or crisis?*, Routledge, London

Selected readings on teaching and learning about the nature of science in schools:

Driver, R, Leach, J, Millar, R and Scott, P (1996) *Young People's Images of Science*, Open University Press, Buckingham

Mathews, M (1994) *Science Teaching: The role of the history and philosophy of science*, Routledge, London

Nott, M (1994) Practical approaches to teaching and learning about the nature of science, in *Secondary Science: Contemporary issues and practical approaches*, ed J Wellington, Routledge, London

Osborne, J (1998) Learning and teaching about the nature of science, in *ASE Guide to Secondary Science Education*, ed M Ratcliffe, Stanley Thornes, Cheltenham

4 Learning science

Steve Alsop

Teacher: *Gravity is the force that keeps things on the ground and at the surface of the Earth it exerts a force of 9.81 Newtons, nearly 10N, on a one-kilogram mass. This is the figure you have been measuring today. Actually, the further you go away from the Earth the weaker gravity becomes...*
James: *Yes... I get it sir. Yes, that makes sense because that's how aircraft fly – when they get up in the air they have less gravity acting on them.*

(An exchange recorded during a year 9 science lesson on forces)

Objectives

This chapter facilitates critical reflection on how children learn science. More specifically, the chapter introduces, in relation to science:

- constructivist models of learning including:
- Piaget's theory of learning;
- children's ideas;
- learning as conceptual change;
- Vygotsky's theory of learning.

Introduction

Many pupils find science demanding – they find it difficult to understand relatively fundamental concepts. They can develop confused ideas even when a teacher feels they have explained a subject clearly and precisely. Teachers are often surprised at how little pupils know at the end of a module. They are also frequently concerned with underachievement in examinations.

Recent research has questioned the way that we view teaching and learning. In the past, and possibly to a lesser extent today, the curriculum or subject content dominated how teachers thought about science teaching. Teaching was viewed mainly in terms of the science concepts to the exclusion of how children think and learn. Recent studies have highlighted the importance of teachers understanding how children learn. To teach children successfully requires an understanding of how children think and construct scientific knowledge as well as a thorough understanding of science.

There is a considerable difference between teaching and learning – it is possible to teach and there not be learning, conversely it is possible to learn when there has been no teaching. It is also possible, as any teacher will tell you and as the opening quotation illustrates, to teach one thing and for pupils to learn something quite different. Learning is an internal process that takes place within the mind, whereas teaching is an external, social event that is usually classroom-based. Nevertheless teaching and learning are clearly connected – an understanding of science might be attributed to previous teachers' instructional ability or perhaps considerable patience.

Understanding how children learn has an important part to play in successful teaching because it provides the basis for successful planning and evaluating. There are many claims about science teaching, for example that science is intrinsically a hard subject, that it is always important to start with concrete examples and then move to more abstract concepts. Without an understanding of learning it is difficult to judge the validity of such claims.

We all have our own preferences for learning and teaching; how we learn best for an examination or perhaps a favoured teaching style or approach. However, often the theories underpinning these preferences remain tacit. When starting to teach it is important to articulate and explore your own views of learning as these will influence how you teach. As the psychologist Von Glaserfeld (1991: 22) maintains 'to lead pupils, children and students to some form of understanding, the teacher must have some notion of how they think'. This is the focus of this chapter.

Before starting, you might wish to reflect on your best ways of learning science. You might also reflect upon how science could be taught to nurture your learning preferences. In the following quotation, Vicky, a trainee science teacher, articulates her early thoughts on science teaching and learning:

> Prior to my practice, I thought that teaching would involve telling students about my favourite subject, biology. I guess my view of learning was simply that I would say something and the class would learn it. This is my memory of my biology classes, but as a pupil, I guess, you have little idea about what goes on behind the scenes. I now realise that there is much more to teaching than simply telling pupils a load of facts about your favourite subject.
>
> (Vicky: Trainee science teacher)

Theory Task Evaluating your own views on science teaching and learning

How do your views contrast with Vicky's? What is the model of learning and teaching that Vicky initially advocates and then rejects?

This chapter aims to give a brief introduction to a number of contemporary theories of learning – theories that have had a significant influence on school science education. In addressing such a complex question as how people learn, it should not come as a surprise that there exist a range of conflicting and competing theories. The chapter starts by discussing 'constructivism', presently the dominant way of thinking about learning. So, what do we know about how children learn science?

Observation Task Talking and listening to children

Although this chapter covers a number of contemporary theories we cannot stress enough the importance of combining your reading with classroom observations. You need to seek opportunities where you can listen, watch and talk to children about their learning. You should observe and talk to children while working at science, ask them to explain their ideas as well as how they prefer to learn. Try to arrange time to talk to a group of pupils about their scientific interests, the parts of science that they find conceptually difficult (or easy). You might also explore any concerns or anxieties they might have about learning science, or lessons that they have particularly enjoyed. A good way to find out about children is to talk and listen to them!

Constructivism

Vicki's comments give insight into different ways of looking at teaching and learning. Learning could be viewed as simply remembering (recording) and restating what is said. This is often referred to as 'learning-by-rote', or 'drill-and-practise'. It might have been the way that you learned tables in mathematics or verbs in French. Learning, in these instances, was a case of remembering – perhaps repeating something over and over again until it is finally internalized. In this model, there is little need for a teacher to consider what is going on in the learners' minds other than perhaps to monitor whether the learning has occurred (or not). The emphasis here is placed firmly on the subject material. Learning is the *transmission* of information from source (teacher or textbook) to mind – in some ways analogous to information being transmitted via a telephone call (see Figure 4.1).

Incidentally, this way of thinking about learning has become embedded in our everyday language. We often talk about learning as though we are acquiring an *object*: we grasp a concept, capture an idea, or we are consumed by a thought. Is learning simply acquiring something as these metaphors imply?

Looking at learning in this way stresses the passivity of the mind. It has become associated with studies of behaviourism and stimulus response psychology. Skinner's (1976) work on rats' memory, for example, is a perfect illustration of a study (and may be familiar to readers who have studied behavioural biology). Skinner explored how animals can be trained to perform simple tasks by rewarding them. He claimed that this work has important messages for how pupils learn in schools. Would you agree?

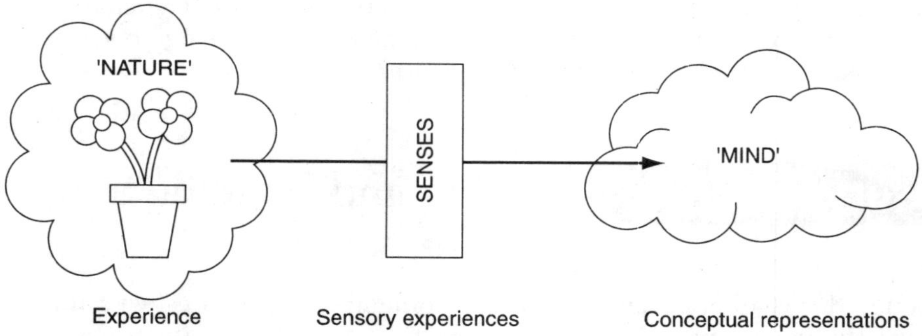

Figure 4.1 A transmission model of learning

In the past, behaviourist views of learning have been popular, however more recently in science education they have been questioned. There has been a shift in thinking about learning and teaching towards a view where learning is seen not as a *passive* representation (a recording) but as an *active* reconstruction and reinterpretation of experiences. We should think of knowledge as being actively built up by learners as they interpret a learning experience – see Figure 4.2. This is a constructivist view of learning.

The educational literature on constructivism is enormous and rapidly growing. Inevitably, there are considerable disagreements in the field. Nevertheless, all constructivists would agree on the principle that knowledge is actively constructed. As Piaget, for example, writes: 'Fifty years of experience have taught us that knowledge does not result from a mere recording of observations without a structuring activity on the part of the subject' (Piaget 1980: 23). Twenty years earlier, Dewey had commented: 'If we see that knowing is not the act of an outside spectator but of a participator inside the natural and social scene, then the true object of knowledge resides in the consequences of directed action' (Dewey, 1960: 196).

For these theorists, learning is viewed as an interaction between the learner and the learning environment. During this interaction, prior knowledge is used as a basis to

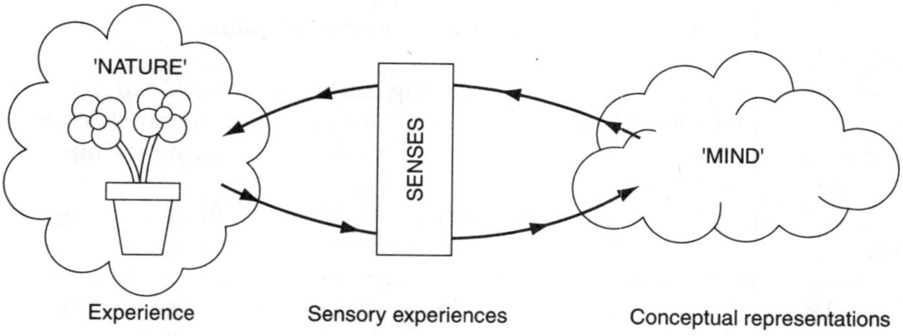

Figure 4.2 A constructivist view of learning

interpret and construct new understandings. In effect, learning is a process in which the learner uses existing knowledge as a basis to interpret and construct new ideas. The science educationist, Rosalind Driver, (1989: 32) writes: 'The key feature of a constructivist epistemology is that humans beings construct mental models of their world and new experiences are interpreted and understood in relation to existing mental models or schemes.'

Observation Task Groups or individuals

Although in educational circles constructivism is warmly promoted, there is considerable diversity and debate in the field. Some authors are troubled by the philosophical basis of the model (see Mathews, 1994), while others debate the importance of the individual or the group in knowledge construction.

Try to spend some time observing children learning science. How important is the learning environment and how does this shape and structure learning? Is learning an individual or social enterprise, or is it both? What is the balance between the individual and social aspects? Do different teachers facilitate learning environments that are more individual or social? Which type of emphasis will you promote in your classroom and why? Do different environments suit different aspects of science?

Despite the continuing debates, during the last decade or so, constructivism has had a profound effect on science teaching and for the rest of this chapter, we consider some prominent constructivist theories of children's learning.

When starting to teach it is easy to get the level wrong, you can assume too much, or assume too little. Often, new teachers fail to recognize the complexity of the science curriculum and the multitude of different ways that pupils interpret their lessons. But how can you get the level right? Is there a right level? What makes science complex or indeed demanding? Would it be possible to simplify a scientific concept in such a way that it can be understood by all – even, for instance, by pupils who have only a limited experience of science or are at a young age? If we had the most perfect educational environment, would primary school children be able to understand Einstein's theory of relativity? Or is learning age dependent and determinate?

The work of Piaget has had a fundamental influence on science teaching and his theories aid an exploration of these questions.

Developmental psychology

Piaget (1896–1980) is perhaps the best-known developmental psychologist. His theories were derived from studies of children, at early ages, as they matured and developed forms of knowledge and understanding. Piaget's work is extensive and contains a rich and detailed discussion of children's ideas of specific areas of knowledge. His writings are extensive (over

50 books) and cover a range of subjects, evolutionary biology, developmental psychology and epistemology. Perhaps for this reason his work is often misinterpreted.

Many science educators have focused on a particular aspect of Piaget's work – his stage theory. For Piaget, learning is developmental and, as children develop, their thinking passes through distinct stages – each stage is characterized by a particular mode of thought. There are four stages in total. The three phases relating to school ages are briefly summarized in Table 4.1.

In some of his writing Piaget attached *indicative* ages to a stage (as included above), however chronological ages, of course, cannot be an *exact* measure of developmental age. Individual children might pass through stages sooner or later depending on their experiences. Recent examples of primary school children achieving Advanced Level qualifications in mathematics and computer science serve as a good illustration of the difference between developmental and chronological age. Although not age dependent, Piaget claimed that his stages were sequential. It is necessary to progress through each of the four stages in the set order – they build on each other. According to Piaget, intellectual development is graduated – what children learn at any given time will depend upon the mental stage of their development.

Piaget's theories gave science educators a new way of looking at learning and his theories have been used as a basis for many school science activities. For example the School

Table 4.1 Piagetian stages

Stage	*Characterization*
Stage 2: Pre-operational (from about 2 years to 6 years)	Being able to represent things mentally enables the child to develop a set of mental operations for acting on the world. In this stage things are believed to be exactly as they are perceived – *modelling for instance is not possible.*
Stage 3: Concrete operational (from about 6 to 12 years)	In this stage the child is consolidating and extending the range of operations. These operations are primarily linked to 'concrete' objects in the real world – however at the end of this stage, it becomes possible for the child to start to 'operate' on 'operations'. In this stage, for instance, children can use models that involve simple comparisons – *simple modelling is possible such as increasing the height of the ramp results in the car travelling further.*
Stage 4: Formal operational (from the age of 12 onwards)	The ability to 'operate' on 'operations', to internally manipulate thoughts about the world, allows the child to deal with abstract and hypothetical scenarios. In this stage, the child develops a system of abstract operations for manipulating the concrete operations developed during the previous stage. *At the end of this stage it is possible for students to design simple experiments and formulate qualitative relationships between variables (such as force = mass × acceleration). They can also think using abstract models such as the particulate theory of matter.*

Council Science 5–13 project adopted a Piagetian framework and these highly influential resources, now perhaps slightly faded, are still in use in UK primary and middle schools. The CASE project also adopts a Piagetian framework and this is explored in more detail in the following pages.

Stages and curriculum demands

Piaget's stage theory can be used to consider some of the questions raised at the start of this section. It offers a way of matching the demands of the curriculum with the conceptual or intellectual ability of pupils. Shayer and Adey (1981) have performed this type of 'matching activity' and their studies highlight a mismatch between the demands of the curriculum and the developmental level of the students. The science curriculum, they note, often requires formal operational thinking while many pupils are still reasoning concretely. Shayer and Adey's observations have been supported by other studies from around the world. Incidentally, it has also been noted that many highly educated adults perform badly on tasks involving abstract formal thinking (see Evans, 1989).

Observation Task Is school science too hard?

Using Table 4.1, consider the intellectual demands of the science concepts that you are teaching. Using your experiences, do you feel the curriculum is too advanced? What aspects in particular require abstract reasoning and when are these introduced?

Shayer and Adey's analysis highlights the potential difficulty of many science concepts. However, it should not be taken to imply that teachers should sit back and wait for children to become intellectually ready before addressing demanding concepts. As Bruner (1986: 29) notes, readiness is something that is nurtured – 'one does not simply wait for it'.

Cognitive acceleration

Building on their previous work, Shayer and Adey have developed an intervention programme based on Piagetian Stages: CASE – the *Cognitive Acceleration through Science Education* project (Adey, Shayer and Yates, 1989, Adey and Shayer, 1994). Materials from the project have been packaged together as a series of teaching activities (entitled *Thinking Science*) and are becoming extremely popular in secondary schools. The activities aim to develop thinking from concrete to formal operational – the requirement, they suggest, necessary to achieve a grade D or above in GCSE science. The claim is that the CASE materials have significant long-term effects on examination results some two or three years after the intervention. The researchers report students who have studied the programme and received higher grades in GCSE science and mathematics as well as KS3 science, mathematics and English SATs when compared with a control group. Other researchers are sceptical and offer alternative explanations for the long-term effects (see discussion in Bliss, 1995). CASE materials are widely available in schools (further details are available on the Web site http://www.case-net.org.uk).

We recommend that you find out more about the CASE project – are the materials in use in your school or in colleagues' schools?

Individual or social development?

Piaget concentrated on the development of individual children's thinking and reasoning about their physical environment. His theories were not concerned so much with social development and this has been an area of criticism. Critics highlight the importance of social and cultural dimensions and the subject-specific nature of learning. Donaldson (1978) claims, for instance, that social and intellectual development are much more intertwined and all Piagetian tasks have important social dimensions that have to be accounted for. When teaching, for example, it is important, as every teacher will tell you, to make science content relevant – both socially and intellectually. You need to make references to situations that children are familiar with. You must cover unfamiliar concepts in familiar contexts. Why? Because we all find it easier to solve abstract problems in familiar contexts and settings. In other words, intellectual demands are also context dependent. By changing the context of Piagetian tasks, Donaldson argues, it is possible for children to display reasoning that is absent in tasks set in unfamiliar contexts.

Observation Task Familiar contexts and unfamiliar concepts

How do experienced teachers make concepts relevant? Can you think of a good instance of relevance from your recent observations?

Multiple intelligences

Howard Gardner (1983) suggests that we should view intelligence in broader terms than simply as logical reasoning. Initially, Gardner proposed seven different intelligences (more recently he has added additional ones, see Gardner 1999). Intelligence, Gardner suggests, can be mapped onto a variety of different human abilities and all humans have differing amounts of and preferences for these abilities. Gardner's original seven intelligences are:

1. logical – mathematical intelligence: the capacity to handle mathematical patterns and long chains of reasoning;
2. linguistic intelligence: the capacity to use language, both written and oral;

3. spatial intelligence: the capacity to perceive the visual spatial world and to transform perceptions spatially;
4. bodily – kinaesthetic: the capacity to control one's bodily movements and to handle objects skilfully;
5. musical intelligence: the capacity to produce and appreciate music;
6. interpersonal intelligence: the capacity to be aware of and sensitive towards the emotions of others;
7. intra-personal intelligence: the ability to understand one's own knowledge strengths, weaknesses, desires and intelligence.

Gardner's theories have become popular in education reform, particularly in primary schools. Curricula materials and whole school programmes have been developed that explicitly aim to develop and enhance each type of intelligence and multiple intelligence assessment tasks have also been formulated.

Practice Task Planning for multiple intelligences

A message from Gardner's work is that we should seek to use different intelligences in our science teaching. With this in mind, consider the intelligences that you foster in your science teaching. How could you enhance your lessons to access a wider range of intelligences?

Children's ideas and conceptual change

In science education, investigating children's ideas has become a popular and rich research pursuit. Over the past two decades or so, studies have revealed that children's ideas are often alternative to standard science. In the past, these ideas might have been dismissed as mistakes or errors, perhaps resulting from confusion, examination nerves or lack of revision time. However, what now has emerged is that these 'errors' are not just random guesses but are children's representations of scientific concepts. From a constructivist perspective, if you recall, learners are seen as developing ideas through an active process in which current ideas have a fundamental role. In this light, children's ideas become highly significant as they potentially form the basis of future thinking and understanding. Researchers have explored, collected and catalogued a vast array of children's alternative ideas (or conceptions) of scientific concepts (see for instance Driver *et al*, 1994 and Pfundt and Druit, 1994).

Osborne and Freyberg (1985) conducted some early research of this type in New Zealand. They asked different groups ('average ability' 11-year-olds, trainee and experienced teachers and biology graduates) the meaning of the word animal. Participants were provided with a series of pictures (a seagull, cow, spider, worm, grass, cat, mushroom, cod, frog, boy, snail, elephant, snake, fire, lion, whale, car, tree and butterfly) and asked 'Is it an animal?' In orthodox scientific terms only the grass, mushroom, fire, car and tree would not be animals. Samples of their data are provided in Table 4.2.

Table 4.2 After Osborne and Freyberg (1985) – Is it an animal? (percentages cited)

	11-year-olds (N = 49)	*Primary teacher trainees* (N = 34)	*Experienced primary teachers* (N = 53)	*University biology students* (N = 67)
Cow	98	100	100	100
Boy	57	94	96	100
Worm	37	77	86	99
Spider	22	65	86	97
Grass	0	0	0	0

The word animal is commonly used in school science, often without formal definition. It seems from these results that many 11-year-olds, as well as a few primary teachers and biology graduates have alternative conceptions of this concept.

The researchers conducted similar studies exploring the questions: 'What is a plant?' and 'Is it living?' Their results also indicate confusion: perhaps surprisingly, many 11-year-olds maintain that a vegetable is not a plant and that the Sun and clouds are both living.

Practice Task Is it an animal, plant or alive?

Try Osborne and Freyberg's activity out with the classes you teach. What are your students' concepts of animals, plants and living things? Can you think of any other common words that we use in science that have potentially multiple meanings?

In some cases, confusions would seem to emanate from our use of language. In everyday language we use terms like animal, plant and fire loosely. We talk about a live electrical wire or a fire that is still alive and smouldering. In science, however, these terms have clear definitions. That is not to say, of course, that in science we are not also guilty of having different meanings for words in different contexts. We use the word *plant* in the context of a nuclear power *plant* and as Hodson (1998) notes *molar, nucleus* and *cell* have quite different meanings in biology and chemistry classes! Chapter 13 explores the use of language in science classrooms in more detail. In other instances, children's alternative ideas seem not to stem from linguistic ambiguities but from everyday informal sensory experiences. From an early age, for instance, we build up models of how objects behave when they are dropped, pushed, twisted and thrown. These ideas, needless to say, are quite different when compared with a Newtonian view of the world.

Sometimes our everyday experiences are useful in science classrooms. However, in other cases our out of school experiences and ideas run contrary to scientific thinking and as a consequence can lead to conceptual confusion. The Children's Learning in Science team (CLIS) (Johnston *et al*, 1990: 21) suggest some children's ideas that science teachers should watch out for (Table 4.3).

Table 4.3 Common conceptual confusions among children

Concept	*Confusions*
Air	• Air is weightless or has a negative weight • Vacuums 'suck'
Heat	• Heat is a kind of substance • The temperature of an object depends on the kind of stuff it is made of (eg metals are cold, plastics are warm) • Heat and temperature are not differentiated
Energy	• Energy is primarily associated with human action/motion • Energy gets used up
Matter	• Matter disappears when substances dissolve or burn
Particles	• Macroscopic properties given to microscopic particles (particles melt, expand...) • The space between particles is not empty
Plant nutrition	• Plants obtain their food from the environment in the same way as animals (ie it is ready made) • Plants take in food through their roots. • Food for plants includes anything they take in, eg air, water, fertilisers and sunlight
Electricity	• Electricity gets used up as it goes round a circuit
Light	• Light travels further at night than in daytime

Experienced teachers may be familiar with many of these ideas – but others they might find surprising. When starting to teach it is essential that you provide opportunities in your classroom to find out about children's ideas, to listen to how children talk and think about different scientific concepts. Do not assume that just because you have not covered a topic that pupils do not know anything about it. We recommend that you find out more about the research on children's ideas – particularly those ideas associated with topics that you are teaching. Further reading, for this purpose, is recommended at the end of this chapter.

Practice Task Finding out about children's ideas

Try to spend time finding out about children's ideas. Schedule some time to talk with children about a topic before you start teaching. You might wish to arrange discussions with a small group of pupils to explore their ideas.

Gravity on the Moon?

Pictures and cartoons can provide an excellent way of initiating discussions about science concepts – try to incorporate them in your science teaching. My personal favourite, after Watts (1983), is depicted in Figure 4.3, entitled *Gravity*. Compare your responses with friends and colleagues. In my experience, this picture never fails to provide a revealing discussion about gravity on the Moon. In this case, perhaps the most interesting question to consider is why different people respond in different ways. What models lie beneath their reasoning?

Teaching with children's ideas in mind

The recognition of children's ideas about science and the important role that these have in learning science has led to a number of innovative teaching initiatives (for example, see Osborne and Freyberg, 1985; Scott *et al*, 1987; Russell and Watt, 1990). These initiatives explicitly recognize the existence of children's ideas prior to teaching, and learning science is considered as a process of changing, restructuring, adapting or adding to these ideas. Viewed in this way, learning science concepts is a process of *conceptual change and addition*. And central to teaching with this agenda in mind is understanding how and why children 'change' their ideas, as Driver (1989: 80) notes: 'If it is accepted that learning involves the restructuring of students' conceptions, then not only do educators need to appreciate the ideas that children bring to the learning situation, but they need to understand the processes by which conceptual change occurs in order that this can be taken into account in the design of learning programmes.'

Driver and colleagues (Driver 1989; Scott and Leach, 1998) suggest a popular 'constructivist' teaching sequence that offers a means of restructuring children's ideas (Figure 4.4).

The Nuffield SPACE (Science Processes and Conceptual Exploration) project and the Oxford Science programme are two, amongst many, teaching schemes that broadly adhere to the above pedagogical framework. They are widely available in both primary and secondary schools.

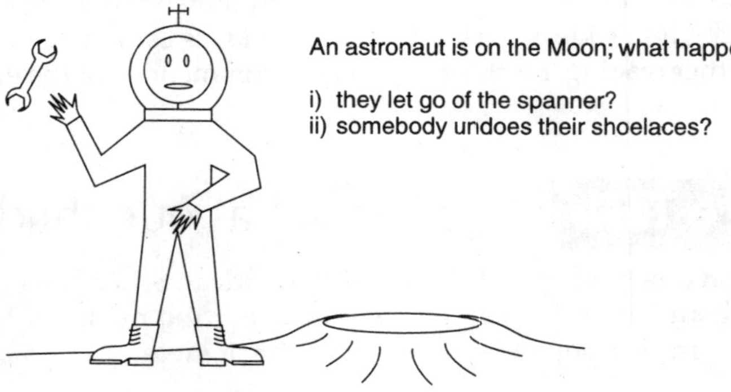

Figure 4.3 Gravity
Source: Watts (1983)

Phase	Overview
Orientation	Teacher introduces the topic
Elicitation of Ideas	Opportunities are provided for pupils to explore and explain their ideas
Restructuring of ideas	
Clarification and exchange	Pupils are given a chance to recognize scientific ideas and examine their own ideas
Exposure to conflict situations	Pupils are provided with situations in which to test their ideas and recognize the limitations of these ideas
Construction of new ideas	Opportunities are provided for pupils to restructure (extend, modify or replace) their ideas
Evaluation	Pupils are provided with opportunities to test out the validity of their newly constructed ideas
Application of ideas	Pupils are provided with opportunities to apply their ideas in new situations – to reinforce these ideas
Review change in ideas	Pupils are provided opportunities to reflect upon how and why their ideas have changed

Figure 4.4 A constructivist teaching approach
Source: Driver (1989: 88)

Practice Task Reflecting on schemes of work and teaching

Consider the teaching schemes available in your school – do they take into account children's ideas? Can you identify phases, such as those above? How does your teaching build on children's ideas?

There is much to commend the constructivist frameworks documented above and we recommend that you try to incorporate the phases into your teaching. However, there have been some concerns raised about the type of restructuring that occurs in science lessons and the overly mechanical image the above framework presents of teaching and learning. It is often implied that successful constructivist teaching involves the replacement of children's ideas with more scientific ones. This is a bold claim that is clearly both impractical and unrealistic. Children's alternative ideas about science enable them to function outside of the classroom. They are ideas that have been tested out and developed from the day they were born. It is simply not appropriate, or for that matter possible, to remove these ideas. Instead as Reiss (1993) notes, as science teachers we should:

> prefer a frame of thinking in which a teacher started from the assumption that all pupils come to science lessons with ways of thinking *that have so far served them well*. The aim of a science lesson would be to enable pupils to see *why* their thinking often works, and to allow those pupils who want to *develop* their thinking, not so much by having it proved wrong to them, but by pursuing it into new ideas.
>
> (Reiss, 1993: 39, emphasis in original)

Another concern is the role of emotions and feelings in learning. Is learning always as logical and emotionally detached as the above framework implies?

Learning and feeling

There is a difference between the ability to learn and learning. There are numerous occasions in science lessons, for instance, where children are able to understand a scientific concept (they have sufficient experience) but simply choose not to. I suspect that there have been instances in all our lives when we have preferred not to embrace an idea or avoided thinking too deeply about something. The important question here is why? For instance, why do some pupils continue to study after a succession of defeats while others give up before even starting? Research has only just started to address this question. To speculate for a moment, there are likely to be a host of possible reasons – a lack of confidence, a fear of failure, low self-esteem, a rejection of the school system, a lack of interest in, or a rejection of science. Each learner has his or her own complex emotional agenda. Emotions can be sparked by an incident – an event – in the playground or in a lesson. As we all know, learning can be difficult if you are upset and have something else on your mind. Conversely, if children are enthused, interested and motivated they can achieve beyond their teacher's expectations. There are some areas of science that arouse strong emotions; animal experimentation, sex education, GMF, radioactivity and pollution are all potentially emotive subjects that can lead to heated classroom discussion and debate. Strong emotions can, in some cases, switch pupils on to science, but for others they can turn pupils away (see Alsop and Watts, 2000). Other areas of science are potentially more emotionally remote; the periodic table, forces and plants, etc, are not topics that perhaps immediately get the blood running! Often the trick in such cases is to make these subjects more emotionally engaging – more interesting and motivating.

It should be emphasized that the science classroom is a social arena with many potential social tensions. Claxton (1989) in an article aptly entitled 'Cognition doesn't matter if you're scared, depressed or bored' describes a set of social stances that give rise to different learning approaches:

- the *boffin* stance – the pupil seeks deep understanding;
- the *socialite* stance – the pupil is as interested in the gossip going on in the classroom as in listening to the teacher;
- the *dreamer* stance – the pupil is involved in his or her own inner world;
- the *rebel* stance – the pupil seeks peer approval by challenging authority.

I can look back at my own experience of teaching and put names to these stances – can you? Perhaps the significant point here is that learners have emotional needs as well as cognitive needs and as a teacher you will need to address these. A 'learning block' can be as much emotional as intellectual (see Alsop and Watts, 2000).

Getting social: The science classroom as a learning community

Learning, up to this point, has essentially been considered as an individual pursuit – almost Robinson Crusoe-like in style. We have explored theories of how individuals learn science and proposed some teaching approaches that originate from these theories. There are many authors, however, who would be critical of our emphasis; they would maintain that above all humans are social beings and learning is quintessentially a social act. The social constructivist, Vygotsky (1988), for instance, maintains that how we think by ourselves as adults is a product of a fundamentally social process. Cognitive development, he claims, originates in social interaction and is inextricably linked with language. We know ourselves, through the interactions that we have with others, that we become *enculturated* into society.

Vygotsky (1988) noted that when children worked under the guidance of a more experienced peer (or adult) they were able to achieve more; they could perform tasks that were at a higher level compared with working alone. This view of learning sees the developing children not so much in terms of what they can do on their own but rather, in terms of what they can achieve when they are given help.

In Vygotskian terms, the child is considered to have a *zone of proximal development* (ZPD); a raft of activities that they can achieve with the help and support of an adult but not on their own. Vygotsky (1978) describes the ZPD as:

> The difference between twelve and eight, or between nine and eight, is what we call the zone of proximal development. It is the distance between the actual development level as determined by problem solving and the level of potential development as determined through problem solving under the guidance or in collaboration with more capable peers.
>
> (Vygotsky, 1978: 86)

One possible representation of a ZPD is depicted in Figure 4.5 (see over). Significantly, viewed in this way, teaching leads to development. As science teachers, Vygotsky would

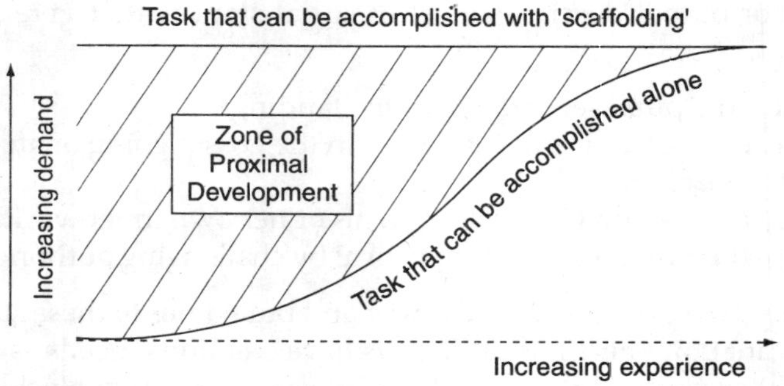

Figure 4.5 A possible representation of a ZPD

argue, we should provide opportunities for our pupils to engage in scientific activities in advance of their current individual achievements but within the boundaries of the ZPD. Vygotsky's views emphasize the importance of teaching; intellectual development is seen as a process of teaching and learning that involves a social exchange in which meanings are shared between teacher and student until the student is able to work on his or her own. In this context, the term *scaffolding* has been used to describe the role of teaching (Wood *et al*, 1976). As Bruner (1985: 25) writes: 'the tutor in effect performs the critical function of "scaffolding" the learning task to make it possible for the child, in Vygotsky's words, to internalize external knowledge and convert it into a tool for conscious control.'

During scaffolding, the teacher does not adjust the task but offers support and guidance in such a way that the learners are able to extend their intellectual range. 'Scaffolding' can come in a variety of forms, depending on the nature of the task. Teachers might, for instance: highlight important features of a task; make the task meaningful in terms of what pupils' already know; establish a familiar context for a task; split a task into a series of manageable stages, or reduce mathematical or linguistic complexity. Furthermore, scaffolding could also entail an affective component – for instance, making a task emotionally and socially appealing, reducing stress and anxiety and creating a classroom environment that is supportive and conducive of learning.

Although the language of Vygotsky may be new, we suspect that these aspects of classroom practice are very familiar from your observations. Throughout this text we will suggest a wide range of techniques that are associated with good scaffolding. Of course, as the competence of the child increases, the teacher needs to gradually remove support (or scaffold) and the timing of this is both sensitive and crucial – judging when learners are ready to work on their own requires considerable care and expertise.

Observation Task A Vygotsky observation task

Try to find time to observe a series of science lessons and think about the Vygotskian framework presented above. Talk to a small group of children about their science lessons and the concepts that they are studying with the aim of trying to conceptualize their zone(s) of proximal development. You might also consider:

- The different mechanisms that science teachers use to scaffold learning.
- How and why teachers use peer interaction and group work.
- How teachers use language as a means of promoting thinking.

Some final reflections

This chapter has covered considerable ground. We have, albeit briefly, considered constructivism and the learning theories of Piaget, Gardner and Vygotsky, as well as exploring learning as a process of conceptual change. So what is the overriding message? Ausubel (1968: 337) provides a much-cited overview of educational psychology: 'If I had to reduce all educational psychology to just a single principle, I would say this: Find out what the learner knows and teach him [or her] accordingly.'

Put another way, you need to find out where pupils are in order to direct them to where you want them to go. Perhaps the single most important message from this chapter is that successful science teaching requires you, above all, to consider pupils' learning. At the start of this chapter a series of questions were posed to get you thinking about your implicit models of teaching and learning. At this point, you might want to revisit those questions and reflect upon your views of learning. You might also wish to consider how you could represent these views in your teaching.

Further reading

Adey, P and Shayer, M (1994) *Really Raising Standards: Cognitive intervention and academic achievement*, Routledge, London

Driver, R, Squires, A, Rushworth, P and Wood-Robinson, V (1994) *Making Sense of Secondary Science: Research into children's ideas*, Routledge, London

Gardner, H (1983) *Frames of Mind: The Theory of Multiple Intelligences*, Heinemann, London

Hodson, D (1998) *Teaching and Learning Science: Towards a personalised approach*, Open University Press, Buckingham

Osborne, R and Freyberg, P (1985) *Learning in Science: The implications of children science*, Heinemann, London

Russell, T and Watt, D (1990) *Primary Space Project Research Report: Space*, Liverpool University Press, Liverpool

Scott, P and Leach, J (1998) Learning science concepts in the secondary classroom, in *ASE Guide to Secondary Science Education*, ed M Ratcliffe, Stanley Thornes, Hatfield

Watt, D (1998) Children's learning of science concepts, in *ASE Guide to Primary Science*, ed R Sherrington, Stanley Thornes, Hatfield

5 The Science National Curriculum

Keith Hicks

Aims for the school curriculum:

Aim 1: The school curriculum should aim to provide opportunities for all pupils to learn and achieve.
Aim 2: The school curriculum should promote pupils' spiritual, moral, social and cultural development and prepare all pupils for the opportunities, responsibilities and experiences of life.

(*The National Curriculum Handbook for Secondary Teachers in England*)

Objectives

This chapter provides an opportunity to reflect on the structure of the Science National Curriculum. More specifically, the chapter explores the following issues:

- the structure of the Science National Curriculum;
- what the future may hold;
- the post-16 science curriculum.

Introduction

In this chapter we will look at the structure of the National Curriculum and more specifically at the science component of that curriculum. We will assess the place of science teaching in schools and its statutory basis. The chapter will explore the structure of the National Curriculum for Science and look at the most recent version of that curriculum. Finally we will discuss issues that may affect the shape of the curriculum in future years.

The Science National Curriculum

The Education Act of 1988 introduced the National Curriculum for schools in England and Wales. The statutory provision of this Act defined the programme of study to be followed by all pupils in maintained schools and also introduced the Standardized Assessment Tasks (SATs) for pupils at the end of Key Stages 1, 2 and 3. The curriculum consists of three core subjects, English (plus Welsh in Wales), maths and science, plus seven foundation subjects: technology, music, geography, history, PE and art, plus, for pupils in the secondary sector, foreign languages. The latest version of the National Curriculum, published in 1999 and introduced in September 2000, has been slimmed down to allow room for schools to introduce other subjects into their timetables.

With science being a core subject it was placed at the heart of the curriculum of all maintained schools for pupils up to the age of 16. The science curriculum covers all the major areas of science including physics, chemistry, biology, earth sciences and astronomy as well as the nature and history of science. It is up to individual schools to decide how they will deliver the science curriculum; some have chosen to teach the three major sciences as separate entities, while others have adapted integrated or modular approaches. By the time a pupil completes year 11 of their education they will have followed a broad curriculum drawing from the three major disciplines that provide an adequate framework for advanced study.

For each subject and for each Key Stage the curriculum specifies a programme of study which the Education Act (1996) describes as the 'matters, skills and processes' that should be taught to pupils of different abilities and maturities during the Key Stage. Also within the curriculum are the attainment targets which set out the expected standards of pupils' performance for each Key Stage. The science programme is presented under four different headings called attainment targets. These are:

Science 1 (Sc1)	scientific enquiry;
Science 2 (Sc2)	life processes and living things;
Science 3 (Sc3)	materials and their properties;
Science 4 (Sc4)	physical processes.

The science curriculum is designed so that scientific enquiry (Sc1) should be taught through the contexts taken from the other three attainment targets. Many schools have adapted the Department for Education and Employment (DfEE)/Qualifications and Curriculum Authority (QCA) workschemes that have been produced for Key Stages 1, 2 and 3 (which are discussed in Chapter 6) to help them deliver the curriculum to their pupils.

Theory Task Familiarizing yourself with the National Curriculum

As a science teacher it is important that you have a good knowledge of the content and structure of the Science National Curriculum across all Key Stages. It is also useful if you are familiar with the content of the curriculum for other subjects taught in the key stages in which you teach. Early on in your pre-service course you should obtain your own copy of the National Curriculum. This can be downloaded from the Internet from www.nc.uk.net or purchased through HMSO, St Clement's House, 2–16 Colegate, Norwich NR3 1BQ.

- Having obtained your own copy of the curriculum documents, carefully read through the science statutory orders to become familiar with their contents.
- Study the attainment targets for science to establish the standards expected from pupils at each level of achievement.
- Spend some time reading the programme of study for other subjects taught in your Key Stage(s).

In Key Stage 4 science there are two programmes of study referred to as the single and double science programmes. Schools may choose to teach either of these two programmes to their pupils depending on the GCSE courses undertaken by the pupils. Pupils who take GCSE courses in the separate sciences (biology, chemistry and physics) would meet the requirements of both of these programmes. Despite the existence of a single programme of study, the government has repeatedly made it clear that it believes that double science or the three separate sciences should be taken by the majority of pupils. The purpose of single science is to allow for a minority of pupils who may be gifted in other areas of the curriculum to spend more time on other subjects (for instance, a second foreign language).

The Education Act (1996) defines the attainment targets for science as setting out the 'knowledge, skills and understanding pupils of different abilities and maturities are expected to have by the end of each key stage'. In the 1999 version of the science curriculum attainment targets are composed of eight level descriptions, starting from the quite simple at level 1 to the more complex at level 8. For pupils who show exceptional ability in science there is an additional level descriptor above level 8. Rather than detailing specific statements of the achievement pupils are expected to demonstrate to reach a particular level (as earlier versions of the curriculum did) the level descriptions refer to the type and range of performance that would typically be achieved by pupils working at that level.

The level descriptions are intended to show progression in knowledge, understanding and skills throughout the four science attainment targets across all Key Stages. It is important as a new science teacher that you realize that the attainment targets are intended to indicate levels of performance of pupils and are not statutory, unlike the programmes of study, which are. The attainment targets will allow you to assess pupils' performance at the end of Key Stages 1, 2 and 3 (assessments at the end of Key Stage 4 are carried out through national examinations).

The expected level of achievement for students at the end of the different Key Stages is given in Table 5.1.

Table 5.1 Expected National Curriculum levels of achievement for pupils

Stage	*Age of pupil at end of stage*	*Range of levels within which the great majority of pupils are expected to work*	*Expected attainment for the majority of pupils at the end of the Key Stage*
Key stage 1	7	1–3	2
Key stage 2	11	2–5	4
Key stage 3	14	3–7	5/6

Source: *The National Curriculum Handbook* (DfEE 1999c: 18)

When assessing a pupil's level of achievement, as teachers are required to do at the end of each Key Stage, judgements are made by comparing the level descriptors with the pupil's performance. When the results of the SAT examinations are published they are done so against the assessment of pupils' performance carried out by teachers. This means that you will be required to be knowledgeable of the levels of attainment so that you can make accurate assessments of your pupils' progress.

Practice Task Assessing pupils attainment

This task should be carried out with a class you have taught for some time and know well:

- Using school and teacher records, establish what level of achievement your pupils were awarded in their last SAT examination. This is good practice for all the classes you teach, as it provides you with valuable baseline data which you can use to plan your teaching.
- Use the level descriptors of the science attainment targets to estimate the current level of achievement of the pupils in the class.
- Discuss your judgements with your mentor or the class teacher.

A detailed look at the National Curriculum

The National Curriculum is structured to ensure continuity and progression throughout the eleven years of compulsory science education in England and Wales. The concepts contained within the programme of study get more demanding as they pass from KS1 to KS4. There has been an attempt in the curriculum to produce a spiral curriculum where themes are revisited as pupils pass from one key stage to another. With the latest revision of the curriculum, material that appeared in more than one Key Stage has been limited to a single Key Stage. For instance, photosynthesis which appeared in Key Stages 3 and 4 now only occurs and will only be assessed in KS3. These changes may mitigate to some extent against the 'spiral curriculum' idea but, as we will discuss later, the Science National Curriculum is composed of a number of key themes that are revisited in each Key Stage. Earlier versions of the science curriculum were criticized for the way in which material was often repeated in consecutive Key Stages; the latest version has tried to specify more clearly what activities belong in each key stage to try and avoid this repetition of work.

Sc1 Scientific enquiry

Scientific enquiry (Sc1) is prefaced by a statement that it should be taught in contexts taken from the other attainment targets (life processes and living things, materials and their properties and physical processes). It is sub-divided into two main components: 'Ideas and evidence in science' and 'Investigative skills'. The pattern throughout all four of the science attainment targets is to move from the concrete in KS1 to the more abstract in KS4. This is illustrated by the content of 'Ideas and evidence in science', summarized in Table 5.2.

Theory Task The nature of science as presented in the National Curriculum

The content of section 1 of Sc1, 'Ideas and evidence in science', presents a particular view on the nature of science and how science progresses. Read through Sc1 for all four key stages and consider the following points:

- Is the pattern of collecting evidence and establishing links between cause and effect a true representation of the world of science or rather a representation of the world of science education?
- To what extent, historically, have scientists tested explanations by using them to make predictions and seeing if the evidence matches those predictions?
- Does it matter whether the 'scientific method' presented by Sc1 is or is not a reflection of reality?

Table 5.2 The development of 'Ideas and evidence in science' through the National Curriculum

Key Stage	*Expectations of the pupils*
1	Pupils are introduced to the importance of collecting evidence through observation and measurement when they try to answer a question.
2	Pupils learn the importance of using the evidence they have collected through observation and measurement to test ideas. Pupils are taught that science is about thinking creatively to make links between cause and effect to try and explain how things work.
3	Pupils are taught how contemporary and historical examples of evidence have been used in the development of scientific explanations. Pupils use explanations to make predictions and then seek out evidence through practical work to test those predictions.
4	Pupils are taught how science is presented and disseminated. Pupils learn how scientific evidence can be interpreted in a number of ways which can lead to controversy. The impacts of social, historical, moral and spiritual contexts on scientific work together with the power and limitations of science are discussed.

For many teachers the problem of delivering Sc1 is the requirement for it to be delivered through Sc2, 3 and 4. This means that the development of content of Sc1 is often very ad hoc for pupils, a fact picked up by Ofsted (2000b) in their report *Progress in Key Stage 3 Science*, which highlights that there is often no systematic development of the skills laid down in the programme of study. The same report also indicates that the requirements of Sc1 have meant that practical skills have often become focused on specific skills to the detriment of open-ended investigations. Recently the QCA have produced schemes of work designed to help deliver Sc1 such as 'Enquiry in environmental and technological contexts' for KS2 and 'Investigating scientific questions' for KS3 (available from www.qca.org.uk). The intention of these schemes of work is not to replace scientific investigations taught through other parts of the course but to supplement them. The danger here is that teachers will adopt these schemes of work as being a place where Sc1 is taught rather than seeing them as a supplement to Sc1 teaching which should permeate the whole science curriculum.

From 2001, in KS4 the 'ideas and evidence' concepts specified in Sc1 are going to be assessed through the terminal GCSE papers of science courses and will contribute 5 per cent of the total GCSE marks available. The remainder of Sc1 will continue to be assessed through coursework with a weighting of 20 per cent of the available marks.

Sc2 Life processes and living things

This attainment target is divided into different subsections at each Key Stage, these subsections are themselves sub-divided at the higher Key Stages. For KS1 the subsections are: 'Life processes', 'Humans and other animals', 'Green plants', 'Variation and classification' and 'Living things and their environment'. As one would expect for such young children, the content of Sc2 is concerned mainly with recognizing the difference between living things and things that have never lived and recognizing key differences between plants and animals.

There are also a number of themes that run through Sc2 across all four Key Stages, one of which is health education. In KS1, in section 2, 'Humans and other animals', there is a requirement to teach pupils about the importance of exercise and diet for good health and also about the role of drugs as medicines. Another overarching theme of Sc2 is teaching respect for the environment through learning about the need to treat animals with care and sensitivity and learning about the need to take care of the environment.

The same subheadings continue from KS1 into KS2 where pupils are to be taught some of the key life processes common to humans and animals such as nutrition, movement, growth and reproduction. Again there is a strong health education content with teaching about caring for teeth and the need for exercise added onto the importance of diet. 'Green plants' is sub-divided into sections on 'Growth and nutrition' and 'Reproduction'. 'Reproduction', which occurs in both the human and plant sections, has a far more detailed content in the plant section than for the human section. In KS2 pupils are to be taught about reproduction in plants while the aspect of human reproduction is limited to the main stages of the human life cycle. This discrepancy in the details about reproduction in humans and plants is accounted for by the sensitivity of teaching sex education in schools. Sex education does not form part of the Science National Curriculum, instead schools are expected to deliver sex education as a separate part of the curriculum.

Within 'Variation and classification' pupils are expected to make and use keys. In learning how to assign animals and plants into groups it is expected that pupils will observe and classify organisms that occur in their environment. Pupils are to be taught about the interdependence of living things in the environment, including humans, by looking at food chains and feeding relationships in a particular habitat.

As pupils move to KS3 the subheadings of Sc2 change to 'Cells and cell functions', 'Humans as organisms', 'Green plants as organisms', 'Variation classification and inheritance' and 'Living things in their environment'. The content of the curriculum starts to contain more abstract concepts and far more detail about biological processes. For instance in 'Cells and cell functions' the relationship between cells, tissues and organs is explored as are the key features of cells and the differences between a generalized animal cell and a plant cell. As an example of the increasingly abstract content of the curriculum 'Green plants as organisms' specifies that pupils are expected to be taught details about photosynthesis in plants and produce a word equation to summarize the process. As pupils are taught about the role of nitrogen and other elements in plant nutrition it becomes clear that links have to be made to Sc3 and Sc4.

Observation Task Links through the Science National Curriculum

Most schools present science in Key Stages 1 to 3 as a single subject rather than as three traditional subjects of biology, chemistry and physics. Observe a science lesson being taught in your school. While it should be clear which attainment target is being addressed in the lesson there are likely be links to other lessons. With a copy of the Science National Curriculum consider the following points:

- **What concepts are being addressed from other attainment targets of the science curriculum?**
- **Is the content from the other attainment targets of a higher, lower or similar conceptual demand as the main concepts being taught in the lesson?**
- **Does the teacher assume that pupils are familiar with the concepts from the other attainment targets?**

The themes of health education and care for the environment are still present in KS3 but occupy a less prominent place due to the expansion of the curriculum content. The health education component includes details about the content of a balanced diet, about the changes to their bodies associated with adolescence and the onset of the menstrual cycle and more specific information about the effects of smoking on the lungs. There is also a requirement to tackle the problems associated with abuse of alcohol, solvents and drugs. Teaching about the effects of drugs may not be delivered in some schools as part of the science curriculum, as all schools are obliged to have a policy on drugs and may choose to deliver this section of the curriculum through a personal, social and health education course, which as a science teacher you may well be expected to contribute to. Environmental education includes the need to protect the environment and the importance of sustainable development as well as teaching how toxic materials can accumulate in food chains.

Sc3 Materials and their properties

This section of the curriculum deals mainly with the aspects of science teaching usually associated with chemistry. There is, however, a major earth science component to this attainment target which is an area of the curriculum many new teachers are not familiar with. In KS1 and KS2 there is notably less content in Sc3 than Sc2 with only two subsections being specified in KS1, namely, 'Grouping materials' and 'Changing materials'. The teaching content of this key stage is primarily concerned with ensuring pupils are familiar with a limited range of materials and are able to describe some of the properties of those materials and how they can be changed by the application of force or heat.

The subheadings in KS2 are: 'Grouping and classifying materials', 'Changing materials' and 'Separating mixtures of materials'. Whilst being taught about the grouping and classifying of materials pupils are to be introduced to a whole range of new concepts used in describing materials, such as their magnetic behaviour, thermal conductivity and electrical conductivity. Underlying these ideas are a number of concepts associated with energy transfer and electricity which are introduced in Sc4. The order in which the whole curriculum is taught is clearly important if pupils are to make sense of the content of Sc3. The QCA schemes of work offer some guidance in this area and present a logical teaching sequence for the KS2 science curriculum that many science teachers will find helpful.

In 'Changing materials', a range of physical and chemical changes are introduced to pupils clearly with the intention of leading pupils towards more formal chemistry teaching in later key stages. Again, most of the examples cited in the curriculum are of materials changing that pupils are likely to be acquainted with from home and which do not require large amounts of specialist equipment to investigate in school. Areas that are more challenging for pupils in this key stage are the water cycle and some of the non-reversible reactions that produce new (often useful) materials. There is plenty of scope here for investigative work for pupils to explore the key concepts being taught.

The final section of this attainment target in KS2, 'Separating mixtures of materials', contains details of a number of separating techniques that will place a higher demand on teachers for specialist equipment in primary schools. Pupils are to be taught about sieving, dissolving, filtering as well as evaporating liquids to recover dissolved solids.

In KS3 the attainment target is divided into the following sections: 'Classifying materials', 'Changing materials', 'Patterns of behaviour'. An overarching concept to be taught here is that of the kinetic theory of matter. This is such an important concept in both KS3 and KS4 science that it is difficult to think of a more central idea. This concept must be grasped in order for pupils to access the science curriculum, impinging as it does on Sc2, 3 and 4.

Kinetic theory is introduced through the first section of 'Classifying materials' which has the subheading, 'Solids, liquids and gases'. Pupils are to be taught the basics of the particle theory of matter and are expected to be able to use it to explain changes in state and diffusion in gases. The second subheading, 'Elements, compounds and mixtures' requires pupils to understand the meanings of the terms 'atom', 'element', 'mixture' and 'compound' as they are introduced for the first time to the Periodic Table. Pupils are expected to be able to represent compounds and elements by formulae and to summarize reactions by word equations. The separating techniques of distillation and chromatography are added to the methods taught in KS2.

'Changing materials' is divided into 'Physical changes', 'Geological changes' and 'Chemical reactions'. The section on 'Geological changes' is an area of the curriculum where other subject areas (notably geography) have also had a teaching input. The earth science that is taught in KS3 includes the process of weathering, the geological time scale and the rock cycle. These are areas that are challenging to teach to children, as processes that may last hundreds of millions of years can be difficult to comprehend. 'Chemical reactions' includes ideas about the conservation of mass in reactions and teaching about the wide range of types of chemical reactions that occur in both living and non-living systems. There is a clear link here to Sc2 as pupils are to be taught about the harmful effects on the environment of burning fossil fuels.

The final section of Sc3 in this Key Stage is 'Patterns of behaviour' which has two subdivisions headed 'Metals' and 'Acids and bases'. Pupils are taught about the way metals react in oxygen, water, acids and the oxides of other metals. This leads onto learning about the reactivity series of metals which can be used to make predictions about other reactions. The section on 'Acids and bases' is a comprehensive introduction to this topic providing another link to the work done on the environment in Sc2 as the effects of acids in the environment are taught.

Sc4 Physical processes

As might be expected, the content of Sc4 at KS1 is quite limited but science teachers in later Key Stages might be surprised by some of its content. It is broken down into three subheadings: 'Electricity', 'Forces and motion' and 'Light and sound'. Many teachers in secondary school fail to realize that basic circuits are introduced to the science curriculum of pupils during KS2. As with all parts of the science curriculum it is important to acknowledge and build on pupils' prior learning experiences before embarking on a new topic.

'Forces and motion' aims to establish with the pupils that forces can be described as pushes and pulls and the effects these have on objects (namely speed up, slow down or change direction). Another feature of the teaching of this section is to ensure that pupils understand the vocabulary of movement so that they can describe the movement of familiar objects. The simple concepts taught in 'Light and sound' are divided into those which concern light, such as that light can come from different sources and darkness is an absence of light, and concerning sound, the different sources of sound and the effect of distance from the source of a sound on its loudness.

At KS2 a new subheading, 'The Earth and beyond', has been added. In the work on electricity, pupils extend their work on simple circuits to use a range of devices and switches and learn how changing the number of components in a series circuit can make bulbs brighter or dimmer. This work represents an introduction to electric current but no currents are measured in KS2 and the ampere is not used. Pupils in KS2 are also to be taught how to draw and use circuit diagrams for series circuits containing conventional symbols.

In 'Forces and motion' pupils are introduced to a range of concepts about forces including magnets and magnetic materials, gravity and forces of friction. In studying gravity pupils are taught that the Earth attracts objects and friction is defined as 'a force which slows moving objects and may prevent objects from starting to move'. Pupils in this key stage are also introduced to the phenomenon described by Newton's third law of motion even though it is not expressed in terms of that law.

The material in 'Light and sound' is extended considerably from KS1 with pupils being taught about light travelling and shadow formation. Under a subheading entitled 'Seeing' pupils learn that we see things only when light enters our eyes. The work on sound is extended to establish that all sound is caused by objects vibrating, and how the pitch and loudness of a sound can be changed. Pupils go on to be taught that sound needs a medium through which it can travel to the human ear.

The first work on astronomy in the Science National Curriculum comes in 'The Earth and beyond'. Pupils are to be taught about the relative movement of the Sun, Earth and Moon. The periodic changes in the position of the Sun are studied and the effect this has on shadows. The movement of the Earth round the Sun every year and the Moon round the Earth every 28 days is also included.

Moving onto KS3, Sc4 looks very much like a typical physics curriculum with sections on 'Electricity and magnetism', 'Forces and motion', 'Light and sound', 'The Earth and beyond' and 'Energy resources and energy transfer'. Work on electricity in KS3 is extended to include parallel circuits and how to measure both current and voltage. Pupils are also taught that current is not used up in circuits and that batteries transfer energy to other components in circuits. The work on magnets is extended to include the concept of the magnetic field and also the making and uses of electromagnets.

The qualitative work done on motion in KS3 includes a quantitative approach in 'Forces and linear motion', with pupils being taught how to measure speed. A concept introduced here which many pupils find quite tricky is the distinction between weight and mass, which seems to pose difficulties for most of the adult population as well! While in earlier Key Stages forces were defined as pushes and pulls, turning forces round a pivot and moments are introduced in KS3. The concept of pressure as a quantitative relationship between force and area is another example of the higher conceptual demands made at this key stage.

When studying 'Light and sound' pupils are taught not only that light travels but also that it has a finite speed. Pupils are expected to investigate reflection at plane surfaces and refraction at the boundary of two different materials. The relationship between light and colour is also taught at this stage. The work on sound contains a subsection entitled 'Hearing' where the working of the ear is taught. When studying sound pupils are to be taught the link between the amplitude of a vibration and the loudness of a sound and also the link between frequency and pitch.

Having studied the movement of the Earth, Moon and Sun in KS2 this is reinforced at KS3 by addressing the issue of the apparent daily and annual movements of the stars as well as the Sun. Other bodies in space which are studied at this stage include the planets of our solar system, relating their movement to gravitational forces. The nature of stars and the use of artificial satellites and probes to observe the Earth and to explore space conclude the teaching on astronomy in KS3.

'Energy resources and energy transfer' makes its first appearance in KS3. Pupils are taught about the nature of energy and the different energy resources that are available and how a variety of these can be used to generate electricity. Under the subheading 'Conservation of energy' pupils are taught how thermal energy can be transferred by conduction, convection and radiation as well as the idea that, although energy is conserved, it may be dissipated, reducing its availability as a resource.

Theory Task The National Curriculum in Key Stage 4

For the vast majority of pupils the study of science in KS4 will take the form of a GCSE course. In order to deliver the KS4 curriculum science teachers will generally rely on the syllabus provided by the examination board rather than the programme of study published in the National Curriculum documentation. Those pupils who opt for a single science course will follow a syllabus based upon the single science programme of study which has a reduced content compared to the double science programme of study.

Obtain a copy of the GCSE syllabuses used by the school you are based in and also a copy of the programme of study for both single and double science at KS4.

- Familiarize yourself with both the programme of study and the GCSE syllabus and study how the two relate to each other. What are the key differences in the ways the two documents are presented?
- Identify the major areas of the curriculum that are omitted from the single science courses.
- Are the concepts omitted from the single science course harder or simpler to understand than those included in the double science course?
- It is generally perceived that the single science option at GCSE is more difficult than the double science option. (This is borne out by significant differences in the percentage of pupils gaining grades A*–C in these two subjects.) Why do you think there is a difference in the degree of difficulty of the two courses?

Discuss this work with your mentor or other new science teachers.

The post-16 science curriculum

The post-16 curriculum is currently undergoing a major revision in its content and its structure. The motivation for this change was an ongoing concern about the narrowness of the curriculum followed by pupils taking A-levels. It was very difficult for pupils to study the three sciences with, say, a foreign language in the post-16 scenario. September 2000 saw the introduction of a major curriculum reform called Curriculum 2000 with a requirement for students to do a broader range of AS-levels before specializing in A-level studies. Most pupils will now study four subjects at advanced level where before they undertook only three. The expected change this will make is that more pupils than before are likely to study a science at advanced level for at least an additional year. The AS and A-level courses are now all of a modular nature with module tests dispersed throughout the course.

The introduction of modular courses is perceived as having a number of advantages over the traditional A-level course structure. The ability to give pupils feedback about their performance during the course may be motivating for pupils and also allow teachers to set short-term goals for pupils to achieve. For some subjects it is intended that a degree of choice will be available as to what modules will be studied. For most schools this will not occur due to the financial, timetabling and staffing constraints that come from having fairly small numbers of pupils studying these courses. The modular system will allow new patterns of teaching and learning to emerge in the post-16 curriculum and there is likely to be a rise in the number of pupils spending three years in the VIth form before moving on to colleges or universities. If as a result of these changes more pupils do go on to further education they must be hailed as a success. In addition to the subject-specific content of the AS- and A-level specifications a number of *key skills* (ICT, numeracy and communications) are being introduced which all pupils will have to study.

The other major change coming about in the post-16 curriculum is the introduction of vocational courses such as GNVQs and NVQs. The drive behind these changes is the perceived need to match the requirements of employers with the education and training pupils receive. In 1986 the National Council for Vocational Qualifications (NCVQ) was established in the UK and that body has been piloting and establishing vocational qualifications in science in schools and colleges for some time now. In a White Paper, *Education and Training in the 21st Century*, published in 1992, the government signalled its intention to make GNVQs and NVQs the national vocational qualifications. While NVQs are linked to specific jobs which are usually undertaken by employees in the form of 'on the job' or day release training, GNVQs are primarily aimed at the 16–19 age group and are available at three levels: foundation, intermediate and advanced. The advanced-level GNVQ is intended to provide an alternative vocational qualification to the more academic A-levels with a parity of esteem between the two. Some schools have introduced foundation and intermediate GNVQs into the KS4 curriculum for a number of pupils, so they can be said to provide a vocational route from the ages of 14–19.

Currently there are GNVQ specifications for science at both intermediate and advanced level. Pupils following these courses have to study a number of mandatory vocational units as well as a number of optional units. The advanced-level GNVQ is intended to be the equivalent of two A-levels. As with the new AS-levels, pupils are also expected to study the key skills – ICT, communication and application of number. Wellington (2000: 52) has suggested that GNVQs have not been without their critics when he wrote that: 'They have been accused of being of lower status and poorer quality than A-levels; they have also suffered from a lack of parity of esteem, meaning in practice that certain schools have not touched them and those pupils choosing them have had (on average) lower grades at GCSE level.'

What is clear is that the post-16 curriculum is in a period of ongoing change and as a new teacher you will need to ensure that you keep abreast of those changes in the years to come.

The hidden curriculum

What pupils learn in science lessons is not limited to what is written down in the National Curriculum or subject specifications and syllabuses. The term used to describe these things is the 'hidden curriculum' and all teachers have a role to play in delivering this curriculum. The ethos and the environment you establish in your classroom or laboratory will contribute to this hidden curriculum in a number of ways. For instance, is your classroom a place where pupils are welcomed and are encouraged to develop a sense of ownership? Are your pupils' efforts respected through well cared for displays of their work? Do you foster a mutual feeling of respect in the way relationships between yourself and the pupils and the pupils with each other develop in your lessons? The answer to these questions will determine what pupils learn in your lessons and will affect their moral and spiritual development as much as the National Curriculum programmes of study.

Further reading

Department for Education and Employment (DfEE) (1999) *The National Curriculum Handbook for Secondary Teachers in England*, HMSO, London

Donnelly, J F (2000) Secondary Science Teaching and the National Curriculum, *School Science Review*, **81** (296), pp 27–35

Office for Standards in Education (Ofsted) (2000) *Progress in Key Stage 3 Science*, HMSO, London

Wellington, J (2000) *Teaching and Learning Secondary Science*, Routledge, London

Part 3

Planning, Teaching and Assessing Science

6 Planning for science teaching

Steve Alsop

It took me hours to plan my first lesson. I was suddenly aware of all the things you have to deal with when teaching science. You need to think about things like giving out lab books, children not having pens and pencils and getting out and packing away equipment as well as researching and presenting your subject in a clear and uncluttered way. When I started teaching, my lesson plans were extremely detailed. I planned for every little classroom event; however, as my practice progressed I was able to focus my planning on key aspects of the lesson. Things like taking the register, giving out books and packing away equipment become automatic after a while.

(Peter, a trainee biology teacher, recorded during a PGCE science course)

Objectives

This chapter facilitates critical reflection on planning for science teaching. More specifically, the chapter is designed to aid you to explore:

- the significance of planning in successful science teaching;
- different ways of planning for the school, department and classroom;
- planning for individual needs;
- the QCA science schemes of work;
- different components of outcome based science lesson planning.

Introduction

The intent of this chapter is to explore the practicalities of planning for science learning. Planning is a fundamental component of successful teaching and its importance is emphasized in recent teacher training circulars (Department for Education and Employment (DfEE, 1998a). Throughout your teaching career, lesson planning will be central to your everyday needs. Irrespective of classroom competence and experience, the importance of planning cannot be overemphasized: it enables you to identify appropriate learning goals and structure pedagogical activities to achieve these goals. Before starting a lesson, all teachers need to have an idea of the structure, content and form of their intended lesson. Successful lesson planning should also increase your confidence, formalize your thinking and enable you to enter the science classroom with a clear image of the lesson in your mind.

Getting started

Peter's comments are common: when starting to teach it is easy to overlook the complexities of managing a classroom with 30+ science students. Careful planning is essential because many potential classroom problems (and catastrophes!) can be detected and ameliorated before lessons get underway. Thorough planning will pre-empt potential classroom struggles and concerns; it will enable you to concentrate on the children's learning rather than being preoccupied with your own performance. It will also reduce classroom stress and anxiety. However, lesson planning can be deceptive. As Wellington (1994) notes, lesson planning is 'a somewhat enigmatic activity in that beginning teachers find it extremely time consuming and demanding whereas experienced teachers are able to give the impression that there is absolutely nothing to it'. Don't be fooled, experienced colleagues have internalized the planning process; they have planned many lessons and they are able to identify and concentrate on any unusual or potentially problematic elements. As Peter suggests, the more procedural components of a science lesson (eg managing transitions, giving out textbooks and packing away laboratory equipment) can become automatic and internalized after a while. However, when starting to teach it is often these procedural components that are a source of much concern and trouble.

This chapter is broken up into a series of sections: the aim is to address issues of science planning at different levels. The chapter explores planning from the whole school level to meeting individual needs in a science lesson. We recommend that you read this chapter through and then periodically refer back to it when covering other chapters. It is largely through your lesson plans that the theory covered in this book becomes translated into practice. In many respects, this chapter has a pivotal role in the text because it provides a framework which pulls together the content of the other chapters.

Planning for the science curriculum

As previously noted, planning is the foundation of successful practice. The Office for Standards in Education (popularly known as Ofsted), for instance, emphasizes the necessity of curriculum planning at all levels:

> Curriculum planning and the preparation of lesson plans help teachers to focus their work, with clear goals and sensible strategies for achieving them. Effective plans for single lessons and for a series of lessons complement and amplify the departmental scheme of work. Good lesson planning translates school policies and subject guidance into informed classroom practice; it identifies learning objectives, making provision for the different learning needs of pupils; and specifies the activities to be pursued in the lesson, the use of time, the resources, any assessment opportunity and any link to cross curricular themes and spiritual, moral social and cultural development.
>
> (Ofsted, 1998b: 30)

In schools, planning usually takes place at four levels – the whole school level, the departmental level, the class level and the level of the individual pupil (see Figure 6.1). Planning at a whole school level will mould and shape departmental planning, which in turn will influence and drive lesson planning and planning for individual needs.

Initially, the curriculum will be planned for the whole school and this will involve allocating curriculum space for science, linking science with other subjects and cross curriculum themes, and developing whole school policies on, for example, equal opportunities (see Chapter 11) and special educational needs (see Chapter 12). In secondary schools, a school timetable will be constructed and a regular allotted time will be allocated to science. In primary schools, the arrangement is likely to be more flexible and teachers will allocate time for science in their long-term plans. However, recent discussions suggest that a regular time slot for science (a 'science hour') is on the horizon.

At the 'departmental' level, planning usually takes the form of a scheme of work, sometimes referred to as a unit of work. This will typically consist of an agreed programme that is followed by all science teachers in the school. The term 'department' is more common in secondary schools that have a departmental structure. Secondary schools will have a head of science and a series of other positions of responsibility, such as a head of biology or a Key Stage 3 science co-ordinator. In primary schools, the science co-ordinator usually has responsibility for the science scheme of work and this is often accompanied by a long-term and a medium-term plan.

Planning at the class level consists of teachers' individual lesson plans (or short-term plans). The purpose of these is to translate the 'intended curriculum' into learning events and activities – the 'taught curriculum'. This is the level where pupils directly experience the curriculum. Put differently, it is the level where classroom pedagogy is formulated.

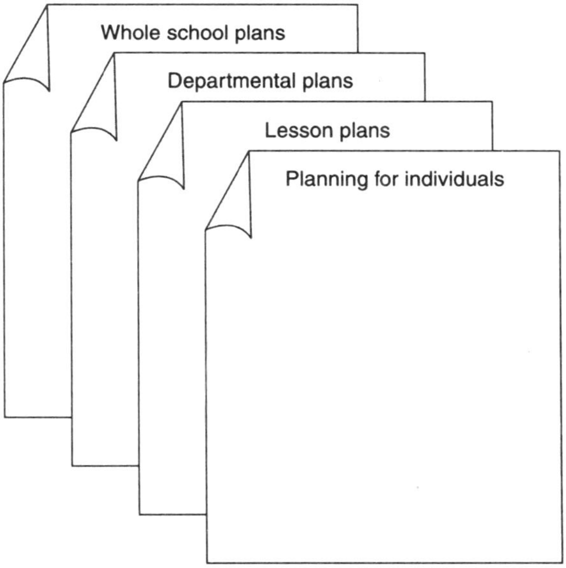

Figure 6.1 School planning for science

Individual planning is the way classroom teachers cater for individual needs. All pupils have different interests, motivations and abilities and, as a class teacher, it is your responsibility to cater for these individual needs. Some pupils' needs are designated as special and these needs must also be addressed in your planning (see Chapter 12 for more details).

Schemes of work, long-term and medium-term planning

A scheme of work is a long-term plan that should be agreed by all science teachers in a school. It is the school's science curriculum and it will embody the whole school plans and reflect the aims, ethos and approach of the school and the science teachers. A scheme of work shows how the content of the science programmes of study (DfEE, 1999a) are sequenced across a year and a Key Stage. It should act as the basis for what is to be taught and should make clear and show the sequence for the skills, content and concepts at each Key Stage. A scheme of work should be planned with lessons and pupils in mind; it will often contain a list of learning objectives, teaching activities, resources and assessment issues. It should also take into account continuity and progression. Figure 6.2 signifies some key factors involved in designing a science scheme of work. Ideally a scheme would embrace all these factors and many more!

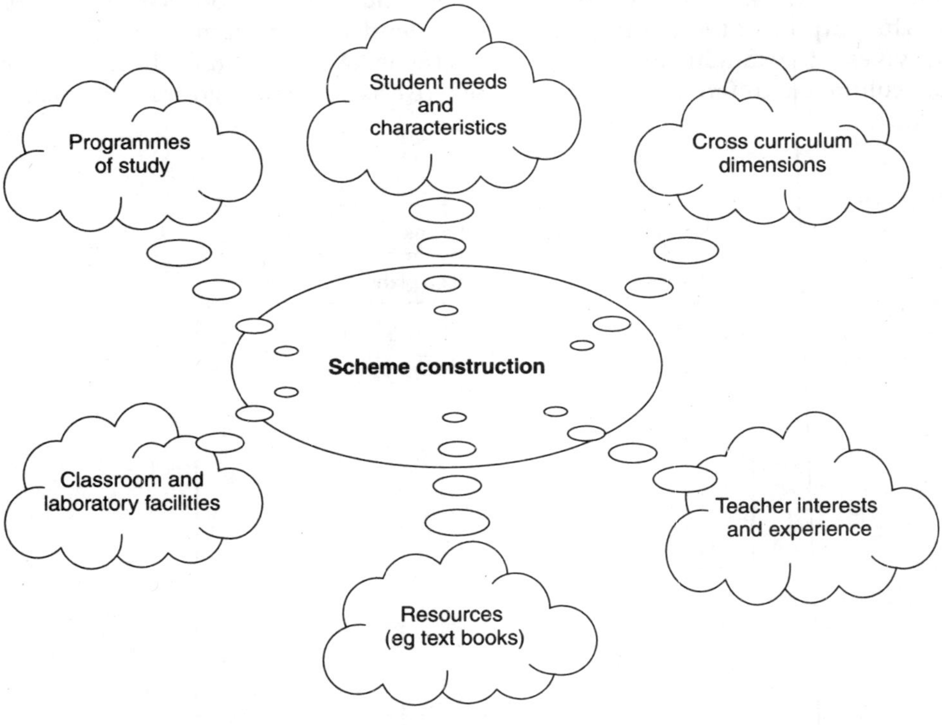

Figure 6.2 Factors involved in designing a scheme of work

The science programme of study provides the basis of what should be taught along with other cross-curricular themes and dimensions (see Chapter 5). As noted above, a scheme of work needs to be carefully ordered to provide progression and continuity. Progression refers to how children's ideas develop – it is to do with pupils' learning. Continuity, on the other hand, is linked to teaching rather than learning and refers to how a curriculum is organized to facilitate learning. As Driver *et al* (1994) write, continuity and progression are quite different – indeed continuity may not always lead to progression:

> Continuity... is something organised by the teacher: it describes the relationship between experiences, activities and ideas which pupils meet over a period of time, in a curriculum which is structured to support learning. Curriculum continuity cannot guarantee progression. Its role is to structure ideas and experiences for learners in a way which will help them to move their conceptual understanding forward in scientific terms.
>
> (Driver *et al* 1994: 8)

An analysis of students' needs, interests and characteristics is also important when designing the school curriculum. In addition, a scheme of work will need to take into account the local education authority and school's particular needs. For instance, a school may have a centre for hearing impairment or a high percentage of children with ESL (English as a second language) and a scheme of work will need to embrace these particular needs. There will be other factors that impinge upon the scheme design, such as the availability of time and resource issues (the accessibility of textbooks and laboratory equipment). If computing resources are required, the availability of computer facilities will also need to be taken into account. Some secondary schools will teach separate sciences (more commonly in Key Stage 4 than Key Stage 3) and a scheme will need to be designed to take this into account. It should enable connection between the separate courses. In some primary schools a specialist teacher teaches science on a rotary basis and this also needs to be considered in the school plans.

Up to now the main focus has been on students and their needs. However, a scheme of work should also enthuse and engage teachers. To achieve this, it is essential that curriculum development is collaborative and should build upon the expertise and experience of all the teachers involved. Above all, it should be a document with joint ownership; it should be something that all those involved feel is pedagogically sound. To this end, a scheme of work will need to embrace the beliefs, attitudes and perceptions of teachers as well as any technicians and administrators involved.

Science schemes of work

Given the above factors, it should not be a surprise that schemes of work vary considerably in structure and style. They are designed with particular schools, staff and classes in mind – not to mention the resources available. Recently the Qualifications and Curriculum Authority (QCA) and the Department for Education and Employment (DfEE) have provided sample science schemes of work linked to the UK National Curriculum. They are available on the DfEE Web site (www.standards.dfee.gov.uk). The schemes are very detailed and break the curriculum up into a series of teaching units sequenced across each Key Stage. They are optional and the accompanying documentation stresses that they offer 'one way that the science programme of study can be interpreted for the classroom'. They are also intended to be flexible resources – 'schools are free to use as much or as little as they find helpful' (QCA 2000: 5).

The schemes have met with a mixed response. For some, the level of detail and the structure has proved extremely helpful. For others, the level of detail and the particular interpretation of the National Curriculum raise concerns. A recent copy of the Association for Science Education (ASE, 2000a) publication *School Science Review* contains a series of articles discussing this very subject (see Volume 18).

As mentioned above, a scheme needs to take account of a school's culture, its pupils, teachers and resources, and the extent to which this can be achieved in a generic document is obviously questionable (see Monk, 2000). That said, the units offer a detailed and structured interpretation that could form a good resource. My personal concern is that in an increasingly busy and scrutinized climate, the schemes offer tempting instant 'documentation'. For any scheme to be meaningful it has to be more than 'documentation', it has to embody the thoughts, feelings and experiences of those who are teaching. There are no short cuts here, curriculum development is a rewarding, essential but, unfortunately, time-consuming process.

Theory Task Using the QCA schemes

We encourage you to download the QCA science schemes and compare them with your school scheme (visit www.qca.org.uk). What do you like about the scheme? How does the scheme interpret the curriculum? How can you use the scheme in your practice?

Individual lesson plans

As previously noted, when starting to teach you will need to spend considerable time planning your lessons. In many cases, early lessons will take you three or four times the lesson length to plan. This requires careful time management and you will need to balance your teaching week – after you have had a busy day teaching you will often not feel like spending the evening planning. Like it or not, Saturdays and Sundays are often prime time for lesson planning!

In secondary schools, class planning will usually consist of a series of discrete plans for individual lessons – a series of lesson plans. These will typically be 40–75 minutes in duration. In primary schools, a short-term plan is more common and this will build on the scheme of work and medium-term plan. A short-term plan will usually structure activities on a day-to-day basis. It is a very good idea to build up a file of lesson plans as well as any additional materials such as curriculum materials, resources and subject notes. This file will be an invaluable resource in future years. A teaching practice file is usually a mandatory requirement of a teacher training course.

An outcome-based model

There have been numerous models and templates advocated for classroom planning. In more recent years, an objective, or outcome-based approach has become popular. Typically this model has four phases. Kyriacou (1991: 17) for example, proposes the following components in lesson design:

1. a decision about the educational objectives that the lesson will be designed to foster;
2. a selection and scripting of a lesson (deciding on the type and nature of activities) and ordering and allocating time for these activities;
3. a preparation of all the props to be used (sorting out lesson materials, arranging the classroom, checking laboratory equipment and setting up demonstrations);
4. a decision regarding how you will monitor and assess pupils' progress and attainment (deciding on how you intend to evaluate whether the intended learning has taken place).

Successful lesson plans will usually have these four components and the following sections place some flesh on these bones. As a new science teacher, we hope the following discussions prove useful in *scaffolding* your planning. However they come with a health warning: not all the components are compulsory and they should only be used when you consider them appropriate. What follows is not a rigid step-by-step recipe – a panacea for instant classroom success. In the end, it is impossible to provide a generic set of lesson components because lesson design is dependent on myriad factors, including your preferred teaching style, the nature of your classes, your school and the resources available. That said, here are some tentative suggestions.

Selecting lesson objectives

An initial stage in outcome-based planning is usually deciding upon your educational objectives. Decisions of this type involve finding out about the previous experiences of the pupils, building on the content of previous lessons and consulting the departmental scheme of work and the national curriculum programmes of study. To select and structure learning objectives, you might ask yourself these questions:

1. What concepts, skills and attitudes will pupils already have?
2. Do some pupils have particular needs?
3. What concepts, skills and attitudes do I want the pupils to grasp?
4. How can I structure these teaching objectives to build on pupils' needs and previous experiences?

Selecting lesson objectives might seem straightforward. Unfortunately it is not as simple as it seems (things rarely are in teaching!). In the past, Ofsted has been critical of much science planning because of a lack of clearly defined learning objectives. Encouragingly, in more recent inspections, they highlight that considerable development has taken place in this area: 'From 1993 there has been a steady improvement of standards in science. In particular, a sharper focus for lessons, clearer objectives identified by teachers, and better use of class-time have contributed to an improvement in pupils' knowledge base' (Ofsted, 1998b: 20).

However, in our experience, selecting clear learning objectives is something that new teachers often find difficult. Vague phrases like: 'it's sort of about...', 'to introduce the basics about ...', 'to give an idea about ...', should be avoided. You should be able to specify clearly and precisely what your learning objectives are: 'In this lesson we are...'

Observation Task Identifying learning objectives

Watch a science lesson and try to isolate and summarize learning objectives. Are these objectives clear – do pupils know what they are?

Also make sure that you can clearly and precisely explain your lesson objectives before starting a lesson.

Building a lesson plan

Selecting and ordering learning activities will need to take account of numerous factors including: the learning objectives, the experiences, the ability and interest of the pupils, your experiences and comfort levels and the resources available.

The following four points offer some suggestions for the main lesson components (please note these are only *suggestions* and should not be followed slavishly).

Starting a lesson

To start a lesson, you might try to select a learning activity that relates to the learner's previous experiences and orientates the learner to the lesson objectives. Many lessons begin with a recapitulation of a previous lesson combined with opportunities to find out about the following lesson by stating the lesson objectives and purpose. Good introductions provide a context for the lesson and make connections between the content of the lesson and what the pupils already know – the lesson should appear relevant to all those involved. In planning an opening activity you may find it useful to consider the following five questions:

1. How can I find out what all pupils know about the lesson content?
2. How can I link pupils' past experiences to the lesson content?
3. How can I introduce the purpose of the lesson?
4. How can I explain my learning objectives?
5. How can I isolate and emphasize the key lesson concepts, skills and attitudes?

An orientation activity usually takes place at the beginning, or near to the beginning of a lesson. Needless to say this is not a hard and fast rule – for example, in some lessons the objectives emerge through an 'open-ended' activity. In this case, the lesson objectives and purpose are left to the final stages of a lesson.

Developing the lesson

A crucial question when considering lesson development is how you might best facilitate your learning objectives. Wherever possible you should try to use a variety of different activities because apart from anything else this provides motivation and increases interest. In outcome-based planning, learning activities should be selected on the basis of your learning objectives.

Two things you might find useful to consider are:

1. *Illustrations*: You should try and provide clear examples and illustrations to illustrate your learning objectives. Explore unfamiliar concepts in familiar contexts. Wherever possible try to incorporate multi-sensory experiences.
2. *Applications*: This refers to opportunities where pupils apply the content and processes they have learned. The teacher should closely supervise initial attempts. As experiences and competence are gained, new situations and contexts should be explored with less and less support from the teacher (Bruner would refer to this process as scaffolding – see Chapter 4 for more details).

Assessment

A consideration of assessment is an important aspect of lesson design. It is important to plan for assessment opportunities of both a formative and summative nature, see Chapter 10 for more detail. The key question here is, how can you monitor student understanding and comprehension during and after the lesson? You may, for instance, ask a series of questions, observe groups performing a set activity, or give a test or examination. Assessment need not be formal but should provide an opportunity for pupil feedback and lesson adjustment. You need to respond to pupils' needs, if you find pupils confused with a concept you need to adjust your lesson plan to respond to these needs.

Ending a lesson

Lesson endings often include a summary of the lesson objectives and should isolate and emphasize the learning objectives. Ideally, classroom activities should be sought that enable the learner to summarize the lesson objectives in their own words. If the final lesson summary is driven by the *learner* (not the teacher) it provides a basis for assessment. You can check the efficacy of the lesson and monitor whether your learning objectives have been achieved. In short, you can evaluate the success of your lesson. For instance, groups of pupils summarizing the learning objectives might facilitate a good lesson closure.

Observation Task Lesson planning

The four subsections above offer a way of conceptualizing a lesson plan. We recommend that you consider these lesson components when you are planning your early science lessons. Try to observe a lesson and then construct a lesson plan. You might wish to compare your representation of the lesson with the teacher's original lesson plan. The important thing in planning is to build up a mental picture of the lesson before starting to teach.

The seven Es

Trowbridge and Bybee (1996: 215) present a lesson structure that you might find helpful. Their structure takes account of recent constructivist research and has similarities with the 'constructivist' teaching model proposed by Driver *et al* (1994 – previously discussed in Chapter 4). The lesson structure is based around seven Es, as shown in Table 6.1.

In Table 6.1 the Es are presented in a particular sequence, however it should be borne in mind that this sequence is flexible. You can play around with the order to suit your particular classroom needs. The components might also be used as the basis of a scheme of work, where each component is the focus of a particular lesson. In this respect the model has potential for both short-term and long-term planning.

Table 6.1 The seven Es of of the lesson structure

Elicit	Structure activities to find out about children's ideas about the concepts and skills you are about to explore
Engage	Use a series of classroom activities that engage students' interest and curiosity
Explore	Provide activities for pupils to explore particular phenomena and generate their own explanations of these phenomena
Encounter	Any misconceptions about these should then be challenged. This can be achieved by setting up a series of activities that promote alternative conceptions and demonstrate the weaknesses in pupils' current understanding
Explain	Pupils should be provided with opportunities to explain their understanding; you should encourage pupils to explain concepts in their own words
Elaborate	This is the application phase: classroom activities should be provided for pupils to apply their new ideas in different contexts and to different situations
Evaluate	Pupils should be given the opportunity to evaluate their own learning. They should be given a chance to explore why they have changed their ideas and the strengths of their new ideas when compared with their old ideas. The importance of this meta-cognitive component in learning has been highlighted in much recent research

Observation Task The seven Es

During your observations, try identifying the seven Es and then reflect upon the following questions:

1 How are the Es sequenced?
2. What makes particular Es successful or unsuccessful?
3. Are some Es more popular and frequent than others?
4. Are any other lesson components evident?

Other important planning considerations

Safety

Science is a subject with a practical dimension and as such it is essential that you consider any potential risks involved. You will need to perform a risk assessment on all your science lessons involving practical work as part of your pre-lesson evaluation. This includes teacher demonstrations as well as class experiments. Safety is of utmost importance – it is essential that you consider any potential hazards and take measures to reduce the likelihood of any accident occurring. There is a simple rule, if you are concerned about the safety of a classroom activity do not do it. Your planning must consider safety issues. Classroom transitions, for instance, need to be planned; you need to consider extremely carefully how pupils can safely and efficiently collect (and pack away) apparatus as well as any dangers involved in performing set tasks. We suggest that you also pay particular attention to the following potential concerns:

- Highlight all safety issues in your lesson plan. If you are using potentially hazardous chemicals, a clear set of safety procedures should be documented. For example, this should include safety precautions that you plan to emphasize as well as any clean-up procedures, for example if chemicals are spilt. Where necessary, safety spectacles *must* be worn; this includes the teacher – for your own safety as well as acting as a role model! You also need to know the location of any eyewash bottles, electrical cut-off switches, emergency exits and the arrangements in the event of a fire alarm.
- Equipment should always be counted-out and counted-in. Before pupils are dismissed you should know if any equipment is missing and then you can act accordingly.
- Coats and bags are always a cause for concern in a laboratory classroom. We have witnessed a number of instances where pupils have tripped over a disregarded bag with potentially serious consequences. Before performing any practical work, we suggest that pupils should be asked to remove their bags and coats.

Chapter 9 explores safety issues further.

Preparation

Successful lessons require careful pre-lesson preparation. You need to make sure that all is set up and working before your lessons commence. The following short list provides a checklist of things to consider. It is certainly not exhaustive, but we hope it is useful.

- Make sure all visual aids, for instance overhead transparencies, are pre-prepared and clearly presented. Put an overhead on the projector and walk to the back of the room to check if it is legible. If using an overhead projector, check that it is working and in focus. They usually have a spare bulb, you should check that this is installed and working.
- If you want to change the classroom layout, do this in advance of the lesson.
- If you are doing a practical or demonstration, you should order all equipment well in advance. You will also need to check the equipment works before the lesson (preferably at least the day before). If possible, set up any demonstrations before the lessons start. By trying it out you will discover important instructions that can save time in the lesson.
- Make sure you have all the equipment; it is not possible to leave the laboratory, for example, to search for a box of matches or some sticky tape.
- If you are using a video or slides they should be at the right place. A class will not sit and wait for you to fast-forward and rewind a video to get the right spot.
- If you are using computer software, again make sure the system and software are working in advance. If pupils are using software, you need to be familiar with this software in order to offer advice and guidance.

Management and control

Management and control are fundamental to good practice. They are often the areas of most concern when starting to teach. The generic text in this series (Nicholls, 1999) explores these areas in some detail and for this reason they are only briefly mentioned here. There are also a number of other texts that deal specifically with these issues; I personally find Docking (1990), Kyriacou (1986, 1989) and Wragg (1993) extremely helpful. These authors all emphasize the need to promote and reinforce acceptable behaviour and pre-empt misbehaviour. Reprimand and punishment should be used as a last resort. As Docking (1990) emphasizes, try and catch the child being good, give praise as soon as possible and use praise to communicate your belief in the child's competence. Plan to promote and reinforce good behaviour.

Outcome-based lesson planning revisited

Up to now, outcome-based learning has been our focus. Indeed, this book exemplifies this approach as each chapter begins by stating a series of objectives. However, many educationalists would argue that this style of lesson planning has weaknesses. Bloom (1998) for instance, highlights the behaviourist origins of objective-based planning. Objectives present a model of learning that focuses on pieces of content that need to be internalized rather than taking children's construction of knowledge into account. There is an important difference between learning objectives and learning outcomes. Learning objectives are specified by the curriculum (the scheme of work and the programmes of study). In contrast, learning outcomes are what the pupils' understand and can achieve. In a nutshell, objectives are teacher and curriculum based and outcomes are learner based. This difference is actually very important. When planning, a crucial question to consider is what should form the basis of my lesson design – learning outcomes or learning objectives? In my mind, there seem to be two major reasons for generating learning objectives. The first is to guide lesson planning and the second is to guide lesson assessment. In this respect, lesson objectives specify the 'conceptual territory' (Bloom, 1998). In designing your lessons, we maintain, you need to consider both objectives and outcomes. Lesson outcomes are linked with pupils' knowledge – your intent should be that pupils are constructing their own knowledge and not simply memorizing and reciting your learning objectives. In writing this text our aim is to provide you with opportunities to explore key issues (our objectives). Our expectation is that in reading this text you will create your own understanding of the issues explored (your learning outcomes).

Suggested formats for a lesson plan

A lesson plan should be constructed as a means of conceptualizing a lesson. There are many templates available and in the end you need to select or develop one that you feel comfortable with. A successful lesson plan can only really be judged within the context of successful classroom practice. Figures 6.3 and 6.4 offer two popular lesson planning templates. In both cases, they encourage the planner to identify learning objectives/ outcomes, resources, safety issues and individual needs. They also provide a means of sequencing and timing lesson activities. Figure 6.3 distinguishes between 'teacher activities' and 'pupil activities'. This type of distinction can be useful because it enables the planner to recognize whether the lesson is teacher or pupil focused. As previously noted, you should try to build in as much variety in pupil activities as possible. Successful lessons tend not to involve long passive periods of time in which the learner sits listening to the teacher! The importance of active learning is discussed in the following chapter.

We wish you success with your lesson planning and hope that the content of this chapter is useful. If you have recently spent many hours planning early lessons, you should bear in mind that lesson planning does become easier after a while!

General Information

Class _____, Grade _____, Date _____, Room _____, Time _____,

1. **Lesson Objectives**

Knowledge, skills, attitudes, social expectations
National Curriculum reference

2. **Resources Needed**

(eg science equipment, text materials and worksheets, visual-audio equipment, room organisation, ...)

3. **Safety Issues**

Risk assessment for any practical equipment
Key safety warnings – eg a reminder to get all pupils wearing safety glasses

4. **Individual Needs**

5. **Homework**

Time Mins.	**Activity (Teacher)**	**Activity (Pupil)**	**Comments**	**Learning Outcomes (and Assessment)**
5–10	Introduction Orientation – a readiness activity	Listening – in class seats	List of key questions…	Pupils' responses
10–15	Exposition		[continued on separate sheet if required]	
15–45	Etc.			
45–60				
etc.				

Lesson Evaluation: How did the lesson go? Why? What would you change next time? How can you build on this lesson?

Figure 6.3 Lesson planning – one suggested format

General Information

Subject: Topic:
Location: Time:

Teacher Objectives

Knowledge, skills, attitudes, social expectations
National Curriculum reference

Student Outcomes: the children will:

Safety Issues

Risk assessment for any practical equipment
Key safety warnings – eg a reminder to get all pupils wearing safety glasses

Classroom Management Issues

Materials and Resources

Introduction

Procedure

Closure

Key Questions

Modifications

Extensions

Lesson Evaluation:

How did the lesson go? Why? What would you change next time?
How can you build on this lesson?

Figure 6.4 Lesson planning – another format

Further reading

Monk, M (2000) A critique of the QCA specimen scheme of work for Key Stage 3 Science, *School Science Review*, **81**, p 297

Nicholls, G (ed) (1999) *Learning to Teach*, Kogan Page, London

Office for Standards in Education (Ofsted) (1998) *A Scheme of Work for Key Stages 1 and 2: Science*, HMSO, London

Ofsted (2000) *A Scheme of Work for Key Stage 3: Science*, HMSO, London

Sherrington, R (1998) *ASE Guide to Primary* Education, ASE Publications, Hatfield

Wellington, J (1994) *Contemporary Issues and Practical Approaches*, Routledge, London

7 Activities for science teaching

Steve Alsop

Teacher: *In today's lesson we are going to explore photosynthesis, can anybody tell me what photosynthesis is? Yes, Cameron.*

Cameron: *Photosynthesis is how plants make food.*

Teacher: *Yes that's right, photosynthesis is how plants make food. Does anybody know anything more about it? For instance, how does it work?*

Latika: *It's something to do with why they are green... isn't it?*

Teacher: *Excellent Latika, yes it is... Does anybody know the link between plants being green and making food? Why do they need to be green to make food?*

Breanna: *Is it something to do with the greenhouse effect?*

Teacher: *Well, yes and no really Breanna. We will cover the greenhouse effect later on after we have looked at how photosynthesis works. Plants are green because they have a pigment called chlorophyll...*

Objectives

This chapter facilitates critical reflection on a range of science learning activities, including:

- active learning;
- effective questioning techniques;
- classroom discussions;
- collaborative learning;
- explanations.

Introduction

The fictional passage above is intended to illustrate an opening sequence in a science lesson; in this case the setting is a secondary school. The teacher is introducing a unit of study on photosynthesis with a series of questions. This activity might be followed by a short explanation and some notes on the board. Perhaps, after the pupils have copied the notes down the teacher would bring them to the front of the classroom and demonstrate today's experiment, testing leaves for starch using iodine solution. In a previous lesson, silver foil was attached to Pelargonium leaves to isolate the effects of sunlight. Typically after the practical has been performed, the lesson would finish with a series of questions summing up the experiment and highlighting the learning objectives. Lessons like this are common in science classrooms; you might have observed lessons with a similar structure.

As the title suggests, this chapter is concerned with activities for science learning. In the terms of the Department for Education and Employment (DfEE, 1998a: 10), we are considering a range of 'effective teaching methods' (Section B of Circular 4/98) In the fictional lesson above, the teacher is using a variety of learning strategies. These include teacher and pupil questioning, explanations, laboratory work, group work and copying notes from the board. Some of these might be more successful than others; in the above extract for instance, the teacher's questions seem rather short-lived. If their purpose was to explore or investigate pupils' ideas in any depth the questioning sequence, we suggest, warrants further reflection and adjustment.

Chapter overview

The intent of this chapter is to offer practical advice about different learning strategies. To avoid repetition this chapter is selective, strategies involving computer technology, practical work, assessment, language and role play are not considered. These are covered in subsequent chapters – Chapters 8, 9, 10 and 13 respectively. The aim of this chapter is to explore, within the context of the science classroom, five different aspects of practice, namely:

1. teachers' questions;
2. children's questions;
3. classroom discussion;
4. learning structures;
5. explaining clearly.

Throughout the chapter an emphasis is placed on active learning. Before exploring these aspects of practice, we pause briefly to consider what active learning is.

Active learning

The significance of promoting 'active learning' is widely recognized. Educational research has demonstrated the success of teaching and learning activities that actively and collaboratively engage children in the learning process (see Chapter 4). Gone are the days when teaching science involved standing in front of the class reading a one-hour lecture to an audience of note-taking pupils. This type of activity too often results in information passing from the teacher to the children's notebooks without bothering the minds of either. The construction of knowledge requires learners to be *active*ly and purposefully involved in making sense of material rather than being *passive* recipients of another person's interpretations.

Active learning has been widely defined and debated; Bentley and Watts (1992) set out a series of useful markers. *Active learners*, they suggest:

1. initiate their own activities and take responsibilities for their own learning;
2. make decisions and solve problems;
3. transfer skills and learning from one context to another;
4. organize themselves and organize others;
5. display their understanding and competence in a number of different ways;
6. engage in self- and peer evaluation;
7. feel good about themselves.

Bentley and Watts also provide a list of measures that promote this 'style' of learning, including: a non-threatening learning environment; getting pupils actively involved in the learning process; making material relevant and interesting; and continuous assessment, evaluation and feedback. Many of these are explored in this and the following chapters. I start by considering the importance of talking and listening in science classrooms.

Observation Task Reflection: active or passive learning

Use your recent observation (and any teaching experiences) to consider Bentley and Watts' markers for active learning. Is active learning promoted? How might children become more involved in their own learning? While observing science lessons make a note of activities that you feel promote pupils' involvement in learning. Do some teachers get pupils more involved than others? Try to isolate exemplary practice and share your thoughts with others. Consider how you can incorporate these aspects of effective teaching into your practice.

Classroom talk and listening

The first three sections of this chapter are about classroom talk, spoken language and listening. More specifically, the focus is upon how teachers can effectively create, structure and maintain verbal exchanges in the science classroom. In an extremely influential publication, several decades ago, a distinction was made between speech-as-communication and speech-as-reflection (Barnes, 1976). This important distinction structures the following discussions. An essential part of learning is sharing our thoughts with others; children need to be given opportunities to voice their opinions, exchange their outlooks and develop their ideas by testing them out. Speech also has an important reflective component; communicating is a means of thinking out aloud – exploratory talk helps us formulate, structure and order our thinking.

The significance of language in science is explored in Chapter 13. In this chapter, our focus is on three aspects of classroom speech: teachers' questions, pupils' questions and class discussions. We start by visiting teachers' questions.

Teachers' questions

Suppose no one asked a question. What would be the answer?

(Gertrude Stein)

Teachers' questions serve a multitude of purposes. For instance, questions such as: 'Why did you put your Bunsen burner on the water tap?' or 'Didn't I say be careful when pond dipping?' [Splash!] act as warnings and reprimands. Other questions serve the purposes of controlling time, controlling learning and controlling the pace of the lesson. Brown and Wragg (1993) suggest twelve reasons why teachers ask questions, these include: to focus attention, to arouse interest and curiosity, to express an interest in a pupil's work, to structure a task, to diagnose particular difficulties and to develop an active approach to learning. The authors contrast this list with the reasons that most new teachers give for asking questions, which focus mainly on checking understanding and diagnosing difficulties. As a new teacher you need to be aware of the range of purposes that your questions serve.

The focus here is on questioning as a means of helping pupils to think, to learn from each other, and to ask questions. The assessment nature of teachers' questions is explored elsewhere (in Chapter 10).

Effective questioning

So what makes an effective question? In the end, quite simply, an effective question is one that achieves its purpose or aim. However, good questioning is not as simple as it might seem, as Elstgeest (cited by Harlen, 1988) demonstrates:

> A child was reflecting sunlight onto the wall with a mirror. The teacher asked: 'Why does the mirror reflect sunlight?' The child had no way of knowing, felt bad about it and learned nothing. Had the teacher asked: 'What do you get when you stand twice as far away from the wall?' the child would have responded by doing just that, and would have seen the answer reflected on the wall.

One of Elstgeest's recommendations is that teachers should try to curb their 'impulse' to ask questions until they have fully considered their purpose. To overcome this impulse, as a new science teacher, you need to prepare key questions in advance. When planning a lesson, you need to formulate questions and question sequences. Try to put questions in a logical order by predicting responses. In the classroom, you will not be able to stick to the list exactly, questions are exchanges and, most importantly, you will need to listen and respond to pupils' responses. Nevertheless a well thought out question sequence can help you to semi-structure these exchanges.

Different types of questions

There are lots of ways of categorizing questions. Perhaps the best-known distinction is between open-ended and closed-ended questions. Open-ended questions enable pupils to respond in a variety of different ways; they encourage pupils to express an opinion and have no right or wrong answers. Close-ended questions, on the other hand, have a single right answer and require the pupil to respond more directly to the teacher. For example:

'What do you observe about the birds' beaks?'

'What happened when the sugar was added to the water?'

are illustrations of open-ended questions that encourage children to express a point of view and open up further discussion. In other words they are divergent. While their closed versions:

'Do the beaks have different lengths?'

'Has the sugar disappeared?'

tend to close down discussions and can limit responses to a single answer. They are convergent. Both closed and open questions can have their merits. However, something that should be avoided is asking an open question with a single right answer in mind. That is, try to avoid instances of pupils having to guess what is inside the teacher's head. You should also be wary of questions with guess-able yes/no type responses.

Another common distinction is made between higher-order and lower-order questions. Higher-order questions promote reasoning and encourage pupils to link knowledge together or apply it to new situations, they promote thinking. In contrast, lower-order questions involve factual recall. For instance: 'What is the relationship between force and mass?' is a factual question, whereas, 'Have you noticed that heavier objects are harder to move than light ones, why do you think this is?' is a higher-order alternative. Be conscious of using higher-order questions in your teaching, research suggests that these are grossly under-represented in our science classrooms (White, 1989). Ofsted's recent Key Stage 3 progress report (Ofsted, 2000b: 6), for instance, notes the significance of 'Why?' and 'What if?' higher-order questions in effective science teaching.

> In the good science lessons observed questions such as 'Why?' and 'What if?' were used to challenge pupils to offer their own explanations or use their own knowledge to predict effects. The

use of such questions enabled the teachers to establish how well pupils were gaining knowledge and understanding, encouraged them to articulate their developing scientific ideas and promoted discussions. Teachers who made good use of this style of questioning were often less occupied with management of practical activity and made interaction with pupils a priority.

Another useful means of classifying questions is to use science process skills (Sc1). Different questions can be associated with different process skills. This categorization is documented in another chapter and consequently is not explored here (see Chapter 9).

Theory Task Different questions for different purposes

The DfEE (1998a: 10) guidelines for new teachers suggest that effective teaching in science involves the ability to 'skilfully frame open and closed, oral and written questions for different purposes'. Different purposes, the DfEE suggests, are to:

1. elicit and make explicit pupils' existing knowledge or ideas, including identifying misunderstandings about scientific ideas;
2. help pupils make connections between new and prior knowledge, eg making connections between existing knowledge of burning and the chemical reactions in respiration;
3. require intermediate steps in a causal sequence to be made explicit, eg explaining how beta radiation can be used to check the thickness of aluminium sheeting;
4. stimulate discussion and require pupils to articulate and consolidate their understanding through prediction, application and making justifications or repudiations based on scientific evidence;
5. focus pupils attention on different features or aspects of the activity, investigation or science being taught by asking for qualitative or quantitative information;
6. require pupils to broaden their understanding by applying their knowledge of scientific ideas and processes in new contexts.

For each purpose try to come up with a series of suitable questions and discuss these with colleagues. How many of your questions are higher-order, lower-order, closed and open? Do different purposes necessitate different question types?

Distributing questions

A standard sequence for a class question–answer session is:

1. the teacher asks a question;
2. pupils who wish to respond raise their hands;

3. the teacher calls on one student; and
4. the student attempts to state the correct answer.

This type of sequence has a weakness because it only involves a few students. A more effective questioning sequence might try to involve as many pupils as possible in verbal exchanges. The above sequence, for example, could be expanded by asking a variety of different pupils the same question, effectively bouncing a question around the science classroom. Alternatively, the teacher need not always be the focus of questioning interactions; pupil–pupil questioning exchanges should be actively sought and promoted. Trowbridge and Bybee (1996) offer a useful depiction of these differing interactions (see Figure 7.1). Further ways of structuring questions are suggested later in the group work section of this chapter.

A gender bias can exist in questioning interactions. Studies in science education have found that boys tend to receive more higher-order questions than girls, who are asked predominately lower-order question types, particularly in secondary schools (see Barba and Cardinale, 1991). Given this, you need to carefully monitor and plan the distribution of questions in your classroom. Try to keep a mental tally of who has answered questions and plan strategies to effectively distribute your questions.

Wait time

Wait time responses have been considered in some detail by researchers with revealing results. Wait time is the time lapse between asking a question and receiving a response. In science classrooms, teachers were commonly found to give pupils considered more able longer time to respond (nearly two seconds), while those who were perceived less able were given much less time (less than one second). However, when teachers consciously increased wait time (to between three and five seconds) more responses of a greater length were received from *all* pupils (Rowe, 1974). The practical message here is to be conscious of wait time when asking questions. Try to mentally count four seconds before requesting an answer. Inform pupils of the need to think and wait before responding. You might wish to

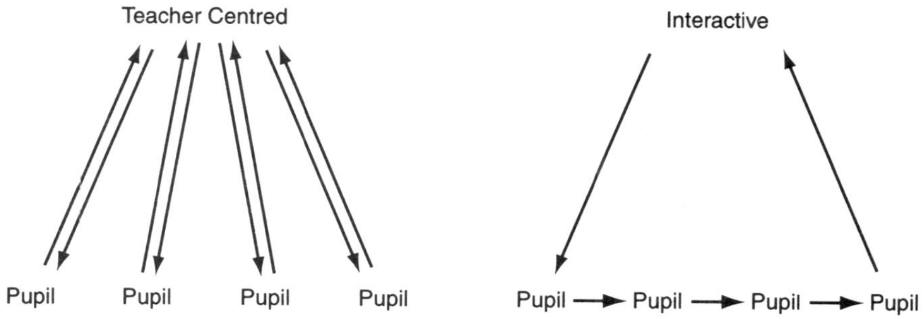

Figure 7.1 Distributing questions
Source: Trowbridge and Bybee (1996)

use phrases such as 'I am going to give you a bit of time to think about this question before we discuss it' to slow down the more impulsive. Reid and Hodson (1987) suggest that by increasing wait time science teachers can break the 'vicious circle' of underachievement.

Practice Task Recording your practice

Try to record questioning sequences in your lessons. You can do this with either an audio or video tape. Play the recording back and analyse your questioning techniques: what types of questions do you ask? How do you sequence questions? How do you distribute questions? And, what is your wait time?

Children's questions

The one thing that stands out from research on children's questions is their infrequency. Teachers' questions dominate classroom interactions and pupil questions are frequently marginalized and often non-existent. This is particularly regrettable because as Watts and Alsop (1995: 94) suggest, pupils' questions have a fundamental role in learning science:

1. Asking questions helps formulate thinking. Children's questions have a fundamental role in reflection and communication. To ask a question is a willingness to seek understanding, an expression of curiosity and therefore an indicator of an effective learning environment.
2. Questions can diagnose areas of understanding and incomprehension. They are diagnostic state of the art indicators of the individual's thinking and can indicate the routes through which pupils are seeking understanding.
3. Science itself is based on asking questions. Some like Einstein's Gedanken experiments led to considerable advances, while experimental science has developed through endless empirical questions. Pupils need to understand the importance of questions in the nature of science and feel that they can ask scientific questions themselves. Pupils' need to understand that different questions require different responses; some stimulate empirical investigations, others necessitate more theoretical pursuits.

Providing an environment that promotes children's questions cannot be left to chance. In the first place, asking questions requires considerable confidence as Lemke (1990) notes:

> It takes a lot of frustration, and not a little self-confidence, for a student to do this. Perhaps this happens more often silently than out loud, but then it does happen and we get a glimpse of the difference in thematic patterns that lie behind so many odd-sounding student questions and so much of the miscommunication and confusion that occurs in everyday classrooms.
>
> (Lemke, 1990: 27)

Encouraging children's questions also requires considerable confidence on behalf of the teacher. Elsewhere, I have suggested a series of classroom strategies designed to help promote children's questions in science classrooms (Alsop, 1992). You might wish to try these out:

1. Explicitly asking children to formulate questions, perhaps after an initial introduction. These questions could form the basis of future topic work. As part of a classroom discussion pupils need to be given the opportunity to propose how they intend to find out answers to their questions. This serves as a means of exploring how different questions require different responses.
2. Using a puzzling situation, perhaps a demonstration, to encourage children to ask questions to explore the phenomena. This could take a form such as a 'twenty questions quiz' where each group takes turns to present their questions to the class discussion. Subsequent groups have to modify their questions in light of the previous responses. For instance, an electric circuit could be presented where the bulb doesn't work (a common phenomenon in physics classrooms!). Groups are then requested to formulate questions exploring why it doesn't work, such as 'Has the bulb blown?' or 'Is the battery flat?' The teacher, or another group could then respond.
3. During a class discussion after a pupil has answered a question they are expected to ask a question. The teacher, for instance, might begin by asking a question and the respondent then asks somebody else the next question. In this case, it is important to have a question in mind as well as knowing the answer before responding. This acts as a means of increasing wait time.

Another way of promoting a 'question rich learning environment' is by encouraging children to keep a journal of their thoughts. This could be completed at home after each science lesson. In this journal, pupils might make a list of all the questions that the science class stimulated. These could be collected together and put up on a 'question-wall' in the classroom. Pupils could then be encouraged to suggest answers, which could also be placed on the wall. Hopefully, a wide range of questions with differing answers will emerge. This would then provide an excellent focus for some reflective classroom follow-up activities.

Ten questions

The following ten children's questions were recorded in primary and secondary pupils' journals. As you read through the questions, we encourage you to consider the validity of children asking more questions in your science teaching – you might also think about the answers to these questions. Sometimes pupils' questions can produce a 'sweaty palm' response in teachers!

1. If oil has energy, why can't barrels of oil move around on their own? If bread has energy for living, why can't a loaf jump off the table?
2. Do insects sleep and why has a spider got eight legs? Do spiders breathe?
3. Meteorites burn up because of friction as they move through the air. Why then, is the wind cold, and why does it feel cold when you stick your hand out of a moving car window?
4. How many times do ants feed in a day? How long can they exist without food?

5. Can you attract light by a magnet?
6. When something falls and hits the ground, it can warm up. If you lift something up, will it cool down?
7. Hot air rises, so why is it so cold at the top of Mount Everest?
8. Does light travel further at night or during the day?
9. Flowers can really brighten a room, do they give off light? When a beam of light comes through the curtains into a room, you can see through to the other side of the room – how is it possible both to see light and to see through it at the same time?
10. Is it really possible to clone a dinosaur?

Classroom discussions

Class discussions, small group discussions and peer discussions provide opportunities to structure and explore understanding. They provide essential opportunities for pupils to formulate, exchange, evaluate and support their viewpoints with classmates and the teacher. We encourage you to incorporate as many opportunities as possible for discussion in your science classroom. However, initiating, maintaining and wrapping up discussions are arguably some of the most demanding aspects of teaching.

The following small group discussion was recorded during a lesson on food safety. Three primary school children (all aged 10), Olivia, Sophie and Marlon have been provided with stimulus material. The material consists of pictures of different foods (roast beef, eggs and chips) mounted on cards. The pupils were asked to consider the dangers involved and arrange the cards in order of increasing danger.

Olivia:	Beef, you know, BSE, isn't it
Sophie:	BSE and the cows
Marlon:	Salmonella
Sophie:	Salmonella, oh yeah... the chicken
Olivia:	Eggs at the top because of the salmonella, I don't know...
Sophie:	The beef is not that dangerous, people still eat it don't they
Marlon:	I know, I eat it
Sophie:	Yeah, I do as well
Olivia:	I don't eat eggs
Marlon:	I do
Sophie:	Chips is just fat isn't it
Marlon:	Why the beef in the middle
Olivia:	Because, if the chips are in the middle, it would be funny – chips are just fattening
Marlon:	You can fry eggs
Sophie:	Or boil them, some people think boiled eggs are nice
Olivia:	Or scramble them, or poach them, but beef has been in the news with all the BSE
Sophie:	I think beef is the most dangerous... because of beef burgers and BSE
Olivia:	Chips are the least dangerous and eggs are in the middle because of salmonella
Marlon:	Finished!

In this rich interchange, the group explores a range of food safety issues. A series of short exchanges act as a forum for pupils to check their understanding, share their knowledge and develop their thinking through the set task. It is difficult to deny that this is a rich learning experience although the teacher, on this occasion, is absent.

There is no doubt that issue-based content (such as food safety) and practical work lend themselves to discussion (see Chapters 9 and 14). Nevertheless, discussion can be used extremely successfully in other ways. For instance, we have observed wonderful small and large group discussions on force and gravity, the digestive system, particles, chemical reaction and plate tectonics. The importance of allowing pupils time to discuss and explore their own ideas is highlighted in Ofsted's review of effective science practice. Ofsted (1999: 12), for instance, provides the following discussion-based primary science teaching sequence as exemplary teaching practice:

> Before starting an investigation [into] dissolving jelly in water, the children discussed with the teacher what questions they would try to answer, how they would go about doing so and what they expected to happen. One pupil suggested that separating the jelly cubes would 'make it easier for the water to get to the bits', another suggested that hot water would make the jelly 'melt more easily', another that stirring would 'help keep the water and jelly mixed up'. The teacher responded positively to all these suggestions but reminded the children about earlier work they had done on melting and made a note to check again later that they understood the distinction between this and dissolving.

You should try to incorporate discussions in all aspects of your science teaching. A well-structured and managed discussion will enable pupils to explore, share, structure and develop their ideas. The following six points are offered as pointers to be considered when contemplating any type of large or small group discussion, we hope they prove useful:

1. *Plan for successful discussion.* Stimulating discussions are often simultaneous and unpredictable; nevertheless, all involve careful forethought. When planning, you need to keep the purpose of the discussion in mind and devise a series of questions to guide and focus the discussions. Discussion needs careful structuring and timing: you need to consider how you can renew attention and heighten interest and allow sufficient time to pull the discussion(s) together at the end. Discussions started in a novel way gain attention and require less maintenance. High impact demonstrations or stories lend themselves to opening up exchanges. You need to have something that the pupils find interesting and can identify with. Before they start, the pupils also need to be clear about the purpose of the discussion and any follow-up activities; they will also need some time to prepare.
2. *Get off to a good start.* At the start of the discussion, provide a series of ground rules for participation. For instance, in a class discussion do pupils need to raise their hand to participate or, in a small group discussion, how can you ensure that everybody participates equally in the conversations? In small group discussions, you might consider assigning roles, such as chair and note-taker.
3. *Promote listening.* Perhaps most significantly successful discussion involves listening, and it is our experience that most pupils are better talkers than listeners. When guiding

class discussions, use non-verbal cues to maintain the flow – prompt pupils to speak and listen by eye-contact. Walk away from pupils who are talking and encourage them to speak to the whole group rather than directly to you. Praise listening as well as talking: 'that is very good listening, James'.

4. *Facilitate discussion*. Keep the discussions focused by listening carefully to what pupils are saying and, where appropriate, summarize their points. Ask questions to clarify pupils' thinking, but try not to impose your point of view. Make sure that pupils are responding to each other and not just repeating a single point of view. Be alert to signs that discussions are breaking down, and prevent arguments. When facilitating small groups, Harlen (1988: 91) suggests the following factors should be considered:
   - joining in as part of the group, without dominating the discussion;
   - listening to children's answers and encouraging then to go on (I see, yes);
   - asking the children to explain their thinking;
   - probing to clarify meaning (what will it be like inside?).
5. *Monitor and increase pupil involvement*. Make sure each pupil has a chance to talk and try to draw all pupils into the discussion. Some pupils will find it easier to speak in small groups, so divide the class into small groups to discuss an issue and then return to the larger class group. Arrange the class so that all pupils can see all those involved in the discussion. Encourage participation by offering support and praising participation. Discourage pupils who monopolize the discussion. In class discussions, use comments like 'I'd like to hear from others in the class' to indicate your desire for increased involvement.

Learning structures

Group work is common in science classrooms; pupils often work in small groups (of perhaps three or four pupils) when performing an experiment or investigation. Group work, however, is less common in other aspects of science teaching. With this in mind, here we offer a range of different ways of organizing the science classroom that you could use in a 'practical' or 'theoretical' context. Our emphasis is on promoting a co-operative rather than a competitive learning environment.

A selection of different learning structures is summarized in Table 7.1 (based on a list proposed by Kagan, 1990). Our advice is simple: try to incorporate as many different learning structures as possible into your practice. Structures should be selected on the basis of their academic, emotional and social usefulness. Different structures support different types of leaning interactions. For instance, an activity such as 'Jigsaw' involves pupils researching information in groups and then reporting this back individually. This requires individual comprehension of new material, informed discussion and working collaboratively with colleagues. In comparison, a round robin discussion of initial ideas helps individuals to formulate these ideas and share them with others. In both cases, pupils are able to get acquainted with their classmates and if the structures are managed sensibly they can create supportive learning environments. These examples promote active involvement for all pupils. This, of course, often contrasts with whole class discussions and expositions where usually only a handful of pupils are actively involved.

Table 7.1 Different group structures

Structure	*Brief description*	*Illustration*
Round robin	Each student in turn shares something with other members of their group.	At the start of a lesson the pupils could explain their initial thoughts about a topic such as food chains and webs with others. This type of structure ensures that all participate.
Corners	Each pupil moves to a corner of the room as directed by the teacher. In their corners they discuss a common theme.	Pupils could be issued with a card with a substance on it (such as copper, ice cream, glass, sugar, oxygen, chlorine etc), corners of the room are labelled as solid, liquid or gas and pupils have to move to a particular corner depending on their cards. Once in the corner they then have to discuss why they went to this corner and what all the substances have in common. Groups could then report back to the rest of the class.
Circus	Stations are set up around the classroom and groups visit a series of stations and then report back.	Pupils could perform a series of experiments on, eg, the circulatory system; this might include stations such as: measuring pulses, direction of blood flow, a computer simulation of the heart and a written exercise.
Question groups	The teacher asks a question and pupils gather in their question groups (or pairs), discuss the answer and report back.	The teacher could ask a question probing understanding such as 'Which of the following are animals?' The groups then discuss a given list or set of cards (depicting for instance a tree, seed, ant, human, spider, cat...) and report back their selection and why. This type of activity can be used to increase thinking and stop impulsive responses.
Research groups	Each group is required to research a particular topic and then report back. The idea is that each group contributes to a common goal.	The teacher provides an overview of the digestive system and each group is assigned a particular component of the system. Groups research for instance the structure and function of the mouth, stomach, large and small intestine, and the bowels. They then produce a summary sheet and report back to the larger group.
Interviews	The pupils interview each other in small groups (or pairs) and then share the information with the rest of the class.	Pupils could interview each other about their understanding of a concept such as evolution by posing a series of questions. This can be useful when reviewing concepts for a final examination.

Table 7.1 *continued*

Structure	*Brief description*	*Illustration*
Roundtable	Each person writes an answer to a particular question when a pen or pencil is passed around a small group.	Pupils gather at a table with a multi-choice question predicting four different responses to an experiment – for instance an extra bulb is added to a simple circuit. Each group member gives their responses and discusses what happens and why.
Jigsaw	Each student becomes an expert on one particular topic by working with members of a group. The groups are then rearranged so that each group contains an expert to provide feedback.	Pupils might explore the life histories of famous scientists and then report their findings back to another group in chronological order.
Brainstorming	Each group is issued with a large piece of paper and asked to 'brainstorm' their thoughts about the topic. This could take the form of a concept map.	Individuals could simultaneously write their thoughts about a concept such as energy on a large piece of paper. As a follow-up activity, the group could discuss these ideas and gather them together into different groups. In the energy case groups might be 'movement', 'living' or 'heat'. The posters could then be placed around the room and form the basis of further class discussion.

Explaining clearly

Clarity of explanation is an essential part of effective science teaching, as Ofsted (2000b) notes in its review of Key Stage 3 classrooms:

> Clear explanation is a vital component of good science lessons yet it is sometimes neglected in the haste to get on with practical activity. In the very good science lessons observed, exposition was the principal means by which the teachers influenced pupils' understanding of ideas. This exposition was, however, an active process; pupils were not passive but engaged in thought rather than simply with the completion of tasks.
>
> (Ofsted, 2000b: 9)

As the above quotation indicates, effective explaining is an *active* process, it is not a simple process of transmitting factual information. Effective explanations:

- direct pupils' attention to important concepts;
- stimulate interest and curiosity;
- isolate and emphasize key concepts;
- make connections between content and pupils' prior ideas;
- develop pupils' thinking;
- involve multiple sensory experiences (listening, seeing, smelling and touching);
- incorporate effective questioning techniques;
- provide opportunities for pupils to ask questions and give feedback.

On the other hand, they do *not*:

- give pupils the basics;
- tell pupils everything you know about a topic;
- make assumptions about what students' know;
- lack structure and focus;
- involve long periods of uninterrupted teacher talk;
- involve limited sensory experiences.

As a science teacher you need to both acknowledge and understand the difficulties experienced by pupils when exploring demanding concepts and plan your lessons accordingly. You need to provide a sense of continuity and meaning by explaining how today's lesson relates to other lessons. You should also provide a sense of purpose by exploring why this content is important and where it is leading. Clear explanations provide a means of structuring pupils' conceptual progression; they should acknowledge and build upon pupils' ideas using familiar examples whenever possible. Clear explanations are memorable, interesting and relevant. Vivid concrete illustrations help pupils understand difficult concepts. HMI have noted that good science teachers use models and analogies well to represent and explain abstract ideas. They isolate the following analogical discussion-based activity as exemplary secondary science teaching:

> Pupils were asked how they pictured electric current and resistance. Suggestions included the flow of water in pipes or a river, cars on roads of varying width, people crowding through a stadium entrance, a 'chain gang', and eels swimming through a swamp! The class discussed the strengths and shortcomings of each of these as representations of electric current. Pupils demonstrated a good understanding of electricity when questioned and used a variety of analogies to explain particular points.
>
> (Ofsted no. 23, 2000b)

Analogies and models are used extensively in science classrooms to explain concepts; they are explanatory tools that seek to aid understanding. For instance, sound waves are often represented by springs (Slinkies) and light waves by water waves in ripple tanks. Other analogies include polystyrene balls and cocktail sticks to represent molecules; a torch and ball to represent the phases of the moon; and egg boxes are often used to represent Villi in the intestine.

Although analogies are commonplace in the science classroom, there is considerable research evidence to suggest that they are not as effective in the classroom as might be expected (see Treagust *et al*, 1996). For instance, particularly in secondary schools, pupils can take an analogy too far and become unable to separate it from the concept that it is intended to represent. Furthermore, pupils can remember the analogy and forget the concept.

Theory Task Classroom reflections on analogies

Make a list of analogies that you have seen used (or deployed) in the classroom. What makes a successful analogy? Are some analogies better than others. Why? How might some analogies be improved?

A teaching audit

One message from this chapter is straightforward: using a variety of teaching and learning approaches can enrich and revitalize your science teaching. Although the 'introduction–practical–summary' formula can be very successful, it can be over used. Indeed recent concerns have been voiced about the lack of variety of teaching and learning strategies in science:

> One of the major difficulties with the current science curriculum is the lack of sufficient variety in the kinds of activities in which learners engage. We feel, therefore, that it is important to emphasise our view that the science curriculum of the future should have much greater variety, not only in the types of activity involved but also in the pace of learning.
>
> (Osborne and Millar, 1998: 5)

In science we are extremely fortunate: we can use all the teaching strategies commonly found in other subject areas (such as maths, English and history) and supplement these with motivating practical work and demonstrations. This chapter has explored a few teaching and learning approaches; there are many others and some of these are covered in the following chapters. We conclude this chapter by providing a list of 72 different teaching and learning activities (Table 7.2 after Hoyle, 1990) – how many do you use?

Theory Task 72 ways of varying your teaching strategies

Review the list in Table 7.2 and consider your own practice: do you use some strategies more than others? If so, devise ways of incorporating different strategies. In the long run, we suggest, it will make your life a lot easier, reduce discipline issues and make teaching more enjoyable.

Table 7.2 72 teaching and learning strategies

1. Worksheets	25. Radio programmes	49. Class practicals
2. Overhead transparencies	26. Making a video programme	50. Demonstrations
3. Board work	27. Group structures	51. Investigations
4. Films/videos	28. Round robin	52. Project work
5. Slides	29. Corners	53. Problem solving
6. Photographs	30. Circus	54. Design and make
7. Newspaper clippings	31. Question groups	55. Computer simulations
8. Television programmes	32. Research groups	56. Databases and spreadsheets
9. Plays	33. Interviews	57. Word processing packages
10. Music – writing songs	34. Roundtable	58. Interfacing
11. Playing games	35. Jigsaw	59. Computer modelling
12. Devising games	36. Brainstorming and sharing	60. Field trips
13. Role plays	37. Listening	61. Day trips
14. Lectures	38. Puzzles	62. Library visits
15. Posters	39. Diagrams	63. Outside speakers
16. Note taking	40. Discussion – teacher led	64. Making a radio programme
17. Report writing	41. Discussion – pupil led	65. Nature trails
18. Creative writing	42. Teacher questions	66. Drama
19. Stories	43. Pupil questions	67. Quizzes
20. Photography	44. Cartoons	68. Tests
21. Rhymes and poetry	45. Textbooks	69. Examinations
22. Art	46. Mime	70. Jokes
23. Historical case studies	47. Analogies	71. Homework
24. Expositions	48. Flow diagrams	72. Concept maps

Source: Hoyle (1990)

Further reading

Alsop, S (1992) Questioning, in *Primary Science and Technology*, ed D Bentley and M Watts, Open University Press, Buckingham

Harlen, W (1988) *The Teaching of Science in Primary Schools*, 2nd edn, David Fulton Press, London

Office for Standards in Education (Ofsted) (1999) *A Review of Primary Schools in England, 1994–1998*, Ofsted, London (http://www.ofsted.gov.uk)

Ofsted (2000) *Progress in Key Stage 3: Science*, Ofsted, London

Osborne, J and Millar, R (eds) (1998) *Beyond 2000: Science education for the future*, Kings College Publications, London

Sutton, C (1992) *Words, Science and Learning*, Open University Press, Buckingham

Watts, M and Alsop, S (1995) Questioning and conceptual understanding: the quality of pupils' questions in science, *School Science Review*, **76**, pp 91–95

A range of excellent activities for science teaching can be found at the Schools Online Science Web site: http://www.shu.ac.uk/schools/sci/sol/contents.htm (supported by Sheffield Hallam University). You can visit the science library, café, project and prep room for teaching ideas.

8 Science education and information and communications technology

Marcus Barbor

Computers can be useful in science lessons. They offer a really good way for children to see the results of their experiments. For instance, in a recent lesson, I got groups of children to monitor their heart rate before and after exercise and plot the results using a spreadsheet.

(Vanessa, a secondary science teacher)

Objectives

This chapter facilitates critical reflection on information and communications technology (ICT) in science education. More specifically, the chapter explores:

- some general and some specific ICT guidance;
- ways to organize and prioritize elements of your ICT learning;
- a range of ICT issues within science;
- ways of avoiding some of the more obvious pitfalls in your early encounters with some of the ICT equipment and software.

Introduction

Using computers and communications technology is not new to science teaching. A very few schools still cherish venerable BBC computers, well over a decade old and still reliably measuring the acceleration due to gravity. What is new, is the insistence by government, through the Teacher Training Agency (TTA), that all teachers become equipped to use information and communications technology (ICT). The full list of requirements for trainee teachers on courses of initial teacher training is provided in Circular 4/98 (DfEE 1998a). In addition, the new Science National Curriculum provides examples of ICT use in science lessons.

There is a view, expressed by the Association for Science Education (ASE) that 'at the end of ITT you cannot produce a fully qualified teacher who is expert in all things' (ASE/DfEE, 1998). This would seem especially to apply to the use of ICT, a view that appears to be acknowledged by the TTA itself when it affirms that throughout their careers teachers will 'continue to improve their skills in using ICT for professional purposes'. The field of ICT just within science education is potentially very large and very few would claim to be expert in all areas of it. So those new to ICT in science will need guidance.

The majority of trainees embarking on science ITT courses already have some skills in the ICT field, but experience is patchy and seldom reflects many of the very specific standards listed under Circular 4/98. ITT institutions are now obliged to monitor their trainees' knowledge but a large proportion of the ICT skills, knowledge and understanding cannot actually be taught within the higher education institution (HEI) itself. As a trainee teacher, you will need to develop much of your ICT competence in school and in your own time.

This chapter will focus exclusively on those areas of ICT that have a bearing on science teaching, in particular elements of:

- word processing and electronic publishing;
- data recording and spreadsheets;
- remote sensing and data logging;
- simulations and modelling;
- presentations;
- multimedia;
- network and Internet opportunities;
- communication.

What is ICT?

The relatively recent change from the term information technology (IT) to information and communications technology (ICT) reflects the accelerating pace at which modern technology is impacting upon teaching. ICT covers not just computers, but any technology involved in communicating such as:

- software;
- CD-ROMs;
- the Internet;
- television and radio;
- image capture devices including still and video cameras;
- sensing, data logging and control apparatus;
- and other equipment, for example even using a video recorder.

ICT is an important teaching tool. Used appropriately it will improve the quality and standard of education in schools in a variety of ways. For example it can:

- enrich the quality of pupils' science classroom experience;
- support you through your continuing education and development;
- make you more effective by reducing time used for administration.

ICT and ITT

The importance the government attaches to ICT, both at primary and secondary school level, is reflected in a number of ways. For the new science teacher perhaps the foremost of these is the way ICT has been made a part of initial teacher training (ITT). It is expected that every newly qualified teacher will have the knowledge, skill and expertise to make decisions about the appropriate use of ICT in school. This will have an impact on your personal and professional development both during and long after your initial training course. Naturally the government has not ignored serving teachers: a New Opportunities Fund (NOF) using National Lottery money is intended to help school teachers and school librarians to make effective use of ICT. These training aims are made explicit in the Expected Outcomes developed by the TTA.

ICT and new science teachers

Many new teachers reveal fears or anxieties, asking 'Do I need to become a computer expert?' The short answer is 'No': ICT is just one of the tools intended to enhance the learning process. Do not be concerned if there appear to be enthusiastic individuals on your course who already seem to know a great deal about computing: your main aim is to learn about teaching, not computers, and to persuade yourself that ICT improves teaching and learning.

On the other hand it is clear that you will need to become familiar with a range of applications and ICT equipment. Set yourself targets in line with your ICT audit. Discuss the possibilities with your HEI tutor and your school mentors to ensure that you become familiar with the key applications. Seek out the opportunities during your block practice episodes (not forgetting to keep records and examples to help demonstrate that you are satisfying the Circular 4/98 standards). It is not essential that you find the latest versions of either hardware or software, indeed one of the refreshing elements of much school science ICT is the way that much hardware and software can remain in service for many years.

Another common question is 'Do I have to buy a computer?' Once again the short answer is 'No' but with some reservations. Clearly satisfying the Circular 4/98 standards cannot be conditional on the ownership of a computer but it does depend upon your professional development. In order to use ICT effectively you will need personal knowledge of ICT, you will need to be familiar with a range of applications that suit your needs and interests and you will need to learn them with a fluency that allows you to use them confidently in a science class of 30 or so lively pupils. The time and energy necessary to acquire this fluency may make you decide that a computer at home is needed. If you do so decide then take plenty of advice, and do bear in mind the often considerable savings that can be made through your being in education. In general hardware costs are so competitive that educational discounts are very low.

ICT in school science

The ICT experiences new science teachers can expect in school are very wide ranging. Different schools vary enormously in their history of spending on ICT provision. So, for example, the number, age and location of computers can vary hugely. It is vital in your training year that you do not allow this to be an impediment to you. If your classrooms have a lonely ageing computer in the corner then make sure your lessons make use of it. If the computing facilities are located in a separate suite then make sure that some of your lessons use the suite – and get it booked.

Theory Task ICT in class

You should become familiar with the ICT standards that you will be expected to demonstrate as a new teacher. These can be found at the TTA Web site (www.tta.gov.uk). The exact manner in which you demonstrate the achievement of these standards will depend on the course you are on and discussion with your HEI tutors and school mentors.

You should, in particular, look at:

- Annexe B, which covers the general ICT standards;
- Annexes E and H, which cover specific ICT issues within science (primary and secondary) including a variety of application types that pupils must use. For example Annexe H Section B c. iii requires that you 'teach pupils to use information technology for more effective collection, analysis and presentation of data, eg data logging; producing graphs from spreadsheets;
- the exemplification material DfEE (1998a).

Data collection

In science lessons you need to use computers to promote learning, not just for their own sake, not just to improve presentation, and not just to entertain. A logical starting point is collecting data. Children at primary level learn how to enter their findings into simple spreadsheet packages. At secondary level this should become routine and science pupils should be able to enter results into a package like Excel. (This can be done with a single, and even quite old computer.) Then you, the teacher, save the results. The results are available next lesson, when you come to revise the topic, to compare with the following years' results, or when disaster strikes and a practical goes awry. More importantly, a set of results gives you a means to discuss with pupils how the results can best be displayed. Is a bar chart appropriate, a pie chart or a line graph? What scales are needed? A spreadsheet allows you to switch swiftly from one to another and to discuss the merits of each. This approach should reduce the time wasted by pupils toiling to produce beautiful but inappropriate graphs. If you haven't used a spreadsheet before doing so should be a top priority.

Interfacing

In science teaching 'interfacing' broadly means attaching an experiment to a computer. The purpose of interfacing is to collect experimental data straight into the computer memory. Apart from eliminating some errors while taking readings, a particular advantage of this approach is that it permits continuous readings from experiments that would otherwise be too rapid or too slow. For example the discharge of a capacitor can be measured, or the fluctuation in temperature and oxygen of a pond can be monitored over a week or more.

The progress of such experiments is detected by sensors and there are many different types, including temperature, light levels, sound and movement. A very few computers, such as the RM Nimbus 'Windows boxes' developed for primary schools, allow sensors to be plugged straight into the machine. However in the great majority of instances direct plugging is not possible and an interface box is needed. You plug the sensors (usually a maximum of three or four) into a separate box and the box into the computer, usually through the serial socket. Some interface boxes work with a wide range of sensors, a few accept only dedicated sensors. Those working with dedicated sensors are often simpler to set up.

The sensors are normally set running by software which is capable of storing, saving, and presenting the data collected. The variety of sensors is ever widening (eg pH, movement, light, temperature, heart rate) and a glimpse through a supplier's catalogue will probably whet your appetite, but there are a few snags. For most science department budgets the sensors and interface boxes are expensive. In your school or college there may only be a few sensors. They may have been bought over several years and so may be from more than one manufacturer, in which case they will not 'mix and match'. To ensure your ICT experience includes teaching with this equipment you may have to use the equipment as part of a demonstration or else have the interfacing as part of a 'circus' of activities. The circus approach will require a particular teaching style that you may wish to discuss with your mentor in school.

The good news is that interfacing is rarely very demanding of the power of the computer. Even an old computer (such as a '386') will usually be perfectly suitable to connect to an interface box to collect data. The problems may arise with the software. Interface boxes require software that you will have to learn how to use. It is quite possible for data to be collected and stored on an old computer running old dedicated software, but you may find that you have insufficient time to educate the pupils in the use of the software. Most manufacturers continue to rewrite and upgrade their software making the packages more intuitive, graphical and user friendly. But then you may find the latest version only works under a more recent operating system (such as Windows 2000) that won't run on an old machine. But don't despair, a fall back position is to use the old 386 with the interface box and its sensors to capture that data, save the data to a file on a floppy disk, and reopen the data under Excel in another machine. The feasibility of this approach will depend on the facilities in school, and your experience and enthusiasm! You should find out how to collect and store data and how to reopen it in Excel. Once learned, the principles will apply to other combinations of hard- and software that you may encounter in future.

Many of the problems mentioned in the last few paragraphs will diminish as pupils get older and may become competent, autonomous users. At this stage, if not earlier, you may wish to take advantage of another feature of many dataloggers: they can be used away from the computer. Several types can be taken out of the lab, for example to make readings as part of an ecological study of a pond. Security and battery life permitting, the interface box can be left to gather data over a protracted period. The box is then brought back to the lab or plugged into a laptop and the data downloaded. In principle this is simple enough but you are strongly advised to try it out several times before undertaking anything important such as examination coursework. An inadvertent touch on a button at the wrong time may bring tears (for teachers and pupils!).

By way of example, Figure 8.1 shows a very simple set up, monitoring the weight of a plant over several days. The polythene bag prevents water loss except through the stem and leaves. The light period was controlled by means of a time switch. Weight, light and temperature were monitored using a Philip Harris datalogger and Philip Harris software. The slope on the weight graph allows you to hypothesize about the action of the stomata and the transpiration rate.

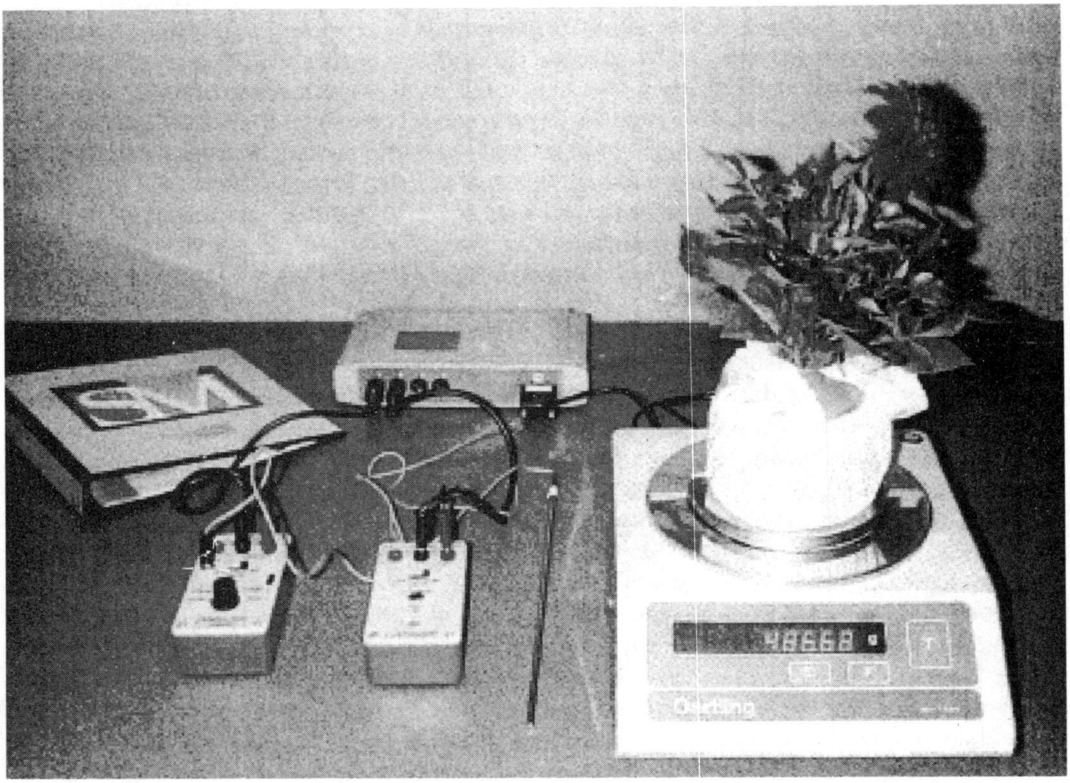

Figure 8.1 Experiment showing data logging in use with a plant monitoring activity

Modelling and experimenting

Scientists make computer models as a way of testing their hypotheses. The results of manipulating the model are compared with reality in order to test their theories. Pupils should be introduced to the idea of modelling in science and at some stage can be taught to create their own models. A useful introduction to this is outlined by Cox (1999).

Computer models have also been used extensively to allow pupils to do 'virtual experiments'. Computer models allow pupils to investigate systems which are too fast, too slow, too remote, too dangerous, too expensive – too anything for the classroom, eg studying radioactive material, exploring a human body in 3-D or trying out variations on an industrial chemical process. Many opportunities will come from specially written software, often on CD-ROM. Visitors to the Association of Science Education annual conference will know that a number of major public companies and utilities in the UK have written software of this type. The Internet also provides another resource point, for example the virtual fly lab allows pupils to do a wide range of Drosophila breeding experiments in minutes rather than weeks (see at www.biologylab.awlonline.com).

You must be selective. The important point is to ensure that the software you are contemplating really delivers the educational objectives you desire, and that these objectives are clear to the pupils you are teaching. Pupils need to know why they are doing the activity and what they should learn from it.

Another important point is that the computer should not get in the way of the learning experience (this is especially true of the next section too). Some pupils, particularly younger pupils or those with SEN, may have very modest keyboard skills. For such pupils you may wish to use software that takes advantage of simplified input devices, such as concept keyboards. ICT in special needs teaching is explored in Chapter 12.

Presenting

Using a word processor is not just about improving the presentation. You can use a word processor in many of the ways you might have used pencil and paper or paper only tasks. As a teacher you can create, for example:

- sequencing activities – pupils use the mouse to drag and drop sentences written by you into the correct order;
- completion tasks – short accounts with phrases missing;
- error correction tasks – you write the account with deliberate errors, pupils find and correct them.

A whole range of text processing activities is available to you, though of course these are not science specific. Many pupils will wish to include diagrams of their science apparatus in their reports. This is potentially a great waste of time. Until pupils have reasonable graphics skills, and probably good and appropriate software, it will be hard for them to create worthwhile diagrams. It is unlikely that science lessons are an appropriate occasion on which to develop pupils' graphics skills. You, the teacher, have a variety of other strategies in this area, including:

1. pupils leave a blank space in their report and draw, in pencil, on the print out;
2. you provide a ready drawn image on the computer for them to incorporate;
3. you provide a photo of the apparatus.

You will find out more about (2) and (3) later in this chapter.

Class management issues and teaching styles

Though ICT should not dominate your teaching style, it will at times have an impact. As we have already seen you may need to adapt your approach to suit occasions when only a single computer is available in a science room. Some schools have networks and others have ICT rooms, so there may be occasions when you have to plan an entire science lesson to fit around an activity in a computer suite. Only in a few schools is it possible to move from a lab to a computer suite and back again in a single lesson.

Practice Task Some possible early priorities for science teachers

As a new teacher you should make it a priority to:

- use an Internet search engine;
- visit a range of science Web sites and make a list of those you find most useful;
- use electronic sensing equipment to capture experimental data (data logging) and use the data logging software to tabulate and chart the results;
- take data from a data logging experiment and transfer it to a spreadsheet package such as Microsoft Excel where the charting possibilities are much greater;
- use a modelling program which allows you to investigate the effect of changing a single variable;
- use a CD-ROM database.

Remember that evidence of doing these sorts of activities may help you to demonstrate achievement of the TTA standards.

Lesson preparation

Many new science teachers are attracted by the idea of using a computer to produce worksheets and transparencies for the overhead projector. This route will allow you to create professional looking pages but, initially, it will probably take you quite a while. As your IT skills improve you will get quicker, but think carefully about whether the computer is most appropriate: cutting and pasting real paper can produce an acceptable product much more quickly. The computer route really comes into its own when you need to produce a series of similar pages, or where you wish to experiment with an idea, perhaps over a series of lessons. If you have chosen to use the computer to create documents containing pictures then you face two sets of problems. First you have to get the image and other components of the document into the computer, and second, you may have to create the hard copy.

Multimedia

The term multimedia can mean practically anything, from a computer that happens to be equipped with a pair of speakers to a complex program capable of driving a laser disk or DVD player and multiple screens and hi-fi quality sound. Multimedia is not an unalloyed joy. CD-ROMs that employ sound can prove to be a distraction in a class. On the other hand anyone who has seen a by-now famous clip of caesium being added to water will know that the impact is lost if pupils cannot hear the splintering crash of the glass trough breaking.

Multimedia, especially with a video projector, can provide real impact in a classroom as your computer becomes a flexible blackboard, a movie clip presenter and more. In your training year, the opportunities to explore this field will depend on the equipment in your placement school and your HEI. However the next subsections discuss a number of areas you should actively investigate.

Presentation application

Many schools will have Microsoft PowerPoint, though there are many other such packages. For teaching purposes presentation packages have many strengths including:

- they allow you to build sequences of images and text which will replace a series of OHTs;
- they will be cheaper than OHTs as there is no printing cost;
- images or text can be 'built up' in stages, relieving you of the need to use a sheet of paper to gradually reveal the contents of your OHT;
- the reduced cost diminishes the temptation to squeeze more text onto a screen than you should: you have no limit to the number of 'slides' that you can display;
- they can incorporate sound and/or movie clips;
- pupils can easily be taught to incorporate text and images for presentation purposes;
- selected 'slides' in a sequence can be printed out;
- a good package like PowerPoint will enable you to print out a page of thumbnails which will aid your audience in note taking.

Whilst there is no doubt that presentation packages have their place in school, the number of occasions is fewer than one might imagine. With many groups of children the linear approach demanded by the presentation sequence may not work, or may not suit your style. The 'slides' are difficult to alter as you teach, whilst you can easily write or draw in an ad hoc fashion on a printed acetate sheet (or preferably on a plain one laid over the top of your carefully crafted *magnum opus*).

On the other hand, when you become proficient, it is surprising how little time is needed (eg over break) to add a few extra slides incorporating, say, a pupil's results or a photograph of a group's experimental set up. Another bonus is that PowerPoint is relatively easy to learn.

Multimedia packages

Serious multimedia 'authoring' packages can be extremely complex and difficult to learn. However a few are simple enough to be used by primary school children.

An analogy is of a series of post cards in a pack. Each card can contain text, images or even a short movie clip, plus one or more buttons. When clicked, using the mouse, the button will navigate you to a new card – not necessarily the next in the pile. The actual authoring – compiling the cards and writing instructions for the buttons – can be simple but the result can be astonishingly effective. The user need not be aware that the card has changed: instead he or she may get the impression that his or her button click is simply adding atoms to a molecular model that is on the screen – or won't grow if the wrong type of atom is selected.

Digital cameras

Digital cameras take photographs and store the information as a computer file. Though relatively expensive to buy, the cost of taking a single photograph is negligible. They allow the science teacher a fantastic range of opportunities. In addition to their use as a means of trasferring data onto the computer, the cameras are also useful:

- in field work, eg directing pupils to a specific place;
- in creating assembly instructions such as for a motor;
- for illustrating how to use a microscope;
- in creating records of pupils' work;
- for monitoring the progress of a project;
- simply for making a set of photos of a class to learn their names.

Better digital cameras take larger pictures (usually measured in pixels). These bitmap files may be very large – sometimes too large to fit on a floppy disk. Once taken, a photo can be 'squirted' into your computer and then saved, freeing up space in the camera for more snaps. Many digital cameras connect via the computer's serial port. Downloading via the serial port can be extremely slow. One picture may take about a minute, so you can imagine how long a set of class snaps will take. Many cameras have quicker ways of downloading, for example the Kodak cameras use small flash cards to store the images. These cards can be popped out of the camera, placed in a special flash card reader and downloaded 20 or 30 times more quickly.

If you wish to use a digital camera in class, live, then you will certainly need to enquire about the download routine and the software it uses.

Links with other schools

Communication by e-mail is becoming commonplace. It provides a simple effective and inexpensive way of communicating. The Internet provides a variety of other communications opportunities. Many television programmes, particularly those with a science theme, offer a chance to 'talk' to a scientist after the programme. The BBC Web site provides many such opportunities (see at http://www.bbc.co.uk/science/). There are also science chat rooms: though you will want to check these out before recommending them to your pupils. The ASE co-ordinates the Science Across the World initiative where pupils exchange data via e-mail on common science projects. Further details can be obtained from the ASE Web site (www.ASE.org.uk).

The Internet is also a route by which schools can communicate with each other. It is probably fair to say that this is still an enthusiast's activity, but many schools can and do exchange ideas, views, opinions via Web sites established for this purpose. Some schools communicate with partner schools on the continent, often with a desire to promote language skills but science topics may provide the content. In your training year it is more a question of 'watch this space'.

The Internet

The explosive growth of Internet connection indicates a sea change in our society. It is a commonplace that the next generation will do things differently. A real danger is the growing difference between the educational possibilities of those who have and those who lack, access to the Internet. Schools can do something to redress the balance by allowing pupils adequate access. For obvious reasons this will not be entirely unrestricted.

One positive endeavour you can make is to find appropriate teaching activities on the net. Ebenezer and Lau (1998) have compiled the following 11-point checklist of criteria for selecting Internet resources suitable for pupil use:

1. The lesson plan should match the goals and objectives of student learning.
2. The science content must be at an appropriate developmental level.
3. The reading level must also be appropriate.
4. The Web site must present meaningful information and activities for both teachers and students.
5. Lesson plans and activities must reflect scientific inquiry, the curriculum connections (science, technology and the environment), integration and multiple approaches to teaching and learning.
6. The Web site must have links to other related Web sites.
7. The Web site must have background information with lesson plans.
8. The Web site must provide connections to experts, peers, teachers, or mailing lists.
9. The Web site should have a variety of activities available, either online or downloadable to disk.
10. Information must have a multimedia approach: sound, movie, animation and good graphics.
11. Articles and papers must have complete references.

We would also add to this list the following points:

1. The Web site should enable pupils to explore their own ideas – it should have a 'constructivist' philosophy.
2. The Web site should involve pupils in active thinking and problem solving.
3. The Web site should be gender, ethnically and culturally appropriate.

You will also need to think about the extent to which a Web site suits your teaching and learning style and is appropriate in terms of race and gender. The points made by Ebenezer and Lau have more force in relation to science activities done away from the classroom. Web-based activities carried out in your presence can be properly contextualized, fully explained and, if need be, adapted.

Some useful Web sites are listed in Table 8.1.

As with all Web sites these are subject to change and modification of address. For this reason, rather than giving a comprehensive list we suggest that you use the search engines available to track down other resources.

Trainees will need to keep abreast of developments in the National Grid for Learning (NGfL) (http://www.ngfl.gov.uk/). This will be a way of finding and using online teaching and learning material. The government plans that the NGfL will be a public–private partnership providing a national service aimed at raising standards for teachers and learners. It will include online advice for pupils and teachers, GCSE revision and differentiated support including special needs. The target date is 2002, by which time it is planned that all schools will be connected to the 'superhighway' and both pupils and teachers will be ICT literate.

How ICT is making teaching more problematic

The sheer quantity and availability of information through CD-ROM and the Net can provide problems for teachers, especially in relation to homework. It is so easy to look up in Encarta (the Microsoft CD-ROM and Internet-based encyclopaedia) and print off a section without having to understand, or even read, the extract. Teachers need to think carefully about the implications of the new ICT technology for the type of activity that they should set. One of the biggest problems remains the inequality between those who have Internet access at home and those who do not.

Because of the open nature of the net there is little control over what is published. Many pupils are now publishing their own GCSE coursework. So current GCSE pupils will have ready access to other pupils' work. The implications are obvious: the precautions schools should take are less so. It would be unfortunate for science teachers to become cynical and to perceive real imagination or innovation by their pupils as undiscovered plagiarism.

What of the future?

The government intends that the UK will be among world leaders harnessing new technologies to raise educational standards and thereby to increase the UK's international

Table 8.1 Useful science Web sites

Web site	*Comments*
www.justforteachers.co.uk	A site of educational news, examples of good practice and classroom resources for teachers
www.ASE.org.uk	The site of the Association for Science Education. A 'must have' site for all science teachers
www.iob.org	The Institute of Biology
www.iop.org	The Institute of Physics
www.rsc.org	The Royal Society of Chemistry
www.sciencemuseum.org.uk	The Science Museum, London
www.nhm.ac.uk	The Natural History Museum, London
www.quest.arc.nasa.gov	The main site of the NASA agency, full of useful images and information for teaching about space
www.inform.umd.edu/UMS+State/UMD-Projects/MCTP/Technology/Minority.html	A multicultural science site
www.volcano.und.nadak.edu	Everything you want to know about volcanoes
www.teachernet.com	A site of resources for teachers
http://flybase.bio.indiana.edu	Genetics or inheritance for KS4 science
Landau1.phys.Virginia.EDU/Education/Teaching/HowThingsWork/	Answers all those scientific queries that you never asked
www.reticule.co.uk/flora/	A site for the identification of British wild flowers
www.unmuseum.mus.pa.us/dinosaf.htm #stop1	Information on dinosaurs
www.innerbody.com/image/skelfov.html	A site useful for getting information about the human skeleton
www.engagingscience.org/lpe/lpe/htm	A range of science classroom activities for KS1 & 2
www.ollaquicksource.com/resources/science/Physical/magnets.htm	A large site full of ideas and information about magnets and suitable for all Key Stages
www.illusionworks.com/	A KS4 site on the human eye
www.astr.ua.edu/4000WS/4000WS.html	A site dedicated to the 4,000-year history of women in science
www.crocodile-clips.com/education/crocphys/index.htm	A site dedicated to physics simulation software
www.chem4kids.com/	A useful site for exploring chemistry with KS 3 & 4 students
http://tqd.advanced.org/16600/beginer/	Online physics textbook – useful for addressing gaps in your subject knowledge
www.eurekascience.com/ICanDoThat/dna_rep.htm	A site dedicated to DNA and its replication

competitiveness. The rate of change in ICT in general and the intention to embrace all teachers means we can expect rapid developments. How will your professional development keep up with the expected changes? Clearly the government expects that the NGfL will have an important influence. Meanwhile there are other centres that can help keep you up to date. Three useful starting points are:

1. ASE publications, meetings, conferences and Web site;
2. British Education Technology and Training (BETT) – an annual London-based show hosting exhibitions, seminars etc, usually in January;
3. Education Show – an annual Birmingham-based (National Exhibition Centre) show with a strong ICT vein.

Details of these can all be found on the Internet, quite easily, or, easily when someone has shown you how!

Further reading

Cox, M (1999) Using Information and Communication Technologies (ICT) for Pupils' Learning, in *Learning to Teach*, ed G Nicholls, Kogan Page, London

Department for Education and Employment (DfEE) (1998) *Requirements for Courses of Initial Teacher Training*, Circular 4/98, DfEE, London

DfEE (1998a) *Requirements for Courses of Initial Teacher Training*, Circular 4/98, DfEE, London (exemplification materials see http://www.teach-tta.gov.uk/itt/supporting/ ict_exemp.htm)

Somekh, B and Davis, N (1997) *Using Information Technology Effectively in Teaching and Learning*, Routledge, London

9 Practical work in science

Keith Hicks

I like science because we do practical work. (Joe, a year 8 secondary school pupil)

You have to do practical work otherwise the kids go mad. (Joanne, a secondary science teacher)

Objectives

In this chapter we will discuss and reflect on the role of practical work and investigations in science education today. More specifically this chapter explores:

- the reasons for carrying out practical work in school science lessons;
- the types of practical work undertaken in science;
- the role and nature of investigations in science;
- the assessment of investigations;
- safety in science lessons.

Introduction

Since the introduction of the Nuffield science projects in the 1960s, practical work has been a common feature of science education in the UK. However, practical work may mean different things to different people. Within the context of the Science National Curriculum it is often taken to mean investigative work, which means that it is a statutory requirement for you to assess your pupils in this area of the science curriculum. This hands-on approach to science education is a particular feature of science teaching in England and Wales where large amounts of resources are devoted to the building of science laboratories in schools and to the provision of technical staff to support science teaching. This is especially true in the secondary sector. In recent years this emphasis on practical work in school science education has been questioned. People have talked about the 'hands-on, head-off' approach of pupils to practical work and the great motto of Nuffield science from the 1960s of 'I do and I understand' has been parodied as 'I do and I'm even more confused.'

For most pupils the move from primary to secondary school sees the move from doing science in the classroom to doing science in the laboratory. Science becomes marked off from other curriculum areas and pupils are inducted into the strange and mysterious world of Bunsen burners and conical flasks. To what extent does that move hinder or enhance effective science teaching? There is an acute danger that this demarcation of the subject devalues the work done in science in the primary sector, with the impression given by many secondary science teachers that what they are now embarking on is 'real' science because you cannot really do science without a science laboratory. In reality, much effective science education is carried out in the primary sector and this is evidenced by the enthusiasm the pupils have for the subject when they arrive in secondary school. Within two years much of that enthusiasm has evaporated – could this be due to the presentation of science as being something set apart from the rest of the curriculum and a subsequent sense of alienation in pupils to the rituals and practices of the school science laboratory? These are questions we want you to consider as you work through this chapter.

Theory Task Why do practicals?

Reflect upon your understanding of the reasons for doing practical work in science. Brainstorm a list of reasons for carrying out or benefits from doing practical work. What arguments can you present to justify the resources demanded for practical science in school? If possible share your ideas with other trainees or new teachers. Try and sequence your ideas in order of importance.

Repeat the exercise with a group of pupils. Ask them why we do practical work in science. Again ask them to sequence their reasons in order of importance. Use the opportunity of this exercise to discuss the idea with the pupils.

Compare your list with the list compiled by the pupils. How do they compare in terms of content and sequence?

The role of practical work

In recent decades the role of practical work in science has been very heavily influenced by the Nuffield science teaching projects of the 1960s which aimed to make pupils 'scientists' as they worked in their science lessons. To facilitate that aim many new experiments and apparatus for school science were devised and still remain part of the standard repertoire of school science lessons. It was assumed by this approach that if you allowed pupils to make the appropriate observations of selected experiments and procedures then they would be able to infer and conclude scientific laws and theories by themselves. The idea that explanations emerge from a series of observations was presented to pupils as the way that scientists work. This assumption now seems slightly ludicrous. No matter how guided and structured those observations are, it most unlikely that pupils will arrive at the laws of science by a process of some sort of natural intuition. This is clearly not the way that real scientists work or that new theories are generated.

Many science teachers feel that the laboratory is central to the task of teaching science, but as this chapter will make clear there have been many studies on the effectiveness of practical work on science teaching and the results of those studies are by no means conclusive. As Joseph Novak states:

> The science laboratory has always been regarded as the place where students should learn the process of doing science. But summaries of research on the value of laboratory work for learning science... show an appalling lack of effectiveness of laboratory instruction... Our studies showed that most students in laboratories gained little insight regarding the key concepts involved or toward the process of knowledge construction.
>
> (Novak 1988: 77–101)

If practical work does not allow students to 'discover' the laws of science, what then does it do? Many practical activities carried out in lessons are designed to allow pupils to make connections between the concrete things they can see and touch and the more abstract ideas or theories that may account for the observations they make.

When science teachers are asked the question 'why do practical work', why is it necessary to have an answer? A knowledge of the reasons why you do practical work in science is important so that you can effectively state the aims of your lessons and also plan more effectively the practical work so that it meets those aims. It is also important to be able to justify the resources that are spent providing support for practical science in schools. Wellington (1998: 6) presents three arguments for doing practical work which he calls: the cognitive argument, the affective argument and the skills argument. For each of these arguments Wellington presents the case that there is also a counter-argument which we should be aware of. These three areas recognize that as science teachers we are concerned with both the content of science and its process.

The cognitive argument

The premise of this argument is that by doing practical work pupils' understanding of the theories and abstract concepts of science education can be better understood and visualized. By doing theory work, it is hoped that the concepts are made more accessible to the pupils and that those theories can be confirmed by their own experiences. Science teachers talk of practical work backing up the theory taught in their lessons or illustrating the theoretical component of the lesson. By doing practical work teachers can give pupils a first-hand experience of the abstract concept they are trying to communicate to their pupils. Wellington (2000) argues that in reality practical work may cause pupils to become confused just as easily as it may clarify their understanding. There is little argument that practical work can aid pupils to elicit the theories of science as envisaged in the Nuffield science projects of the 1960s, rather, it is now believed that practical work has a place in the learning scheme after the theory has been taught.

The affective argument

This is the belief that practical work helps to generate interest and motivation for the subject. Some science teachers argue that by doing practical work things become easier to remember and pupils become more enthusiastic about their lessons. Most science teachers will tell you the first question asked by pupils at the start of the lesson is often about the possibility of doing practical work, but to what extent is this a reflection of the hands-on head-off approach mentioned earlier? Johnstone and Wham (1982) noted that 'pupils enjoy practical work, pick up hand skills with varying degrees of proficiency, but learn little of the theoretical information which practical work is alleged to illustrate or to initiate'. It would be wrong to assume that all pupils are motivated by practical work; some appear to be very demotivated by it, preferring to take on the role of the passive learner rather than the active learner. It is the nature of school practical work that it does not always 'work' and this too can demotivate pupils despite our best explanations of what went 'wrong'.

The skills argument

Some science teachers would claim that practical work helps to promote the development of skills such as observation, inferring, investigating and hypothesizing (see Chapter 3) and that these skills are intrinsically valuable and transferable. While some measurement skills are clearly of value and transferable it could be that the other skills have, in reality, little use in future life.

In order to assess the purpose of practical work in a science lesson we suggest that you cannot give blanket definitions and aims but rather need to evaluate the particular exercise being undertaken in a particular lesson with a particular class. It could well be that in certain circumstances the same practical exercise may serve different functions with different groups of pupils. If you carry out a practical exercise in a lesson it is important that you know why you do so and that its aim is communicated to the pupils in your care.

Observation Task Practical work in action

Observe a science lesson that involves an element of practical work. Before the lesson starts discuss and agree with the teacher the aims for including that piece of work in the lesson. As the lesson progresses, evaluate the extent to which the agreed aims are being met. Is the practical activity justified or could its content have been delivered more effectively without the activity? Are there individuals or groups of pupils for whom the aims of the practical exercise are not clear or for whom the aims are not met? Discuss with your mentor how you would run the lesson to make the practical exercise a more valuable learning experience for all the pupils.

Demonstrations

Demonstrations are defined as the process of showing something to another person or group (Trowbridge and Bybee, 1996: 184). There are many ways in which you can give a demonstration: it could be that you present the demonstration as an exercise for your pupils of observation or verification. For instance you may show sodium reacting in water and say, 'This is sodium, it reacts with the water to produce hydrogen gas and sodium hydroxide.' Alternatively a demonstration may be given inductively where the teacher asks many questions but gives very few answers. This second approach has the advantage of being more motivating to the pupils as it is presented to them as a series of riddles or puzzles, taxing their minds and inviting them to think. It also provides better information for the teacher of the pupils' understanding and comprehension of the demonstration.

As well as being an exercise in observation and verification or induction, demonstrations can also be experimental in nature. If a problem is being presented to a class for which the solution is not immediately apparent, such as determining the reactivity series of the alkali metals or investigating the sink or float properties of a number of objects, then the demonstration is experimental. Experimental demonstrations can be particularly motivating to pupils as they involve more action than words, allowing them to see the answers to questions with their own eyes.

Learning how to give good demonstrations is clearly an important skill for new science teachers. It is also important to know when it is best to demonstrate and when to allow individual experimentation in the laboratory. Individual laboratory work promotes a whole range of process skills in a way that a demonstration does not, but demonstrations can be justified for the following reasons:

- *Expense.* Carrying out a demonstration of a procedure or experiment is cheaper in terms of the cost of apparatus and equipment used.
- *Equipment.* Some procedures require apparatus that may not be available in sufficient amounts for class use. It is unusual for a primary school to have class sets of glassware or microscopes for instance, while in secondary school it is unlikely that class sets of ripple tanks are available.
- *Time.* It is usually much quicker for a teacher to carry out a demonstration than for a class to carry out a class experiment. It is important to ask if the time taken for an exercise is justified in terms of the increase in knowledge it brings about in your pupils.
- *Safety.* Some procedures or materials are too dangerous for pupils to use.
- *Effective teaching.* In a skilled demonstration the teacher can direct the thinking process of the class to challenge their conceptual frameworks.
- *Demonstrate procedures.* When you need to teach pupils how to use a new piece of apparatus or carry out a new procedure a demonstration is usually the most effective way of doing this.

If you are giving a demonstration for the first time it is vital that you practise the procedure first. Giving a demonstration is a performance and as such needs good rehearsal. If possible you should rehearse in front of a critical friend who can comment on your performance to ensure that things are visible and that you speak loudly enough. Remember that you need to convey a sense of excitement and drama about the demonstration to your audience.

Throughout the demonstration you need to ask questions about what you are doing, what is happening and what is going to happen. Invite pupils to respond to the apparatus and events on show and remember to give plenty of positive reinforcement to the pupils' responses. At the end of your demonstration ask a pupil to summarize what the purpose of the demonstration was and what has been learnt.

A demonstration should not be a teacher-centred activity as this does not allow for enough pupil involvement. Try to involve pupils in the demonstration as much as possible, working as a team. This approach will lead to pupils paying greater attention to the activity as they would much rather watch their peers than you! In this way a demonstration can be used to power forward a class understanding of a particular concept and allow the teacher to skilfully assess the extent to which the class and individuals have assimilated the required knowledge.

Practice Task Presenting a demonstration to a class

Seek out an early opportunity to carry out a demonstration to a group of pupils you teach. Before you carry out the demonstration consider the following points:

1. What the aim of the demonstration is.
2. Whether the demonstration will be a process of verification, induction or experiment.
3. How you will ensure all members of the group can see and hear the demonstration.
4. To what extent you will involve the pupils in the demonstration.
5. Prepare a script of questions that you will use in the demonstration.

Arrange for your mentor to be present during the demonstration and discuss how effective it was with your mentor following its delivery.

Individual laboratory work

Individual laboratory work or whole-class practical work is the mainstay of practical work in secondary science. In the primary sector the advent of the National Curriculum resulted in a wider range of practical work being done in KS2 and we include that work under this heading while acknowledging that such work is rarely done in laboratories. The effective use of individual practical work requires a high level of skill from science teachers who need to be competent themselves in the tools of inquiry. At this point we will make a distinction between the individual laboratory work and investigations as defined in the context of Attainment Target 1 (AT1) which we will discuss later in this chapter. Learning how to run an effective practical session is a key skill the new science teacher must acquire.

In view of already stated concerns doubting the effectiveness of practical activities in promoting learning during science, let us consider how the organization of those activities can enhance learning. Johnstone and Wham (1982) suggest that this poor performance is due to an information overload on the 'working memory' of pupils during practical work and suggest three key steps that teachers can undertake to counteract this:

1. The aims and goals of the practical work should be made very explicit by the teacher at the start of the activity.
2. Pupils need to be informed about what is 'preliminary', 'peripheral' and 'preparatory'.
3. Manipulative skills should not be taught at the same time as data collection to avoid possible overload.

These steps are sensible precautions to follow in any practical work situation and will help to enhance the learning that takes place. Whatever the ability of the pupils you teach, the practical work needs to be differentiated to meet the needs of the pupils. Hofstein (1988) suggests the following guide for differentiating practical work to meet the needs of different abilities:

- *Lowest level*: pupils report the results of one simple experiment using units of measurement specified by the teacher.
- *Medium level*: pupils report the results of several replications of the experiment, choosing for themselves the units of measurement and justifying their choice.
- *Highest level*: pupils report the results of several treatments and replications, determine not only the units of measurement but also the most efficient and visually expressive organization and presentation of the complex results.

By acting on these basic guidelines for doing class practical work you will be able to plan practical activities which are enjoyable and useful for both yourself and your pupils.

The setting up and delivery of whole-class practical work poses problems that have to be dealt with by careful classroom management as it inevitably involves moments of transition from one activity to another which occur more frequently in practical lessons. These points of transition are key points in the lesson that must be thought about and planned for in advance of the lesson. The distribution of apparatus around the laboratory can prove a problem for the smooth running of a lesson, especially if it is all located at one point in the room where it has to be accessed by all pupils. As you introduce a practical exercise and the apparatus that the pupils are going to use it is good practice to show the pupils the apparatus and explain its use while you distribute it around the laboratory. Remember that you need to arrange the pupils into groups, ensuring that all groups are visible to you and you must plan in advance how these groups are to be arranged. Just as the distribution of apparatus needs careful planning so does the collection of materials at the end of the practical activity. Pupils need to be allowed time to clear away equipment and you will also need to allow time at the end of the practical exercise to discuss the results and draw out the significance of the exercise with the class. From what you have just read it is clear that the key to a successful practical lesson is careful planning, just as this is the key to all good lessons.

Practice Task Planning a whole-class practical lesson

Using a forthcoming lesson that you have to teach, draw up a plan for a whole-class practical. In your plan you should make clear the following points:

1. Carry out a risk assessment for your proposed activity (see later part of this chapter on safety).
2. What is the aim of the practical activity and how will this be communicated to the pupils?
3. How will the pupils be given instructions for the practical work. How will you check their understanding of those instructions?
4. How will pupils record the results of the practical work? Will they each record their own result? Will they design their own results table? Will there be a class record of each group's results?
5. Plan the method by which the apparatus will be distributed around the class.
6. Decide how much time the activity will need, what extension material you can provide for those who finish early and how much time clearing up will take.
7. How will you discuss the results with the pupils and elicit conclusions (when appropriate)? How will you prompt the pupils to evaluate their own results?
8. What written record of the activity will you expect the pupils to make? What guidance and instruction will you give the pupils on this?

Before you teach this lesson discuss it with your tutor and after the lesson evaluate the lesson and how you would change your plan in the light of experience.

Developing skills through practical work

There is a requirement in both primary and secondary science to teach about the process of science as well as its content. Indeed we argued in Chapter 3 that teaching the process skills of science could be presented as one of the goals of the science curriculum. Being competent in the skills of science develops pupils' confidence to undertake the practical work already discussed. An observation skill that requires the use of unaided senses is easier than one that requires the use of a piece of apparatus. We see this developing of skills occurring as pupils progress throughout the four stages of the National Curriculum. When groups of simple skills have been mastered they can then be used in a more complex skill activity, for example drawing a graph relies on simple skills of measurement and using a ruler.

While there was great emphasis placed on the teaching of skills in the 1980s it is an area that tends to be overlooked in schools today but still needs to be planned into science work schemes. The mistake made in the 1980s was to try and teach science process skills in what amounted to an almost concept-free framework and what we have learned from that time is that teaching skills requires concepts to act as a vehicle to drive the process forward. As pupils become more sophisticated with their use of science process skills then the concepts through which they are taught can also change. To implement a programme for teaching science process skills there are a number points that must be borne in mind during the planning stage:

- Skills are developed through practice, pupils will not become proficient in a skill through one-off activities.
- Practical exercises must be presented in such a way that all pupils have the opportunity to use the apparatus and materials required to learn the desired skill.
- It is important not to overload an exercise with too many skill requirements, this leads to the working memory overload referred to earlier in this chapter.
- The assessment of the proficiency of a pupil's skill needs to be based firmly on the pupil's manipulative ability in carrying out that skill, not on a paper exercise about the skill.

Science teachers, having identified the skill to be taught, have to match the skill to suitable learning experiences in a structured way that will promote the development of that skill. For most skills, which are learned by doing, the practical science lesson is the place where those skills are going to be learned by pupils having hands-on experience.

Investigations in science

What is an investigation? Once again we have a question with a far from simple answer but we are going to use the term to refer to open-ended practical activities carried out by pupils in science lessons and addressed through Attainment Target 1 (AT1) of the Science National Curriculum. Wellington (2000: 157–60) provides a useful typology of investigations carried out in science lessons where he defines five types of investigations as follows:

1. *'Which'* type investigations where questions such as 'Which design is best for...?' or 'Which X is best for...?' are posed for pupils to investigate and answer.
2. *'What'* type investigations which involve questions like 'What happens if...?' or 'What is the connection between X and Y?' are asked.
3. *'How do'* investigations involve ideas such as 'How does X vary with Y?' and 'How does X affect Y?'
4. *'General investigations'* which may be surveys or long-term projects possibly involving the significant use of secondary sources.
5. *'Problem-solving activities'* which have an element of design and make in them to solve a practical problem.

Examples of each of these types of investigation can be set in the context of science lessons in all Key Stages and allow a more open-ended approach to practical work. The degree of teacher involvement in these investigations depends upon the nature of the task, the age of the pupils and the complexity of the ideas involved. What they do allow pupils to do is to carry their science work over a series of lessons in a way which is not usually allowed for in the day-to-day life of school science lessons. As such they represent a change from the normal diet of learning in science and can be very motivating for both pupils and parents. At A-level there is often a requirement for pupils to carry out a longer project of their own design and this can be one of the most enjoyable parts of the school year for both the pupils and the teachers.

Many new teachers fear the openness that investigative science exercises can create in the classroom. Despite the length of time that Sc1 has now been established, it is surprising how much debate remains in the interpretation of the standards for Sc1 assessment. Doherty, Dine and Gardner (1998: 81) were surprised at the spread of marks awarded to a group of year 7 pupils' work when it was presented to a group of experienced science teachers. The version of the National Curriculum their study was using (1995 revision) allowed for a wider interpretation of the level of achievement of pupils. This flexibility has caused problems for teachers and GCSE examination at KS4 where there is a requirement for a moderation of Sc1 marks and this problem is ongoing, with new guidelines issued in 2000 to help teachers assess levels of achievement in Sc1 work, which are *Guidance GCSE Science: Sc1 Coursework: Managing the Assessment of Sc1*, available from Edexcel.

Practical assessment in Key Stage 4

The assessment of practical work in KS4 is done under the guise of 'coursework'. The work is divided into four skill areas, namely:

1. Planning and experimental procedure – skill P;
2. Obtaining evidence – skill O;
3. Analysing evidence and concluding – skill A;
4. Evaluating evidence – skill E.

The assessment of coursework under these skill headings is a common component for the GCSE science syllabuses published by the Examining Groups who have a Joint Council for General Qualifications Sc1 Working Party which meets on a regular basis to review and regulate procedures associated with this component of the GCSE examinations. The same requirements for coursework are made by all the GCSE science syllabuses.

Teachers are expected to devise their own tasks and mark schemes for the assessment of Experimental and Investigative Science (Sc1), basing their work on the general assessment criteria shown in Table 9.1. Samples of the students' work are then moderated by examination boards.

The examination boards make a distinction between 'investigations' and 'experimental tasks'. As already alluded to, the investigations are studies carried out by the pupils which provide evidence from all four skill areas. An experimental task is an activity which requires pupils to carry out work which produces some evidence in either one, two or three skill areas. In order to assist teachers with the setting and marking of these tasks and to help to ensure a standardization of the marks awarded, the examination boards produce training materials which are sent out to school science departments. These materials often contain suggested activities and marking schemes for practical work assessment. You should seek these publications out in your school and make yourself familiar with them. In the case of the Edexcel board, the materials are also freely available to be downloaded from their Web site at www.edexcel.org.uk.

Table 9.1 Mark descriptors for GCSE science coursework

Mark	*Skill Area P: planning experimental procedures*	*Skill Area O: obtaining evidence*	*Skill Area A: analysing evidence and drawing conclusions*	*Skill Area E: evaluating evidence (maximum mark available is 6)*
2 marks	P.2a plan a simple safe procedure	O.2a use simple equipment safely to make some observations or measurements	A.2a explain simply what has been found out	E.2a make a relevant comment about the procedure used or the evidence obtained
4 marks	P.4a plan a fair test or a practical procedure, making a prediction where appropriate P.4b select appropriate equipment	O.4a make appropriate observ-ations or measurements which are adequate for the activity O.4b record the observations or measurements	A.4a present findings in the form of simple diagrams, charts or graphs A.4b identify trends and patterns in observations or measurements	E.4a comment on the accuracy of the observations or measurements, recognizing any anomalous result E.4b comment on the suitability of the procedure and, where appropriate, suggest changes to improve the reliability of the evidence
6 marks	P.6a use scientific knowledge and understanding to plan a procedure, to identify key factors to vary, control or take into account, and to make a prediction where appropriate P.6b decide on a suitable number and range of observations or measurements to be made	O.6a make sufficient systematic and accurate observations or measurements and repeat them when appropriate O.6b record clearly and accurately the observations or measurements	A.6a construct and use appropriate diagrams, charts, graphs (with lines of best fit), or use numerical methods, to process evidence for a conclusion A.6b draw a conclusion consistent with their evidence and relate this to scientific knowledge and understanding	E.6a comment on the reliability of the evidence, accounting for any anomalous results, or explain whether the evidence is sufficient to support a firm conclusion E.6b propose improvements, or further work, to provide evidence for the conclusion, or to extend the enquiry
8 marks	P.8a use detailed scientific knowledge and understanding to plan an appropriate strategy, taking into account the need to produce precise and reliable evidence, and to justify a prediction, where appropriate P.8b use, where appropriate, relevant information from secondary sources or preliminary work	O.8a use equipment with precision and skill to obtain and record reliable evidence which involves an appropriate number and range of observations or measurements	A.8a use detailed scientific knowledge and understanding to explain a valid conclusion drawn from processed evidence A.8b explain how results support or undermine the original prediction when one has been made	

As a science teacher it is vital that you provide your pupils with an opportunity to carry out assessment tasks with the appropriate level of demand to allow them to achieve the highest marks within their capability. This is a very skilful task for the teacher, especially in a mixed ability situation. In such situations it is almost inevitable that you will need to set a number of similar activities and allow students to make a guided choice as to which level of activity they embark upon. If you teach in a set or streamed situation it is much easier to differentiate by the outcome of pupils doing a common task.

Tasks carried out as part of a GCSE practical assessment also have to be set so that the scientific content of the investigation is consummate with the pupils' ability. If a pupil has the potential to get an A or A* grade then the practical test should be based around a more demanding scientific concept than that for a student with the potential for a D or E grade. For example, an investigation into the solubility of sugar may be suitable for pupils likely to achieve in the C–G range, as this type of investigation is unlikely to contain the academic rigour the more able candidate is capable of. Setting tasks suitable for the A*–C range is tricky, but might include an investigation into the properties of thermistors over a wide temperature range or the energy yield obtained by burning different alcohols.

The marks for Sc1 contribute 25 per cent of the marks for the entire GCSE course and, as such, time spent on Sc1 is often a good investment for your pupils' future grade. (In 2001 new GCSE specifications will be introduced to be examined for the first time in 2003, under these new arrangements the mark for Sc1 coursework will fall to 20 per cent of the total GCSE mark.) A scientific investigation takes a considerable amount of lesson time to complete and you need to be aware of this as you plan your lessons for KS4 pupils. A top year 11 class is likely to require at least two weeks worth of lessons to complete an investigation that gains them the highest marks; this will be in addition to homework time. On the issue of homework, you will have to make careful decisions on the amount of the investigative work that is done as part of homework. Some of your pupils will be clearly advantaged by being able to seek out and gain additional help at home with their 'coursework' and it is important for you to consider the extent to which this may affect the provision of equality of opportunity for your pupils. There are many sites on the Internet where pupils can post up their completed coursework and this makes it even more difficult for teachers to determine what is original work completed by their pupils.

Practice Task Completing GCSE coursework

Becoming familiar with the assessment requirements of the GCSE syllabuses is an important part of your training to be a science teacher. Work with your mentor and carry out an assessment activity with one of your KS4 classes. Decide on a suitable exercise that falls within the scope of the current work scheme you are teaching and plan an experimental task which will provide evidence in either one, two or three skill areas. It is not recommended that you attempt a full investigation over all four skill areas for your first attempt, but do seek out an opportunity in your school science department to observe an experienced science teacher set up such an investigation with a class.

Having planned the experimental task write a marking scheme that details the expected level of performance for the award of marks for the skill areas you are hoping to assess. Discuss this marking scheme with your mentor.

When your pupils have completed the task, assess their work using your marking scheme. Be sure to annotate the pupils' scripts to highlight the evidence for which you award marks. Show a sample of the marked scripts to your mentor to ensure you are in agreement over the marks you award.

It is very important to give the work back to your pupils at some stage to allow you to explain the reasons for their marks and to discuss what actions they need to follow to gain higher marks the next time they do science coursework.

Practical work in Key Stage 3

The most recent revision of the National Curriculum has removed some of the content of the curriculum in order, partly, to free up more time for practical work in KS3 where Ofsted had expressed concern about a general lack of practical work. The fall off in practical work in KS3 has partly been due to the emphasis placed on the SAT results at the end of this Key Stage. However, a careful analysis of the SAT examination reveals that many of the questions are set in the context of practical exercises that pupils will be expected to have carried out in their science lessons. In the *Progress in Key Stage 3 Science* report published by Ofsted in 2000 (available from www.ofsted.gov.uk) there is clear concern expressed that Sc1 (Experimental and Investigative Science) is not sufficiently integrated into the science teaching of many schools, despite the fact that this attainment target is seen as something which can motivate pupils and raise standards. While many studies report a fall off in standards for pupils as they transfer from Key Stage 2 to Key Stage 3 it seems salient that we take on board issues that could help raise motivation and achievement in our pupils during KS3. Ofsted feels that the disappointing progress made by pupils in experimental and investigative science may be due to the difficulties teachers had with the earlier version of the National Curriculum and especially with the assessment arrangements for Sc1, where many teachers felt that they had to train their pupils to jump through hoops in order to exhibit their achievement.

It is important that we take on board the fact that this assessment target has been changed and now gives a structure and purpose to teaching practical work in an investigative context. Visits by HMIs to schools where science achievement is high identified the teaching of Sc1 as being a major contributory factor in raising achievement and motivation in KS3. Clearly this is an area of the science curriculum that needs to be improved in our schools to encourage a greater degree of motivation in our pupils. The 1999 revision of the Science National Curriculum opens up new opportunities for experimental work and for teaching pupils the part that evidence plays in scientific enquiry.

The teaching of practical work in Key Stage 3 needs as much care and planning as does the teaching of any other scientific concept to our pupils. Too often when a lesson incorporates a practical exercise the initial explanation and input from the teacher is rushed or truncated in order to get onto the practical exercise itself. The result of this is that pupils are frequently unsure of what they are doing the practical work for, and the skills of planning and evaluating the strength of evidence are neglected. It is important to appreciate the distinction between being busy and having a lesson with a good pace of learning. A good pace of learning does not imply that a teacher has to rush in order to cover the content of the lesson. Getting the pace right during your exposition will determine how effective pupils' learning will be in a practical lesson. That exposition has to be more than a simple giving of instructions but should be an active dialogue with your pupils that elicits their constructs and ideas about the underlying concepts of the investigative science.

Practice Task Marking a KS3 investigation

Figure 9.1 is an example of an investigation carried out by an average ability year 9 pupil. Using a copy of the National Curriculum, assess this piece of work and assign it to a level of achievement for Sc1. Identify the evidence in the work by which you determine the level of achievement. Discuss your decision with your tutor.

Ofsted inspection findings suggest that pupils are most motivated in KS3 science when they are engaged in practical work and they are least motivated when writing up experiments in a prescribed, habitual manner. This is a powerful argument for not only increasing the amount of practical work in KS3, but also for thinking imaginatively about the ways in which this practical work is recorded by the pupils. You could set your pupils a variety of imaginative ways of recording practical work in their books, from writing newspaper reports of their experimental work, to producing posters, drawing cartoon strips or writing a letter to a friend (see also Chapter 13.)

For many schools, practical work in KS3 is not an integral part of their work schemes but a special additional activity designed to assess pupils in terms of AT1 levels of achievement. As the Key Stage progresses this picture often becomes more and more typical, with students in year 9 carrying out little real practical work until the completion of SATs when there is a frantic rush to assess their progress so an end of Key Stage level for AT1 can be recorded. However if practical and investigative work is properly integrated into work schemes it can be a powerful tool for enhancing pupils' understanding of difficult KS3 concepts and for motivating pupils in their work. It is particularly important for the more able pupils who can be easily extended and stretched by practical investigations. Another problem with KS3 practical work is that a large amount of it is based on closed investigations, with teachers undermining the excellent open-ended investigations carried out by pupils in KS2. Too often teachers in KS3 will give the impression that 'real' science begins when pupils have their lessons in science laboratories and the work done in KS2 is not valued or referred to. This is particularly unfortunate where pupils are then subjected to a tedious range of closed practical exercises that are sterile compared to their KS2 experiences. It also means that pupils are denied the opportunity to show what skills in investigative science they developed in KS2.

Stuart Nurdin 9KH

An investigation into the effect of surface area on the rate of reaction of marble chips with hydrochloric acid (HCl)

Prediction In this investigation I am going to see what effect increasing the surface area of marble chips has on the speed at which they react with HCl. I predict that as the surface area of the marble increases so will the rate of reaction because with a larger surface area more of the marble molecules will be exposed to the acid molecules so increasing the chances of a collision occurring between the two. For a chemical reaction to occur the molecules involved have to collide with each other.

Plan

1. Put 5 gm of marble chips in a mortar and grind them down with a pestle (this increases their surface area). Place them in a beaker.
2. Add 25ml of 1.0M acid to the beaker and time how long it takes for the marble to completely disappear.
3. Repeat the experiment but this time do not grind up the marble chips.
4. Repeat both experiments again so I can take an average result.

Risk assessment

I must wear goggles and dilute any acid spills with lots of water before wiping them up.

Fair test

To make sure this was a fair test I used the same strength acid, the same concentration of acid and the same mass of marble for each experiment. I also did the experiments in the same lesson so the temperature was about the same.

Results

Size of chips	Mass of chips	Strength of HCl	Amount of HCl	Time taken for chips to disappear		
				1st go	2nd go	Average
Small	5g	1.0M	25ml	6m3s	8m30s	7m30s
Large	5g	1.0M	25ml	22m0s	26m0s	24m0s

Figure 9.1 Example of an investigation carried out by an average ability year 9 pupil

Conclusion

As the marble chips get bigger the time it takes for the reaction to happen gets longer. This is what my results show and also other groups in my class got similar results. Particles must hit each other for a reaction to take place. The smaller the pieces of marble are the more surface area there is so the greater the chance there is for a molecule of marble and HCl to collide. With the bigger pieces of marble most of the marble molecules were deep inside the chips so the acid could not get to them until the outer molecules had all reacted, this slowed down the reaction.

Evaluation

This is just one reaction and even though other people in my class got the same results it does not mean that all reactions happen like this. We need to investigate other reactions to see if the same things happens. I also noted that the beaker got warm during the reaction, this could mean my results are inaccurate because I know that temperature also affects the speed of a reaction. I need to find a way of keeping the temperature steady during the reaction.

Figure 9.1 *continued*

The teaching of experimental and investigative science is dependent upon a well-planned programme of practical work that needs to be built into workschemes with an overarching eye on the development of skills across all the Key Stages. As such it is an important area of long-term planning which is the responsibility of the department as a whole as opposed to the short-term planning of an individual teacher. The investment of time in this planning will pay off in better motivated pupils who are capable of working and thinking independently and who will have developed a good foundation to the skills assessed in later public examinations. Especially motivating for the more able pupils is to be given some element of choice in the investigations they undertake. Among the examples we have seen have been pupils investigating how the musical instruments they play work and the effectiveness of sports equipment such as trainers and squash balls.

Safety and science practical work

While pupils (and science teachers) are carrying out practical work in science lessons they are going to be exposed to a risk of injury due to exposure to dangerous apparatus and materials. While this may be a disincentive to some to embark upon practical work, we would expect you to seize the opportunity it presents to teach your pupils how to work safely in a hazardous environment.

Accidents will possibly occur when pupils have not been taught the correct skills and procedure for handling materials and apparatus and you have a duty to teach these skills. Accidents can be prevented by a proactive safety education programme which should be an integral part of any science learning scheme. All schools should have a health and safety policy, which covers science lessons, and you will be expected to familiarize yourself with this policy and to follow it at all times. In addition to this policy, science laboratories in schools will have their own lists of rules for pupils to follow, which it will be up to you to enforce. Although the school governors may have the overall responsibility for the safety provision in the school it is you, as a science teacher, who is responsible for the supervision and safety of pupils in the science class. For pre-service teachers undertaking teaching practice the responsibility for the safety of the pupils in the class remains at all times with the qualified teacher who normally takes the class. If during a teaching practice you undertake practical work that involves some degree of hazard to yourself or pupils it would be a reasonable precaution for the usual class teacher to be present during the lesson. Individual science teachers can be and have been fined for breaches of health and safety legislation.

The primary piece of legislation governing safety in your science lessons is the Control of Substances Hazardous to Health (COSHH) Regulations 1994. COSHH provides a legal framework to protect people against dangers caused by hazardous substances used at work. The Act requires that you assess the risks to health arising from your work and decide what precautions are necessary. You must not carry out any procedure that could expose yourself or your pupils to risk unless you have carried out a risk assessment. You must have evidence that you have carried out a risk assessment in your lesson planning and this usually means you should have some written reference to it in your planning. In some school science departments risk assessments are detailed in schemes of work where details of practical activities are recorded. Clearly it is incumbent upon you to read and act on these risk assessments. A useful guide to COSHH is available from http://www.hse.gov.uk/pubns.coshh2.htm.

Over 95 per cent of the education authorities in England, Wales and Northern Ireland are members of the Consortium of Local Education Authorities for the provision of Science Services (CLEAPSS) whose function is to support the teaching of practical science through a range of publications and the provision of in-service education for teachers and technicians. CLEAPSS produces much helpful material covering health and safety in school science including the publication of Hazcards. Hazcards provide detailed risk assessments of the vast majority of chemicals used in school science and are widely available in school science departments. The possession of these cards does not in itself constitute an adequate risk assessment under the terms of COSHH but they should be used when you prepare your risk assessments.

Useful addresses and publications for safety information in school science

CLEAPSS School Science Service, Brunel University, Uxbridge UB8 3PH

- Hazcards (CLEAPSS, 1995)

Association for Science Education, College Lane, Hatfield, Herts AL10 9AA

- *Topics in Safety*, 2nd edn (ASE, 1988)
- *Safeguards in the school laboratory*, 10th edn (ASE, 1996)
- *Be safe! Some aspects of safety in school science and technology for key stages 1 and 2*, 2nd edn (ASE, 1990)

Summary

The ranges and types of practical work in school science have been discussed in this chapter. What is clear is that practical work, like much else in science education, is constantly changing, but there remains in schools and among science teachers a commitment to a laboratory approach to science teaching. We believe that practical work has a positive role to play in science teaching and as a new science teacher you should be aware of the motivating ability that good practical work has and be skilled in using it. Through practical work pupils can become active learners in the search for knowledge and meaning and not passive receivers of facts. We all have a duty to promote a sense of awe and wonder in our pupils – what better setting is there for this to occur than in the science practical lesson?

Further reading

Office for Standards in Education (Ofsted) (2000) *Progress in Key Stage 3 Science*, Ofsted, London

Wellington, J (1998) *Practical Work in School Science*, Routledge, London

10 Assessing science achievement

Keith Hicks

I think I might have enjoyed science but I never did very well in the tests.

(Nazia, a former science student aged 17)

Objectives

This chapter facilitates critical reflection on issues of assessment in science education. More specifically, the chapter explores, in the context of science education:

- the influence of assessment on the curriculum;
- formative and summative assessment;
- how we can assess more effectively;
- the role of assessment in teaching and learning.

Introduction

All parts of teaching involve assessment, which may be formally integrated into a teaching programme in the form of set piece tests and exams or as informal reviews of the learning and understandings of individual pupils. Rowntree (1977) makes the following broad definition of assessment that is a useful starting point for our chapter: 'Assessment in education can be thought of as occurring when one person, in some kind of interaction, direct or indirect, with another, is conscious of obtaining and interpreting information about the knowledge and understanding or abilities and attitudes of the other person.'

There are lots of reasons why we assess, these include:

1. to allow teachers to set meaningful learning targets for their students;
2. to improve the self-confidence of pupils undergoing learning;
3. to provide useful information for pupils, parents, higher education and employers about the attainment and progress of pupils;

4. to help define and maintain standards;
5. to provide information to place pupils in teaching groups or sets;
6. to create a sense of competition;
7. to assess the effectiveness of our own teaching of a programme of study;
8. to provide a diagnostic aid to identify an individual pupil's conceptual misunderstandings;
9. to provide pupils with useful information to allow them to make informed choices about the future course of their education or career choices.

Whenever you are in the classroom you will be engaged in some sort of assessment for some purpose or other. This will form the foundation of your practice and you will be expected to build constantly on the knowledge you gain from this assessment to plan your lessons to meet the needs of both individuals and groups of students. Clearly you need to become competent in the assessment of your pupils (as well as an assessment of yourself) to plan your teaching. As we discussed in Chapter 4, a fundamental feature of 'constructivist' teaching is the requirement to understand pupils' prior knowledge in order to gauge the extent to which learning has taken place and plan for future teaching.

School assessment

Over recent years there has been a much greater emphasis placed on assessment in schools, with schools keen to measure their own performance in terms of local league tables of results as well as an increasing use being made of more sophisticated valued added measures that seek to measure performance in relation to intake. The nature of formal assessments in schools now extends across all phases of the science curriculum with Standard Attainment Tasks (SATs) at KS2 and 3, Certificates of Achievement, GCSEs and GNVQs at KS4, and AS- and A-levels at post-16. In a speech to the North of England Education Conference in January 2000 the Secretary of State for Education and Employment made clear the government's intention to introduce a new raft of assessments in science for 12- and 13-year-olds in response to concerns about KS2 to KS3 transfer. In addition to the formal written assessments across the Key Stages, science teachers are also expected to carry out their own assessment of practical skills in science.

The influence of assessment on the science curriculum

As noted in Chapter 5, the advent of the National Curriculum was a move towards a more centralized education system in England and Wales. While the responsibility for the provision of education rests with the local education authority (LEA), curricular decisions are now made centrally through the Department for Education and Employment (DfEE) and its offshoots such as the TTA, QCA and to some extent Ofsted. There may be a tendency to look back to a 'golden age' when schools were free to determine their own curriculum. However, secondary schools in England and Wales had much of their curriculum determined by the formal end of schooling exams. Control of curricula was largely brought about by the syllabus content published by the examination boards. While this did not have such a direct effect on the primary sector there was a trickle-down effect from the larger secondary schools which influenced curricular decisions in the primary sector. Today the position is far more clarified, the curriculum is defined through the statutory orders of the National Curriculum and the SATs define the interpretations of that curriculum. At Key Stage 4 the freedom of the examination boards to set their own syllabuses has been severely curtailed by the QCA, which must approve all syllabuses and their assessment methods. This control has now been extended to A-levels and the new AS-levels, with courses introduced in September 2000 being subject to strict controls and an enforced modular system.

These changes have led to a substantial reduction in the number of examination boards and a decrease in the number of syllabuses and public examinations on offer. A far more homogenized curriculum is now offered throughout the schools of England and Wales and the publication of the results of summative assessments in league tables has led to schools placing far more importance on them. The moves to incorporate an element of performance related pay into teacher salaries, with at least some acknowledgement of pupils' results, is likely to cause an even greater emphasis to be placed on the assessments carried out on our pupils. The reforms of the formal assessment arrangements in schools have not only been the natural accompaniment to the curricular reforms, but have often also had a pernicious effect on the nature of science teaching itself in many instances. The emphasis placed on conceptual recall in SATs has led to many teachers adopting a far more didactic approach to teaching and to some stifling of the important debate on constructivist learning. This move is to be regretted, but there are signs of a renewal of the debate of the place of assessment and the need for effective assessment that forms part of the learning process in science teaching. This impact of summative assessments on teaching styles was recognized as long ago as 1979 in a report by HM Inspectorate which stated that 'In about one third of schools the teaching of science was always or nearly always overdirected, with insufficient pupil activity. Similarly, dictated or copied notes were prevalent in about half the schools. Some schools achieved good external examination results by these methods but nevertheless it was felt that the excessive use of them detracted from the overall quality of science lessons.' There is a great temptation for science teachers to 'teach to the test' due to the perceived demand for recall in statutory assessments and public examinations. To do so though is a grave mistake; if we adopt a constructivist approach to learning we are educating to promote understanding of science concepts and not to produce rote learning.

The criticisms of summative assessment as demonstrated through SATs are highlighted in an evaluation exercise carried out by a group of teachers unions and the ASE (2000b). This exercise produced a number of recommendations to the QCA that included the suggestions that the style and range of questions in science SATs should be broadened. It was felt that the tests need to be written so that pupils have a greater opportunity to use their science knowledge in data analysis questions rather than being written with too much reliance on factual recall. Black (1998) outlines how teachers' tests promote rote and superficial learning, while the Ofsted report on secondary schools (1998c) commented that teacher assessment of pupils' work often failed to give guidance to pupils on how their work could be improved. The same report went on to state how the information teachers received about their pupils' performance was insufficiently used to inform subsequent work.

Some of these less desirable aspects of summative assessment can be mitigated by effective teaching and the use of formative assessment. To this end we need to be clear as teachers what our aims and objectives are (as we have outlined in Chapter 3); passing examinations is not one of the main reasons we teach science. We need to take a sense of ownership over the assessment of our pupils and make assessment a tool of the curriculum and not the driving force of the curriculum.

What we assess

We can group assessments in science into two main areas. The first area is the assessment of pupils' conceptual understandings of scientific concepts, theories and applications that may be assessed by a wide variety of techniques including formal essay type examinations, short answer structured questions, multiple-choice tests and oral questioning. The second area for assessing pupils in science is the assessment of process skills associated with practical work primarily defined by Sc1 of the National Curriculum as discussed in Chapter 9.

Observation Task Assessing pupils achievement

Learning how to assess pupils effectively is a key skill for all science teachers and one that has to be learned. Seek out opportunities to observe assessment taking place in your school. Remember assessment does not only take place in formal tests but every time a question is asked in the class. Discuss with the teacher taking the class which pupils are being assessed and also whether science skills or content is being assessed. When the formal part of the assessment is over go through the marking of any written responses with the teacher to see how marking schemes are used.

The assessment of progress in Attainment Target 1 (Sc1) is a particularly demanding task. Usually the assessment will take place over several lessons (possibly several weeks in KS4). Before you attempt to carry out your own assessment of Sc1 make sure you have observed such an assessment taking place with a class and discuss how the outcomes are assessed by the science teacher.

Summative and formative assessment

Kempa (1986) suggested that assessment tasks could be classified in relation to the context in which the assessment takes place. He suggests that there are two possibilites:

1. *Summative*: the assessment is based on an evaluation of the students' performance on tasks or assignments that are specifically designed for the purpose of assessment.
2. *Formative*: the assessment is based on an evaluation of students' performance on tasks or assignments that are primarily planned as an integral part of the learning experience.

The suggestion made by this division is that the first type of assessment would be made following the completion of a course or sequence of lessons in a summative way.

Assessments such as module tests, SATs or GCSE final papers (or end of year tests) fall into this first type of assessment. Bloom, Hastings and Madhaus (1971), for instance, define summative assessment as being designed to establish the extent to which pupils have learned the material of a course to allow for the certification or grading of pupils and to assess the effectiveness of the delivery of the curriculum. As such, this type of assessment contributes little (if anything) to pupils' learning in science but is much beloved by those outside the educational establishment as it allows pupils (and schools) to be ranked and given a number or grade to which some sort of value can be applied. In other words, the assessment is concerned with pupil performance rather than pupil improvement.

In contrast, Kempa's second type of assessment forms part of a pupil's learning experience and is designed to promote a pupil's learning and in the end improve his or her performance. This is commonly referred to as formative assessment. In science there have been attempts to marry formative and summative assessment. For example, in the final aggregation of marks for SATs, GCSE and A-level examination results, the assessment of science coursework (Sc1) is usually carried out as a learning experience where one piece of work can be used to show pupils how to improve on their next piece. At AS- and A-level the old final practical exam has largely been replaced by teacher-assessment of practical skills that are carried out on an ongoing basis during the course. The relative value of Kempa's classification of assessments is perhaps reflected by the fact that the formative assessment never accounts for more than 25 per cent of the marks awarded for a science GCSE examination. Once more summative assessment dominates formative assessment.

Using summative assessment

The annual publication of summative assessment results is received with some trepidation by headteachers and teachers as it allows the construction of league tables which are used to compare school with school. Over recent years the league tables have been supplemented with the publication of the annual Performance and Assessment (PANDA) report by Ofsted which shows how a school's performance in national summative assessments compares to schools in similar contexts. By showing how a school's attainment data changes over several years, the PANDA is a very useful tool for schools to evaluate their own performance and make improvements. As a new science teacher you will find the PANDA report useful to you in that you will be able to make valuable judgements about the performance of pupils in science in your school.

Swain (2000) outlines how science departments can use the information from SATs to analyse patterns of achievement in the school over periods of time. However, what the results do not readily provide is a breakdown of the success of the teaching in different parts of the course (such as chemistry or biology teaching). To gain such information from the results requires a substantial effort in terms of time if there is to be an effective evaluation of schemes of work, quality of teaching and pupil understanding. Swain (2000) argues that the 'national tests provide only a limited sketch of pupil performance at a particular point in time. It is the teacher who is in a much better position to provide a more coherent picture.'

Tools for summative assessment

A variety of techniques can be used for the summative type 1 assessments, each of which has its strengths and also weaknesses that you need to be aware of. You should evaluate the assessments you carry out to determine what type of assessment it is and what its weaknesses are. The following subsections explore some of these issues for the different assessment techniques available.

Essay questions

Generally these are used for assessing higher-level skills and are becoming increasingly rare in science examinations. The last bastion of the essay type question is in the synoptic papers of the A-level biology course where essays with titles such as 'Discuss the structure of the eukaryotic cell' or 'Compare and contrast the process of mitosis with meiosis' can still be found.

In addition to assessing a pupil's knowledge of a subject, the essay question demands that the pupil provides a longer and more extensive answer. This requires the pupil to organize ideas in a coherent and balanced way and to demonstrate a high level of written communication skills. As each answer takes a significant amount of time to complete there is only a limited amount of knowledge that can be assessed through this technique and the essay question is only likely to refer to a short part of the course. To overcome this problem it is usual to offer the pupil a range of questions which they can answer. As a teacher it is clearly apparent that one of the advantages of this type of question is the ease with which they can be written. Problems arise with this type of question when it comes to marking them, as the range of possible responses to the question is usually very large. This can lead to teachers making subjective comments about the work that makes the reliability of any final mark open to question. Examination boards overcome this problem by producing very detailed and structured marking schemes which will often have several components broken down into subheadings such as scientific content, breadth, balance and coherence. The basic weakness remains, however, that it is often unclear to what extent you are assessing pupils' scientific knowledge or their ability to construct an extended piece of written prose.

Short-answer questions

These questions can be presented in a number of ways; if they are written to test a single concept or a group of related concepts they may be 'structured questions'. These structured questions can often be skilfully written to differentiate between students, as they get harder as the question progresses. This is the format preferred in the SATs and increasingly in the GCSE examinations. Examples of SAT papers and GCSE papers are widely available in schools and you are encouraged to familiarize yourself with them.

Short-answer questions can be used to test a large number of concepts in a relatively short time period. Pupils have to write their own answers to these questions, so to some extent they still do test literacy skills rather than scientific knowledge but clearly less so than for essay type questions. Teachers often become very skilled in writing assessment items such as these and they are the most widely used type of assessment used in school science education. Marking these questions is relatively straightforward and with an agreed marking scheme a high degree of accuracy can be achieved. In the case of GCSEs, the final list of agreed answers usually emerges following meetings of large groups of examiners, all of whom will have carried out a preliminary marking of a significant number of papers. An analysis of a pupil's papers allows teachers to assess not only the extent to which an individual pupil has got to grips with the subject but also to analyse strengths and weaknesses in the teaching of the subject.

Multiple-choice tests

These tests can be used to test knowledge and to some extent comprehension at many levels of the science curriculum. They include test items that can test higher-level skills to do with reasoning and are widely used in GCSE science module tests.

Using a multiple-choice format can allow a very large number of concepts to be assessed in a relatively short time. Pupils are not required to construct their answers (they simply select what they believe to be the correct answer) so they cannot be used to asses the pupils' communication skills. It is widely believed that these questions can easily be objectively marked but it would be wrong to assume that this is the case. The degree of objectivity is reliant on the choices of answer available to the pupils and many teachers who have administered these tests will be able to cite examples where pupils have argued logically and correctly why a 'wrong' answer is indeed 'correct'! Writing multiple-choice questions is a high-level skill as it is often difficult to give a choice of wrong answers that do not give clues as to which is the correct response. This means that, while time is saved in the marking and administration of these tests, the writing of them takes considerable time. Care also needs to be taken in the interpretation of these tests, correct answers can often be gained by a good guess on the part of the pupil and may not necessarily be a reflection of the pupil's knowledge of the subject.

Practice Task Preparing summative assessments

Look back at the material you have taught one of your classes over the past two weeks. Prepare a number of summative assessments to gauge pupils' understanding of the concepts you have taught. Try to make three tests covering the same material, one requiring longer answers, one requiring shorter answers and one based on a multiple-choice format. Try to construct these tests so that each one lasts no more than 10 minutes and they all test the same conceptual understanding.

Administer these tests to your class in the same lesson. You could explain to the class that you are trying to see what type of question suits them best and that all three parts of the assesment are assessing the same ideas.

When the pupils have completed the tests collect them in and compare pupils' performance on each type of test. Use a spreadsheet for your results so you can sort pupils into rank order to see if some pupils were advantaged by one test format more than another.

Developing formative assessment

Formative assessment is a useful tool enabling us to promote learning for understanding. We need to develop ways of producing effective methods of formative assessment. Daws and Singh (1996) argued that formative assessment can deepen learning by encouraging pupils to:

- reflect on their learning in a structured and systematic fashion;
- discuss their progress with their teachers and focus on what they need to improve;
- develop greater confidence in their knowledge of science.

These claims for formative assessment can be supported by our knowledge of pupils in later Key Stages but are not necessarily so useful with younger pupils, although the development of greater confidence in their own learning is a most desirable aim for all pupils of any age. Further evidence for the effectiveness of formative assessment was given in a review of the research on the subject by Black and William (1998) which illustrates how the development and practice of formative assessment can produce significant and substantial learning gains. The evidence presented in this review also suggests that the group of pupils who gain the most from the effective use of formative assessment are the low-attainers. This suggests that formative assessment has the power to reduce the spread of ability in a group of students whilst raising standards overall.

The complexity and time involved in developing formative assessment techniques is a problem for many teachers especially when faced with the abundance of material available for summative assessment. However Daws and Singh (1996) have argued that material developed for summative assessment can be adapted and utilized in a formative way.

A summative assessment carried out with a group of pupils can easily be turned into a formative experience by carefully going through the papers with the pupils after the exam. Pupils can be encouraged to mark their own exam papers if you return them to the students and get them to decide in small groups what the key points from each question are. The teacher can then guide pupils through each question making clear references to the marking scheme for the paper. Pupils will often demand explanations of the principles behind the 'correct' answers and will attempt to articulate their reasoning for their examination responses. In a lesson like this there are ample opportunities to explore students' alternative frameworks and misconceptions to ideas tested in the assessment and to promote enhanced understanding through a shared dialogue with the class. The maintenance of a supportive atmosphere for pupils is essential in this situation if the pupils are to have the confidence required to explain their reasoning and interpretation of questions. In a second case study Daws and Singh (1996) described how a group of year 8 pupils were given a simple self-assessment sheet to stick in their exercise books at the start of a module that contained the learning objectives for that module. Pupils were encouraged to tick off when they had achieved those objectives and identify the evidence from their exercise books to support their decision to tick off each objective. This exercise carried out alongside a science homework is a useful formative self-assessment that forces pupils to reflect on the learning aims and objectives of their lessons and helps them to recognize weaknesses in their own understanding of the content of the module they have been taught. It has a secondary advantage of helping pupils who have been absent from lessons to recognize what has been missed and needs to be caught up on. This type of self-assessment is dependent upon pupils having some sort of criteria for judging their own understanding of the learning objectives. Teachers need to help pupils to understand these criteria and to help the pupils develop metacognition (an awareness of their own learning) in order for this formative and self-assessment to be successful.

Any formative assessment exercise is generally more time-consuming than a summative assessment and may require changes to curriculum planning and practice. However, as we claim formative assessment promotes better learning and understanding in our pupils these changes can be justified on educational grounds. Black and Harrison (2000) in a review of the literature on formative assessment cite 20 studies where research has shown that formative assessment produces significant learning gains for pupils. We also need to recognize that formative assessment is a high-level teacher skill and as teachers we need to develop our own skills in target setting and negotiating with pupils. In a review of the literature on formative assessment by Black (1998) the point is made that the effectiveness of formative assessment is dependent upon its quality rather than its existence or absence. The results of formative assessment are also likely to call into question the nature of our teaching practice as they starkly highlight the effectiveness of what we do in the classroom. However, if this results in more effective learning by our pupils it is a job well worth doing.

The use of formative assessment in a constructivist framework

A constructivist model for learning and teaching has implications for our use and understanding of any assessment of our pupils. With a constructivist approach we put the emphasis on encouraging pupils to develop and organize their own conceptions of scientific knowledge and encourage them to reform those conceptions so that they fit into the patterns of scientific knowledge and phenomena we present to them. In this context the idea of a typical assessment designed to elicit a narrow 'correct' answer seems at odds with a constuctivist teaching approach.

The typical summative assessment is not designed to allow pupils to explore ideas and show off their thinking, rather it is designed to close doors and direct thinking down narrow corridors. These assessments do not allow pupils to show what they know but are rather set up to allow the children to play the game 'Guess what the teacher is thinking'. Not only is this to be seen in formal assessments, but observation of many science teachers' lessons will often reveal question and answer sessions where pupils are trying to guess what the teacher is thinking rather than explain their own understanding. Such a regime of assessment is likely to have a serious impact on learning activities in the classroom and moves the focus away from the pupils as learners to the teacher as provider.

We know that pupils do not simply take on the correct answers as taught in the classroom in an instant but rather that their scientific understanding is in a constant state of flux and development. If, as a teacher, you want to move your pupils' understanding on, it means you have to be constantly aware of the conceptual frameworks in which they are operating. To this end, assessment is required to be a continuous process that is firmly built into our teaching methodologies and schemes rather than a bolt-on activity placed at the end of a course or module of work. This leads to the development of a sense of continuous assessment throughout each and every lesson, with carefully crafted questions that allow pupils to express their ideas in a non-judgemental atmosphere. These assessments may take place in a wide variety of situations. Bell and Cowie (1997) cite how practical work, posters, charts, written work and pupils' speech can all be used as sources of formative assessment. This provides information to us as teachers that allows us to adjust the pace and nature of our teaching, allowing us to respond to where the children are and not to where we think they ought to be. The very act of carrying out this kind of assessment becomes a learning activity in itself if pupils have to relate their own constructs to the learning objectives of lessons or sequences of lessons.

Summary

There is still a place for the summative and traditional end of course assessments and their use in grading the performance of pupils at the end of Key Stages and other appropriate times. Since the introduction of the SATs there have been clear improvements in the quality of the questions they contain and their construction, although it is still arguable whether they give an accurate account of a pupil's ability in science. The use of summative assessment is too well established in current practice and in law to be uprooted and abandoned on the basis of the arguments presented in this chapter. However, having read this chapter you should reflect on your use of assessment in the classroom and compare how well it supports a constructivist view of teaching and learning.

A key aim of your training is to produce teachers who are reflective about their practice. In terms of assessment this means you should be capable of breaking away from the models of assessment you have been subjected to throughout your own school days and aim to introduce more effective assessment methods. Assessment is a rapidly developing area in education and, as Gipps (1994) has stated, we need to move on to developing new ways of thinking about assessment which deal with the new issues that are emerging in schools as a result of looking at the way our pupils learn.

Further reading

Black, P and Harrison, C (2000) Formative Assessment, in *Good Practice in Science Teaching*, ed M Monk and J Osborne, Open University Press, Buckingham

Daws, N and Singh, B (1996) Formative assessment: To what extent is its potential to enhance pupils' science being realised?, *School Science Review*, **77** (281), pp 261–71

Swain, J (2000) Summative assessment, in *Good Practice in Science Teaching*, ed M Monk and J Osborne, Open University Press, Buckingham

Part 4

Issues in Science Education

11 Science teaching and equal opportunities

Mike Watts

Interviewer: *Is there something in boys that is beneath them to like biology?*
Teacher: *Well, that's part of the macho thing – the real students go on and do physics and chemistry and that's the way it's been ever since I can remember – ever since I went to high school. Now, a lot of that is being broken down, but it's very gradual. The thing is that girls, for example, didn't go into physics and chemistry.*

(An extract taken from an interview performed by Butler Kahle (1990))

Objectives

This chapter facilitates critical reflection on science teaching and equal opportunities. More specifically, the chapter explores, within the context of science education:

- a discussion of some research about equal opportunities;
- implications of equity for science teaching and learning;
- practical advice for the new science teacher.

Introduction

What are the issues? The two main arguments in this chapter are that, first, the teaching of science in schools is unequal, unfair and exclusive and, second, that it is a major part of the science teacher's role to help make it more equal, fair and inclusive. That may seem fairly straightforward at first sight but the issues are complex.

Taken one at a time, school science can be said to be unequal because for many (many) decades science has been almost exclusively a male preserve. While in recent years there has been an increase in the number of women entering into the sciences, this has been both a slow and very partial process. The same can be said about science as about divisions in society: science tends to be a very middle-class occupation and mono-cultural. At one extreme the study of science – particularly outside of compulsory education – seems to attract white middle-class boys and, at the other extreme, seems to repel black working-class girls. This is a broad generalization of course, however the patterns and detail which lie beneath this overall picture are quite specific.

No one has planned that science should be this way. In fact, quite the opposite – for many years there have been numerous concerted attempts to make science much more open and inclusive of all people. For example, people have pointed to the outstanding achievements of some women scientists and of science in other cultures. These attempts have had mixed success. Whatever happens in the world outside of schools, the key points of this chapter are to examine some of the causes of these divisions in and around science classrooms, and to explore just how the science teacher can make a difference.

Observation Task Classroom time

During your lesson observations see if you can spot any difference in interactions between teachers and their male and female students. On average do male or female students occupy more of the teacher's time? During question and answer sessions, for instance, do more boys or girls ask questions and answer questions? During practical sessions, who dominates the group interactions, boys or girls? If you have the opportunity to observe different classes, are the interactions in the classroom different if there is a male teacher or a female teacher?

When educational researchers have observed science classrooms systematically, their research shows that there are different interactions between teachers with male and female pupils so that there are differences in expectations, and therefore in pupils' own motivation to succeed. These two ingredients may not be the whole answer to providing equal opportunities for all, but they are certainly important: teachers' expectations of young people have a very strong impact on their will to learn and succeed. Research results have shown that attitudes and achievements are strongly connected: learners' positive attitudes are linked to positive results and vice versa. In the case of science, boys tend to have more positive attitudes (and therefore greater achievements) than girls, particularly in the physical sciences (Kenway and Willis, 1990).

There is an additional concern: it is clear from this research that – seemingly in contradiction – boys of some ethnic minority groups systematically under-performed everyone else in school. This means that teachers' expectations are not the only influences at play here, there are many other factors. High on the list come parents' expectations and peer group pressures. So, for example, where black teenage boys are concerned, there is sometimes thought to be an 'anti-achievement culture' operating in schools, where 'macho peer groups' may disrupt schoolwork and generate low expectations among themselves, a situation which is sometimes coupled to a loss of traditional male jobs in the immediate area.

That is, a combination of factors in people, in schools and in society at large, can add together to produce under-performance by girls and some boys – particularly in science-related subjects. 'Bright' and intelligent girls can sometimes develop 'learned helplessness' when they 'give up' because they feel they are making too little progress in the lesson – particularly where boys in the class are taking the lead and dominating the lessons.

Observation Task Expectations and achievement (after Thorp, 1991)

Based on your own practice or recent observations, consider the following questions:

1. What are the expectations of individuals and groups and how are these conveyed by the teacher?
2. What are the students' expectations of themselves and teachers?
3. How does the teacher enable students to recognize their own strengths and promote self-esteem?
4. How do teachers ensure that the language used in their classrooms enables every individual to have equal access to the curriculum?
5. How do teachers, departments and schools monitor the performance of individuals and groups of black, bilingual and other students?

Recently, the debate about equal opportunies has taken a different direction, which relates to the under-achievement of boys (both white and black): it has been renamed the 'gender gap debate'. The UK's league tables show clearly that most single-sex girls schools outperform boys schools in terms of examination results. Furthermore, the official analysis of examinations in 1998 showed girls from all schools increasing their lead over boys in terms of the proportion achieving five or more high-grade passes at the national GCSE examinations at age 16. On the one side of the debate it is argued that the results for boys must rise at nearly double the current rate in order for schools to meet government targets over the next few years, and that more teacher time and resources should now be directed towards boys in order to improve the situation. On the other side, it is said that girls' success in examinations at 16 is only a small achievement for young women when viewed against the generally hostile working conditions and social disadvantage into which they will emerge, and that the notion of 'under-achieving boys' is simply spiteful male backlash against the successes of the 'women's movement' during the last few decades. What is needed, it is said, is a cool head and the continued emancipation of girls in schools in order to further equalize their chances in society as a whole (Flam, 1991).

Observation Task Girls' and boys' test results

Why are single-sex girls schools leading in examination performance? What are your thoughts about girls' increasing performance? Do girls out perform boys in your school results or science results? How do girls and boys perform in your science tests and examinations?

So, what can be done? First, the importance of a clear policy and guidelines at school and departmental level cannot be overstated. Having positive policies is generally common practice in schools but there are many good reasons why these should be taken out and 'dusted down' every so often.

Theory Task School policies

Find all the school documentation and policies concerning equal opportunities, particularly where they relate to anti-sexism, multiculturalism, anti-racism and class inclusivity. There may be many sources, such as school brochures, internal curriculum and policy statements, and science department policies.

It is interesting to look at the Association for Science Education's (ASE, 1997a) policy on 'Gender and Science Education', which includes the following recommendations:

1. Teaching and learning styles should explore and build upon the personal experiences of learners of both sexes and provide compensatory experiences in order to avoid reinforcing existing bias.
2. Assessment schemes should support equal opportunities policies, enabling all young people to recognize their own strengths and weaknesses and thus to influence their own learning.
3. Resources and displays of learners' work should reflect the principles developed in the equal opportunities policies. Display and other materials should ensure that racial stereotypical views relating to adult roles and to aptitude and ability in science are not reinforced.
4. Opportunities should be provided for girls and boys to interact with women and men in employment areas with a scientific and technological base. Both traditional and non-traditional roles should be presented. Role models in the form of secondary sources about the place of women in science in past ages should also be promoted.

Similar recommendations appear in the ASE's policy on 'Race, Equality and Science Education' (Thorp, 1991). In particular all racist, sexist and other abuse and discrimination should be challenged as and when it happens. Teachers, and ideally any adult on school premises, should make it abundantly clear – not only to the perpetrator(s) and the victim(s) but also to any onlookers – that such behaviour is completely unacceptable.

Good tutorial work and classroom practice can help reduce this kind of unacceptable behaviour.

These are basic guidelines for good practice and are probably at the forefront of most schools' everyday work. The ASE's (1997b) policy on 'Access to Science Education' suggests some appropriate science experiences, which might involve:

1. using a range of teaching and learning strategies;
2. developing concepts and skills gradually;
3. matching the demands of the activity to the learners;
4. allowing different outcomes to different individuals;
5. building on the learners' strengths;
6. allowing time for learners to reflect on their work;
7. using a range of methods to monitor learning;
8. ensuring written material is at an appropriate level for each learner;
9. explaining new vocabulary;
10. using first-hand examples to reinforce understanding;
11. using a range of communication methods;
12. adopting a consistent presentation for written work;
13. ensuring safe working conditions;
14. making effective use of learning support assistants.

While policy is vital, this still leaves the difficult ask of realizing the practicalities of this in the classroom.

Practice Task Being challenging

This task relates to 'acting fairly'. Being 'fair' in a classroom, or in the school surroundings, is a difficult issue since bending over backwards to be fair to some will, to others, seem like special and undue care and attention. Having good intentions is not enough – children and other teachers make judgements on words and deeds.

- Find all the school documentation about bullying. It will come as no surprise that bullying commonly has a basis in sexism or racism that must be challenged early.
- Make yourself aware of the school actions and procedures for dealing with and challenging sexist and racist bullying as well as bullying on other grounds.
- Understand from colleagues and senior staff in the school what they mean by the term 'to challenge' inappropriate behaviour, where they draw the line between acceptable play and unacceptable conduct, between healthy robust interaction and distasteful, injurious treatment.
- Now turn to a trusted friend and discuss all this, in particular in relation to the way you work – and want to work – in your science classroom. What does it mean for the day-to-day ways in which you are 'fair' in your portrayal of science, of how you organize and manage the classroom, how you deal with particular students?

At the classroom level

Many children, but particularly boys, benefit from having well-established routines and rules, otherwise they tend to be disorganized or disenfranchised within the lesson. Tasks need to be made very clear and teachers need to set out consistent rules about what children should bring with them to lessons, etc. In some instances, competition and challenge is fun and healthy. In many other instances, though, it helps to reduce competition and encourage group work as much as possible, rewarding perseverance and ingenuity wherever possible.

Second, it also follows that the content and context of all science classroom work must be relevant for males and females of both majority and minority groups. This is no easy task, to relate serious academic science courses to the various interests and everyday lives of groups of young people. However, using their experiences and prior knowledge is vital to engaging them in the subject of the lesson.

A third theme to emerge from the discussions above is the need for teachers to use a wide range of approaches to teaching and to encourage a variety of learning styles in learners. For example, it is important to encourage group work so that there is sharing and synergy, discussion, debate and explanation. There should be a mix of hands-on activities, mini-research projects, presentations of writing and displays, role-play activities, games, video material, broadcast materials, demonstrations, experiments and so on. Conversation and discussion groups, practical work and investigative teams can be mixed in some lessons and single sex in others.

Fourth, practical investigations, project work and problem-solving activities should be designed to encourage personal experience and interests. Ideally, these should be at least a few weeks long so that learners develop a connection with the subject of their study (Edwards, Watts and West, 1993). Students can be asked to produce a plan of action before actually beginning a task. They can be given examples of careless work (poor spelling, errors and poor planning), and be asked to judge these with a view to them reviewing and planning their own work more carefully. The teacher will need to be prepared to talk work through at several stages with learners, so that discussion is supportive rather than overly critical. Where possible, it is important to seek activities to which there are no single right answers, that is where the correct answer is not the aim, but instead the development as a shared understanding, an explanation of the pattern inherent in the data, and an interpretation consistent with the data should be the primary goals of their investigation. Where possible, students should collect data at home or elsewhere out of the laboratory. They might be able to use household materials for their projects to enhance the connection between scientific endeavour and life experiences and to help them realize that science experiments concern real life issues and can be embedded in day-to-day life.

Theory Task Being a reflective practitioner

This task is, in the first place, an individual activity. Here are ten statements, and you are asked to place yourself on a continuum that runs between 'Strongly agree', 'Agree', 'Disagree' and 'Strongly disagree' for each of them. You can position yourself between these labels if it helps:

- Always having positive expectations of girls in science will foster positive attitudes from girls.
- One should expect exactly the same quality of science homework from boys and girls.
- Girls should always have first use of apparatus and experimental materials in class to encourage visuo-spatial skills and avoid them being marginalized in practical work.
- Textbooks must show girls as well as boys in active enjoyment of science, otherwise they are not to be used.
- Problem-solving skills and an experimental approach should be introduced early to science, through group work and co-operative teaching styles which avoid a 'right versus wrong answer' approach.
- Group work should be used where pupils discuss (and listen to each other) about science, and how they feel about some controversial issues in science.
- Always avoid praising neatness and tidiness in girls' work for its own sake.
- Ensure there is a 'girls-only' science club after school hours.
- Women teachers in other subject areas (such as English) must be encouraged to portray themselves as confident and happy with science.
- Being a teacher involves taking a leadership role, of being in authority. This relates to taking a clear lead in equal opportunities through teaching science as it does in other areas of school life.

The second part of the activity is to ask the question 'Why?' If you are at either of the 'strong' ends of the continuum for one of the statements, then why do you feel this way – and not (say) the other pole of opinion? If you are somewhere in the middle, then why do you not feel more strongly about this issue?

Now you need to find a friend or colleague with whom to discuss all this, someone with whom you have a good, trusting relationship. Where do you agree in your views and why? Where do you disagree? What are the implications for your classroom practice? How difficult would it be to radically alter your approach to teaching?

Observation Task Categorizing learners

Choose a class with whom you have a good deal of teaching contact. For this class you will have a class list for which, apart from gender, you may have an ethnicity breakdown, possibly by language need and so on. This task is to categorize each one of the children on a series of rating scales, which run as follows:

Easygoing	⟷	Irritable and quarrelsome
Concentrates on work easily	⟷	Finds concentration difficult
Seldom distracted	⟷	Easily distracted
Well behaved, obedient	⟷	Naughty and disobedient
Works well with others	⟷	Spiteful or a bully to others
Gregarious and a group worker	⟷	Isolated and a loner

The activity now lies in exploring your perceptions of the way you categorize the pupils: do the same kinds of descriptors recur for certain members of the class? Are these all negative perceptions? Is there a clustering of perceptions which are sex-stereotypical, or culturally stereotyping – either positive or negative? When you categorize pupils this way are you simply tapping into your feelings or could you muster more objective evidence? If so, what is it evidence of? Important, too: do other teachers in the school see the same pupils in similar ways? To what extent is it your role to change things?

At the personal level

Because boys in a mixed school can dominate so much of classroom life, teachers must be aware that they pay equal attention to girls and to boys, have similar expectations concerning abilities in science, neatness and presentation of work, giving positive feedback both in lessons and in personal conversations. The aim here is to demonstrate equity and inclusivity for all concerned, and to encourage a sense of self-empowerment. Encouraging 'I feel good about myself' and 'I feel positive about learning science' means that students lose their initial apprehensions, feel capable, feel ownership and an increase in confidence. In this sense it is important to praise girls not only for their diligence and hard work but also for their abilities in science.

Head (1999) maintains that the characteristics of many young men choosing science are typically authoritarian qualities, they are emotionally reticent, like certainty and show a degree of dogmatism. A young man facing the emotional turbulence of adolescence might find the emotionally neutral field of science with its masculine image offers an appealing career. With a colleague, Head conducted an experiment in which the secondary school teaching of physics was modified to make it more 'girl friendly' (Head and Ramsden, 1990). Not only did more girls who experienced the new course opt to continue their studies of physics but the use of psychometric personality measures revealed that a wider spectrum of personality types was attracted to the subject. In other words, says Head, the modified physics course yielded both quantitative and qualitative changes in the girls continuing their education in this field.

Observation Task Preferred learning styles

Considering classes that you have observed or taught, do you find that girls are more conscientious and punctilious than boys? Or are the more significant differences between individuals rather than sexes?

Do you have your own preferred learning style in science? What are your thoughts about preferred learning styles and issues of gender? From your observations of science classrooms are there differences between boys' and girls' preferred learning styles or are there greater differences between individuals? Discuss your thoughts with friends and colleagues.

Finally, a point about language. Care needs to be taken too that pupils for whom English is an additional language have opportunities to talk about science in other languages – pupils can provide their own labels for some of the cupboards and equipment in the laboratory. They can even develop their own list of rules and classroom regulations. Safety rules in Chinese and Bengali are provided in Figures 11.1 and 11.2 (pages 156–57) – these are drawn from an excellent pack of equity materials available from the North and South London Science Centres (contact the South London Science Centre, Wilson Road, London SE5 8PD; e-mail: www.slstc.southwarklea.org.uk). If you speak neither Chinese nor Bengali we suggest that you ask one of your pupils for assistance in translation! Teachers need to be alert, too, to the possibility that some children may need specialist facilities such as spectacles, hearing aids, pocket tape recorders and so on. Much of this can be catered for by thoughtful discussion and liaison with classroom support assistants.

Further reading

Association for Science Education (ASE) (1997a) *Gender and Science Education: Policy Statement*, ASE, Hatfield

ASE (1997b) *Access to Science Education: Policy Statement*, ASE, Hatfield

Edwards, P, Watts, D M and West, A (1993) *Making the Difference: Environmental problem solving in school science and technology*, World Wide Fund for Nature, Goldalming, Surrey

Head, J (1999) *Understanding the Boys: Issues of behaviour and achievement*, Falmer Press, London

Kenway, J and Willis, S (1990) *Hearts and Minds: Self-esteem and the schooling of girls*, Falmer Press, London

Reiss, M (1993) *Science Education for a Pluralist Society*, Open University Press, Buckinghamshire

Thorp, S (ed) (1991) *Race, Equality and Science*, ASE, Hatfield

Bengali

Your Safety Rules

তোমার নিরাপত্তার জন্য কয়েকটি নিয়ম

ল্যাবোরেটারীতে তুমি নিজেই বিপদ – অর্থাৎ তুমি নিজেই বিপদ তৈয়ারী করতে পারো, যদি তুমি সব খবর না জানো এবং সাবধান না হও তবে তুমিই বিপদ আনবে। মনে রাখবে যে তোমার কোনো একটা ভুলের জন্য তোমারই সব থেকে বেশী ক্ষতি হবে।

১। টিচার অনুমতি না দিলে ল্যাবোরেটারীর মধ্যে যাবে না!

২। ল্যাবোরেটারীর মধ্যে কখনই দৌড়াদৌড়ি কিম্বা ঠেলাঠেলি করবে না।

৩। ল্যাবোরেটারীতে কখনই কিছু তোমার মুখে দিবে না, কিছু খাবে না।

৪। ল্যাবোরেটারীর যন্ত্র কিম্বা কোনো কেমিকালে কখনই হাত দিবে না, কোনো কিছু নাড়াচাড়া করবে না।

৫। টিচারের অনুমতি ছাড়া ল্যাবোরেটারী থেকে কখনই কোনো জিনিস বাহিরে নিয়া যাবে না।

৬। ল্যাবোরেটারীর ভিতর কোনো জিনিস ছুঁড়বে না।

৭। টিচার যখনই বলবেন তখনই চোখে নিরাপত্তার (সেফটি স্পেকটাকল) চশমা পরে নিবে।

৮। লম্বা চুল থাকলে মাথার পিছনে চুলটা বেঁধে রাখবে, টাই কার্ডিগান ইত্যাদি জামার মধ্যে ভাল করে ঢুকায়ে রাখবে।

৯। যদি টেস্ট টিউবে কোনো অল্প পরিমাণ জিনিস গরম করো তবে তোমার চোখ সব সময় সেই টেস্ট টিউবের দিকেই রাখবে, খুব মনোযোগ দিয়া সেটা দেখবে। টেস্ট টিউবের খোলা মুখ তোমার দিকে কিম্বা অন্য কারো দিকে রাখবে না। টেস্ট টিউব কখনই তোমার চোখের কাছে এনে তার মধ্যে দেখবে না।

১০। ল্যাবোরেটারীতে ছোট বা বড় দুর্ঘটনা কিম্বা ভাঙাচুর হলে তখনই সেটা টিচারকে জানিয়ে দিবে।

১১। যদি তোমার মুখের ভিতর কিছু ঢুকে যায় তবে তখনই সেটা বার করে দিবে এবং প্রচুর পরিমাণ পানি দিয়ে তোমার মুখের ভিতরটা ধুয়ে ফেলবে।

১২। যদি তোমার চামড়া কোথাও পুড়ে যায় কিম্বা চামড়ায় কিছু পড়ে যায় তবে তখনই সেই জায়গাটা প্রচুর পরিমাণ পানি দিয়ে ধুয়ে ফেলবে।

Figure 11.1 Safety rules in Bengali

Chinese

Your Safety Rules

安 全 規 則

實驗室内最大的危險是你.當你無知或不小心或二者兼有之時.你便是危險的來源.請記着.因你犯的錯誤而蒙受損害的人將會是你自己.故此

(一) 未經許可.不得擅自進入實驗室.

(二) 不要在實驗室內奔跑.

(三) 在實驗室內不要隨便放物入口中.

(四) 不得隨便搞擾儀器或化学製品.

(五) 未經許可.不得擅自從實驗室拿走任何物品.

(六) 在實驗室內不得亂拋物件.

(七) 如教師吩咐.必須帶上護目鏡.

(八) 必須束起長髮.領帶、外套等必須扣好.

(九) 當加熱時.用少份量.並全神貫注工作.小心不要將試管指向自己或別人.不要直接望入試管.

(十) 一切意外或破損.無論大或小.都必須立即向教師報告.

(十一) 如誤將物品放入口中.必須立刻吐出.並以清水洗口.

Figure 11.2 Safety rules in Chinese

12 Science education and special educational needs

Robin Luth

It is as much a sin to treat an unequal as an equal as it is to treat an equal as an unequal. (Socrates)

Objectives

This chapter focuses on special educational needs and science education. It provides an overview of:

- the legislative basis of SEN and its meaning for the new science teacher;
- the main difficulties encountered by newly qualified science teachers in planning and delivering successful lessons to a diverse cohort of students;
- the role of the science department and its members in meeting the needs of all pupils within the school;
- strategies and sources of help and information for the new science teacher in dealing with students with SEN.

Introduction

In 1985, the Department of Education and Science (DES) released a seminal document in science education. The document, *Science 5–16: A statement of policy* (DES, 1985), was an important steer in the sense that it was the precursor to a full national curriculum and detailed the process, content and methodologies of science education that pervades our schools today. The paper was also important because it was one of the first science education documents to demand that science be taught to *all* pupils to the very best of their ability and demanded that curricular access should be based on equality of opportunity and treatment (DES, 1985).

Some 16 years on many of the tenets of that paper are still with us in a variety of curricular and legislative formats. Despite a multitude of National Curriculum revisions and alterations, the document's concentration on the content and process structure of science teaching remain today. The 1993 and 1996 Education Acts and the recent Green Paper entitled *Excellence for All* (DfEE, 1998c) confirm the place of students with disabilities within our mainstream schools. The legislation ensures that a place in a mainstream school must be offered to an individual evidencing a physical, emotional, cognitive or sensory impediment, before a special school is considered: a shift in policy that reflects a movement to build a truly inclusive education system and society.

This means that the new science teacher coming to the classroom for the first time will have an increasingly complex and demanding work place in which to practise. It is clear that, with the political debate on social inclusion, issues surrounding equality of opportunity and treatment abound within those challenges and present science educators, and their institutions, with issues as diverse as designing curricular appropriate to the physical accessibility of laboratories and classrooms.

This chapter will explore issues associated with teaching science to pupils deemed to have special educational needs (SEN) in the context of mainstream schools. By its very nature, the chapter will embrace the philosophy of inclusion and hopefully clarify and improve the new science teacher's ability to identify, assess, plan and monitor appropriate curricular material and teaching styles relevant to those pupils exhibiting additional learning needs.

Special needs: an overview

The SEN policy document, *The Code of Practice for the Identification and Assessment of Students with SEN* (DfEE, 1994), makes it clear that it is the responsibility of all teachers to identify, assess, plan and monitor the education of students with SEN. In most schools, students whose learning causes concern are usually placed on the Special Needs Register and their progress is regularly monitored by the school's Special Educational Needs Co-Ordinator (SENCO), parents, class teachers and outside specialists. Students placed on the register will fall into two categories: school support and support plus.

School support

The additional needs of the students will be met within the existing resources of the school. All teachers will be expected to assess, plan and monitor the progress of these pupils and contribute to any discussion about their future provision and resources.

Support plus

Students causing further concern will be seen by external agencies and may receive a Statement of Special Educational Needs. The LEA will provide resources in terms of money or equipment to help the school meet the needs of the pupil.

Theory Task Getting started by making contacts and collecting information

Find time to talk to the SENCO in your school. If you are in a secondary school, your science department usually has somebody with SEN responsibilities and you should also liaise with this person. Collect copies of SEN school policies and details of any support that you might be able to use in your science lessons and planning. As a new teacher, you should be aware of the school's SEN register and acquire copies of any Individual Education Plans (IEPs) relating to the students you teach. These will tell you which stage the student is on and suggest strategies you will find useful in your lesson planning. The school SENCO will be an invaluable source of help and support to any young teacher and will advise on strategies and support to help you come to terms with an often emotive and complex cohort of students within your classroom.

The term *special educational needs* is very often defined as a broad spectrum of difficulties that result from a range of biological/psychological and social circumstances that may combine to impede the student's progress in the curriculum. Particular needs are summarized in Table 12.1 (additional details are available in Alsop and Luth, 1999), but be very aware of the dangers of labelling students in such strict and definite terms. Although the designations of SEN seem to be fairly well delineated, students may exhibit a combination of need and this should be taken into account when planning appropriate curricula.

Assumptions about ability and performance should never be taken for granted and should be based on sound assessment procedures and information available within the school. It must not be assumed that because a student has a special educational need, there is any degree of impaired intellectual ability or that disability has any associations with cognitive deficit: we are dealing with many students who evidence difficulties in sensory, cognitive, emotional and physical faculties which directly impact upon the usual vehicles of teaching and learning, and an effective and frequent means of identifying need and ability is needed. It is good practice to refer regularly to the SEN register and Individual Education Plans to keep abreast of individual progress as changes in the biological, psychological and social systems of the pupil will affect his or her ability to learn.

When dealing with all special needs pupils it is *imperative* that you liaise with other colleagues in the school as special educational needs can only be met by a consistent, whole school approach.

A brief note on labels and disability

A great deal of legislation has been produced to guide the identification, assessment and planning of special education. DfEE Circular 10/99 (DfEE, 1999d) deals with the issues of social inclusion and equity, and challenges schools to provide meaningful curricular experiences for all students. Whilst the above taxonomy is a useful conceptual framework to gain an understanding about SEN, we would hope the new science teacher would always look

Table 12.1 Categories of need

Category	*Comment*
Sensory difficulties	A sensory need usually refers to a visual or aural impediment and presents a significant barrier to the student experiencing it. Such a need usually requires the extra professional support of specialist advice from teachers and/or technological devices to help overcome its effects. One of the greatest advantages afforded to these students is that of the benefits of modern technology and its ability to record and enhance any language task required in a lesson. It is also quite likely that a teacher will receive some help from a learning support assistant employed to enlarge print, modify materials and act as support to the sensorially impaired student within the lesson.
Cognitive difficulties	A cognitive impediment may present as an inability to spell correctly, record at an appropriate pace for the chronological age of the pupil or may inhibit the retaining and retrieval of information by a student. It may also affect ambulatory or co-ordination skills and severely inhibit an individual's capacity to learn. Cognitive impediments include: profound and moderate learning difficulties, moderate learning difficulties, dyspraxia and speech and language difficulties.
Physical difficulties	Many students will present with difficulties in gross or fine motor control and require help to access laboratories or the small pieces of apparatus needed to function successfully as a scientist in your lessons. They may either have ambulatory needs that require careful thought to address or require specialist help within the room to complete curriculum requirements.
Social, emotional and behavioural difficulties	You are likely to experience students who present you with challenges in terms of their behaviour and attitudes within the classroom environment. It is far too easy to forget that many of these pupils will evidence emotional difficulties as a result of past experiences that drive their responses to other students and teachers. Their disability is difficult in the sense that it cannot be seen or easily understood and can be so problematic to deal with. It must be remembered that, although many students with emotional and behavioural difficulties can present the student teacher with their greatest challenges, they are often some of the most deserving members of society. A sense of humour and empathy goes a long way to facilitate relationships with such students.
Social and communication difficulties	Pupils with difficulties in social and communication skills require a great deal of help in dealing with their responses to teachers and their peer group. Increasingly many students with, for instance, Asperger's syndrome are being educated in mainstream schools and their behavioural needs require monitoring if they are to succeed. It must be remembered that such difficulties do not in any way inhibit their intellectual functioning, with many Asperger's students gaining places in universities.

beyond the label and appraise the needs and interests of the student individually and empathetically.

Practice Task Removing sensory barriers

Think about the difficulties a physically and sensorially disabled student would encounter in a school science laboratory. Discuss how changes in the science department's culture might increase the accessibility for such a student's experience. For instance, how could you plan a practical lesson for a visually impaired student?

Planning for different needs

There are numerous strategies that science teachers can use to cater for children with different needs. All these strategies involve differentiating your teaching and learning environment. In the literature there are many definitions of differentiation. If we focus on pupils, differentiation is about meeting the needs of individual pupils and accepting that individual needs are many and varied. In your planning, you need to devise science activities that provide curriculum access. When starting to plan, ask yourself a series of questions about inclusivity. These might include, for instance:

- Have I identified the needs of all the students in the class?
- Is the learning environment I have created inclusive?
- Is the curriculum appropriate for all the students in the group?
- Are all parts of the room accessible for all students?
- Is the classroom or laboratory safe and hazard free for all my students?
- Does the physical layout of the room/laboratory allow all pupils to participate in the planned activity?
- Can all pupils engage with the activity without feeling left out or frustrated?
- Have I undertaken a risk assessment to ensure the room and activity are safe for all pupils?

Once you have identified particular needs, you will need to structure your lessons to enable access. The National Curriculum Council (1992: 4) has suggested that in science lessons this might involve:

- using a multi-sensory approach to give pupils the opportunity to learn effectively in a way suited to their abilities;
- ensuring that pupils' strengths are used to build their confidence and maintain motivation, eg involving a physically disabled pupil in observing and recording of results while others carry out manipulations of equipment;
- helping pupils overcome learning difficulties, eg by simplifying the language of instructions for pupils with reading difficulties (we explore this in more detail in the following sections);

- including the possibility of pupils' work and reports being recorded in different ways to suit their capabilities, eg on computers, in written form, video and audio tapes;
- using adaptations of communications for the particular special educational need, eg enlarged print, simple and consistent language, clear uncluttered illustrations;
- making effective use of classroom helpers and technical support whilst maintaining pupil control of the work;
- organizing some work to be done in groups and in pairs, create groups such that pupils are able to demonstrate to each other what they can do;
- matching the demands of the activity to pupils' level of attainment;
- ensuring that the pace of the lesson takes account of the differing work rates of individual pupils.

This list is far from exhaustive, but provides some indicative ways that you might structure science lessons for all. Differentiated programmes of study might be available in your school for particular groups or individuals and these will be an invaluable aid to you by cutting down the amount of planning certain groups need to facilitate curriculum access. The department may have pre-differentiated banks of resources and these may help you come to terms with the major features of differentiation.

Theory Task Understanding individual needs

Using any policy statements that you have available, consider how you as a science teacher can meet the needs of Alison described below.

Alison is in care as a result of being severely physically abused by her family. She has acute temper tantrums and demonstrates a great deal of hyperactive behaviour. She has few real friends in the class and often bursts out crying and runs out to seek the solace of the department head with whom she has a very positive relationship. Alison does not have any learning difficulty and is in the top 10 per cent of ability in the classroom. However, she has a very short concentration span and works reluctantly. The school's educational psychologist has advised you that she has emotional and behavioural difficulties and is currently undergoing statutory assessment for a Statement of Special Educational Need.

- How can you ensure that Alison's emotional and behavioural difficulties do not impede her educational experience or isolate her from the otherwise positive social learning context of your classroom?
- How can you plan activities that will engage her and keep her on task?
- Do you think you can solve Alison's difficulties by yourself?

Target setting and assessment

Your school will also have a policy on assessment and recording, and information on each student's progress in the National Curriculum should be readily available from the assessment co-ordinator. This will help you plan work for each student with an additional need. Whilst many students with SEN are operating appropriately within their correct Key Stage, a significant number will also be working in Key Stages below their chronological age. A significant number of students may be working towards Level 1 in any attainment task and these students need very careful attention to ensure that progress is being made.

The Science National Curriculum levels are a useful guide to the ability of students under your care and can provide a useful steer in determining your expectations of students in your own lesson planning. By appraising a student's levels in English, maths and science you will have a firm grasp of their reading, spelling, numeracy and conceptual skills. The difficulty comes when you feel some students find it difficult to go beyond Level 1 or find it difficult to reach Level 1!

At the time of writing, the QCA is developing a target setting resource for all core subjects in the form of a complete curriculum for students working below Level 1 (see the QCA Web site for further details: www.QCA.org.gov.uk. The present expectation is that this will include science and will prove to be a useful aid for new science teachers to assess, plan and monitor the progress of those students whose special needs inhibit their progress through the National Curriculum. The assessment criteria will steer teachers through those skills that enable students to access Levels 1 and 2 of the National Curriculum and help guide programmes of study and individual lesson planning.

A limited number of pupils may be 'dis-applied' from the National Curriculum. The headteacher in consultation with the parents, class teachers and SENCO decide that a student's needs require that he or she may be dis-applied from the requirements of the National Curriculum for a specified length of time (or completely) to pursue other more meaningful options. The headteacher will then apply to the Secretary of State for such an order.

In summary, it is important that as much information as possible is available (and used!) for those pupils who present with additional needs. Detailed planning that links departmental schemes of work with individual lesson plans involves the whole department in the whole school solution to SEN and builds up the expertise of the department in meeting the needs of all students. Good practice for educational inclusion relies upon teamwork. You cannot possibly meet all the needs for all the SEN students in your lessons without developing good liaison and communication skills with other professionals. Learn how to identify and approach the key school staff most able to help you with any issue or difficulty you might be experiencing. Meeting SEN in the mainstream can appear daunting to the new teacher and it is easy to be overwhelmed by its complex terms and legislative processes. Learn to communicate and liaise effectively.

Science, language and access

Much research demonstrates that the accessibility of spoken and written language in science lessons is a dominating influence in the smooth running of the classroom. The language used to convey classroom instructions and rules are often too complex for some of the students to respond in an appropriate manner. SEN pupils will often find it difficult to understand instructions, safety rules and the expectations of group work or teacher-led practicals. Some science textbooks seem to be written for teachers rather than pupils. The language of textbooks, worksheets and visual aids often requires a great deal of additional support with scientific vocabulary. The combined difficulties of the subject specific terms and the inability of the student to access the written material lead to off-task behaviour and ineffective teaching. More often than not the readability of the text is way above the ability of many pupils with a hotchpotch of confusing tables, text, diagrams and activities that further confuse those pupils with additional needs. If you are using a textbook as a major source of information, try to produce a simple sheet with the main points included and reduce the reading age to that of the students who will be using it. Many Key Stage 3 science texts, for instance, have reading ages above 13 and students find them particularly difficult to access.

Assessing readability

A good tip to assess readability is to use a word processing package. Microsoft Word, for instance (Version 6 and above – and ensure it has been checked 'show readability statistics' in the Options box), has a built-in package. If you go to 'Tools' and press on 'Spelling and Grammar', the software will you give you the American Grade Level for the text it has just processed – add five and this will give you the reading age in terms of years and months for the UK. You might try typing in a paragraph of a science textbook and then pressing 'Word Count' – the result, which usually surprises, should then be matched against the class you were intending to use it with. It's not unusual to find that it is sometimes too difficult for nearly half the pupils in your class! *And remember the relationship between pupil text access and the behavioural climate of your lessons!*

Other strategies for increasing access to worksheets and tasks for pupils who evidence language difficulties, ie 'dyslexic', dysphasic and those with other moderate learning difficulties include:

- Try to break up long paragraphs of text and include activities that have sentence completion tasks.
- Keep the number of new ideas to only one or two and constantly reinforce them with visual cues as well as written formats.
- Use diagrams to convey information and allow students to conceptualize their understanding in annotated diagrams.
- Produce diagrams where the pupils have to fill in the main labels involved in the diagram.
- Produce 'fill in the missing word' sheets to reinforce the main concepts you are teaching.
- Use familiar language as much as possible: introduce scientific vocabulary carefully and repeat its meaning frequently.
- Lighten the worksheets with cartoons.
- Underline complex terms and bring them to the attention of students in your lessons.
- Keep tables very simple and explain all the content as a class discussion.

Language is the key to many things in successful science teaching. Pitching your spoken introductions to your lessons at the right level, ensuring students can read your worksheets and keeping the number of concepts you are teaching to an effective minimum will ensure smoother lessons and a better behavioural climate in your classroom. Learning the art of doing this is not easy but with careful planning and periods of reflection on your teaching you will soon strike the right balance. And remember it is often the incidental words, the words that we take for granted, that can cause considerable confusion. For instance, a recent survey of year 9 students found that the majority of these pupils thought that contraction meant 'getting bigger'.

Information communications technology (ICT)

ICT has a key motivating influence on students with SEN and will become increasingly important in their education in the coming years. ICT motivates, facilitates and emancipates students with a variety of difficulties and allows them to compete in terms of access, presentation and performance in all skill areas. If you can bring it into your teaching in the form of word processors with auto spelling checks, simple spreadsheets and specialist science curriculum packages, it will be well worth your while. With the growth of integrated learning systems, some schools have specialist science packages that introduce students to the vocabulary of science and present virtual laboratories for students to practise their skills. Do liaise with the school's ICT co-ordinator to assess how ICT can augment your lesson planning and delivery.

Theory Task Successful inclusion

There are many successful stories in science education and special educational needs. The following passage describes Charlie's successful inclusion into mainstream education. Read the passage and contemplate the questions at the end.

Charlie is a 12-year-old boy with ambulatory and visual difficulties that have necessitated substantial time off from primary school for medical reasons. Charlie's parents want him to reach his full potential as he falls in the high average range of ability but is presently performing with a reading age of 9.0 and a spelling age of 8.9. Charlie cannot sit at an ordinary science bench in a laboratory and suffers from brittle bones. He finds the learning and retention of subject specific language problematic but is very highly motivated and has an ambition to be a doctor when he leaves school.

Charlie has a Statement of Special Education Needs and receives some 15 hours of learning support assistance per week. The assistant works half the time in class with Charlie and half the time modifying materials and enlarging the text of books and worksheets to ensure he can read them. He also receives one lesson a week to reflect on his homework for the core subjects. The assistant helps him to move his special seat from room to room. The school has moved two lessons on his timetable to the ground floor because the seat cannot be carried up some very narrow stairs. The class teacher takes five minutes to write down the key words from the lesson at the end of each science period and these are reinforced by his parents at home. Charlie has a laptop with Internet access and has undertaken a touch typing course run by the school's Learning Support Department.

Charlie's parents meet with the school SENCO every month to discuss his progress and iron out any difficulties that might arise. They are very pleased with his progress. Why you think Charlie's integration has been so successful? You might wish to consider the following factors:

1. physical/environmental;
2. social/attitudinal;
3. cognitive/learning;
4. curricular;
5. peer interaction;
6. medical.

Summary

The present global thrust to promote inclusivity in science education provides an array of difficult challenges to the new science teacher. The difficulties in making the curriculum accessible to all are clear and can appear insurmountable to those embarking upon their first tentative steps into teaching. Special educational needs is a highly complex and emotive subject for all those working in education and it should be realized that successful teaching only comes with experience and guidance from those colleagues who will surround you in your first practices and first appointment. It is important to stress that successful SEN science teaching is based on collegiality and teamwork with all members of the department and school working together to support each other and the students. Learn the invaluable skills of communicating effectively and always seek advice and support should you find yourself floundering when planning or delivering your lessons. SEN is not easy. Teaching science to a very diverse group of students with pressing, individual needs is even more difficult but doubly worthwhile when your confidence increases and your skills grow.

Further reading

Department for Education and Employment (DfEE) (1994) *The Code of Practice for the Identification and Assessment of Pupils with Special Educational Needs*, HMSO, London

DfEE (1998c) *Excellence for All*, Green Paper, HMSO, London

DfEE (1999d) *Social Inclusion*, Circular 10/99, HMSO, London

Kincaid, R, Rapson, B and Richards, R (1993) *Science for Pupils with Learning Difficulties*, Simon and Schuster, London

QCA (1998) *Supporting the Target Setting Process*, HMSO, London

Reid, D and Hodson, D (1987) *Science for All: Teaching science in the secondary school – special needs in ordinary schools*, Cassell, London

13 Literacy and numeracy in science

Kendra McMahon and Dan Davies

There are different routes of entry into each child's mind. It is amazing how much can be taught when subject boundaries are taken away.

(Professor Helen Storey)

Objectives

This chapter explores literacy and numeracy in science education. The aspects which will be covered include:

- ways in which pupils' literacy and numeracy skills underpin their scientific learning;
- ways of using language – spoken, read and written – to support the development of scientific concepts;
- ways of enhancing pupils' use of scientific processes through the application of specific numeracy skills such as measurement, data-handling and pattern-seeking;
- strategies for analysing your own and pupils' use of words and numbers in your science teaching, in order to develop these aspects of your practice.

Introduction

In this chapter we discuss the central importance of literacy and numeracy within science education, and offer a series of strategies for developing their use in the classroom. To start, let us turn to a general question: why are literacy and numeracy fundamental to learning science? We will discuss below what we would suggest are two of the main reasons:

1. literacy is at the heart of scientific learning;
2. numeracy is the language of science.

Literacy is at the heart of scientific learning

There has been some debate about the relative importance of practical, 'hands-on experience' and the role of language in children's learning in science (Sutton, 1992). Over the last few decades in science education there has been a move away from the practical 'discovery learning' approach. Many contemporary teaching approaches in both primary and secondary schools are based on a social constructivist view of learning (see Chapter 4). In this perspective, language (talk, writing, reading and listening) are fundamental to the teaching and learning of science.

By using language, children are able to reflect on their scientific experiences and thoughts, restructuring them in the process of explaining to others. Meaning is constructed through language, and although this construction is an individual process, through a social context we can come to a shared understanding. Through language teachers can gain access to children's thoughts and also intervene to 'scaffold' the construction of ideas in the direction of those currently held by scientists.

Science has its own meanings for words; it is a context in which words are interpreted differently from everyday usage (for example the words 'material' and 'gas'). Scientific use of language includes the naming of abstract ideas such as 'energy' and 'habitat' in order to use them as concepts to manipulate and build upon. Imagine the science classroom without the use of language and its centrality will become apparent!

Numeracy is the language of science

Scientists need to be able to communicate their ideas clearly and simply. Mathematics, as a form of symbolic language representing precise relationships between variables, is often better suited to this task than verbal expression. Take the example of Newton's Second Law of Motion. It is much simpler – and more informative – to express it as $F = ma$ than to say something like 'the force needed to make a mass move with constant acceleration is directly proportional to the size of the mass'. Some scientists (eg Wolpert, 1992) have gone so far as to say that mathematics is the language of nature itself, providing a 'mirror for the physical world'. For instance, the Nobel Prize-winning physicist, Richard Feynmann, claimed that: 'If you're interested in the ultimate character of the physical world at the present time our only way to understand it is through a mathematical type of reasoning' (cited in NACCCE, 1999).

So why do pupils (and many teachers!) have such a resistance to using numbers in science? Stephen Hawking (1988) claimed that the sales of a popular science book would be halved for every equation that appeared between its covers. The answer lies in our deep-seated fear of mathematical abstraction, and the perception that it is unrelated to 'real life'. Science teachers have a mission to perform in opening for children the 'secret garden' of a numerical universe and showing just how important a tool mathematics can be.

Numeracy and literacy in the curriculum

In recent years the dominance of words and numbers in the curriculum (in particular) has been much increased by the implementation of National Strategies for Literacy (DfEE, 1998b) and Numeracy (DfEE, 1999). The accompanying documentation has specified in great detail the key objectives, yearly teaching programmes, time allocation and lesson structure for these subjects. The effect upon primary science has arguably been to reduce its curriculum status, but also to highlight the ways in which literacy and numeracy contribute to – and can be delivered through – scientific contexts. There are indications that a similar emphasis will shortly pervade the lower secondary curriculum. Close correspondences now exist between the documentation; we will take numeracy as an example.

The National Numeracy Strategy contains five strands: (i) numbers and the number system; (ii) calculations; (iii) solving problems; (iv) measures, shape and space; and (v) handling data. Each of these aspects is appropriately addressed through science activities, as expressed in the following paragraph from the document:

> Almost every scientific investigation or experiment is likely to require one or more of the mathematical skills of classifying, counting, measuring, calculating, estimating and recording in tables and graphs. In science pupils will, for example, order numbers, including decimals, calculate simple means and percentages, use negative numbers when taking temperatures, decide whether it is more appropriate to use a line graph or bar chart, and plot, interpret and predict from graphs.
>
> (DfEE, 1999: 17)

This emphasis is reflected in the National Curriculum (DfEE/QCA, 1998) requirements for Sc1 – Scientific enquiry, illustrated by the following statements from the programme of study; for example at Level 2.

- Sc1:2f Make systematic observations and measurements, including the use of ICT for data logging.
- Sc1:2g Check observations and measurements by repeating them where appropriate.
- Sc1:2h Use a wide range of methods, including diagrams, drawings, tables, bar charts, line graphs and ICT to communicate data in an appropriate and systematic manner.
- Sc1:2i Make comparisons and identify simple patterns or associations in their own observations and measurements or other data.

A similar emphasis appears at other levels.

There is also, for the first time, a direct correspondence between the coverage of mathematical skills for particular year groups in the National Numeracy Strategy and the application of those skills within units of work prescribed by the Scheme of Work for Science in Key Stages 1, 2 and 3 (DfEE/QCA, 1998). For this reason it is important during science lessons to make explicit the numeracy skills pupils will need to use, since it has often been observed that children do not always transfer numeracy skills developed in mathematics into science lessons (Fouldes *et al*, 1992).

Theory Task Literacy and numeracy in the National Curriculum for Science

Acquire a copy of the Mathematics, Science and English National Curricula: look at the levels of the pupils you teach and compare and contrast the three subject areas. Consider questions such as:

1. What are the key literacy and numeracy skills needed to access the science curriculum?
2. How can your science teaching promote those skills?
3. Is there continuity in skill level across the three curriculum areas? (Ie what level of literacy and numeracy skill is required to access a particular science level of achievement?)

Words and numbers in conceptual and procedural learning

Learning in science can be regarded as comprising *conceptual* (understanding scientific concepts) and *procedural* (eg performing scientific investigations) elements, in addition to the *attitudinal* dimension which is beyond the scope of this chapter. To discuss the contribution of literacy and numeracy, we will consider first conceptual and then procedural elements. Our approach will be to focus on the use of *words* to support conceptual development and then to explore how *numeracy skills* contribute to procedural development. This divide serves to structure our discussions. However it is, of course, an over-simplification because both numeracy and literacy contribute to conceptual and procedural development.

Using words to enhance conceptual learning in science

In Chapter 4, a popular contemporary teaching sequence was discussed which consisted of four stages – orientation, elicitation, restructuring and review. In the following subsection we explore how language might more effectively contribute to each of these teaching and learning stages.

Orientation

Many pupils find it easier to make sense of scientific concepts and activities if they are set in a meaningful context. One way of doing this in the primary context (and to a lesser extent in a secondary context) is to use stories as starting points. Using literature is not only motivating, but by setting science in contexts that can be related to real life, children are helped to see that science is not some strange abstract set of ideas and procedures, but something both interesting and useful for our everyday lives. For example, at KS2 the story of 'The Enormous Turnip' in which first the farmer tries to pull up the turnip, then one by one a series of other people and animals come to help, could be used to initiate a discussion with young children about forces: Why was it so hard to pull up? How did they make the pull bigger? What else do we pull? Which are big pulls and which are small pulls? This could lead into an investigation in which children explore the different strength of pull needed to move different objects. Imagine this activity presented in isolation – it might seem rather pointless! The story also lends itself to systematically adding 'more pull' – another feature that could be developed in an investigation. This type of activity is more common in primary schools but is equally applicable in the secondary classroom.

Poetry also makes a good starting point for science. It is particularly good for setting science within an emotive context For example the haiku below is a short but powerful introduction to work on pollution.

Haiku

Spring falls gently
Crystal clear but acid sharp
Stripping branches bare

Science is often portrayed as unemotional and cold and this can be rather off-putting to many children, so by making the human dimension a part of work on science it may make science appealing to a broader cross-section of the class. Poetry often emphasizes the aesthetic dimension of the natural world, provoking a sense of awe and wonder at the structure of everyday things. Watts (2000) has recently published a collection of children's poems (primary and secondary) for use in science lessons. Alternatively teachers can use a funny poem – children always respond well to humour – and through this science can have more positive associations. In this way, using words in science can contribute towards children's *attitudinal* development.

Practice Task Using creative writing

Take a story or poem and brainstorm the opportunities for science that could be stimulated by it. Select one of these ideas to develop into a short unit of work, or a lesson in science, which includes elicitation, restructuring and review phases. Several publications from the Association for Science Education (ASE) exist to support this work.

Some children find it easier than others to think in abstract ways, and using literature supports those who need a tangible context for their learning in order to make sense of new ideas and experiences. There is some evidence that there may be a gender difference here and that girls in particular may find science more relevant when presented in a human context (see Chapter 11.)

Non-fiction texts also provide a stimulus for science work. This could take a variety of forms – perhaps a letter asking for scientific information. For younger children this could be from an imaginary character; perhaps the class teddy bear writes to complain that it is too noisy and the class could design it some ear muffs, or it could be a real letter for older pupils. Letters of concern about changes to the environment could initiate an investigation of a local habitat. An information text on, say, the manufacture of clothes, may raise more questions to investigate concerning the structure and properties of fabrics. Creating explicit links between English and science lessons makes for efficient use of curriculum time and helps pupils to realize that, although subjects may each have a distinctive contribution to their education, there are areas of commonality between them.

Elicitation

An important way in which teachers can elicit pupils' scientific ideas is through class, group or individual discussion. Careful teacher questioning is vital to maintain a balance between 'opening up' the discussion so that children can express what comes to mind in an uninhibited way, and 'probing' understanding for the purpose of formative assessment. The teacher's use of language needs to communicate to pupils that their ideas are of value, so that they continue to express them without fearing reprimand or ridicule (Qualter and Taylor, 1999). This should not mean that the children have their alternative ideas affirmed, but that these are treated as a valid starting point. Questions have a major role to play in eliciting pupils' ideas; for more details see Chapter 7.

Theory Task Words

The dialogue below presents an example of elicitation through discussion. Read it and consider how the teacher is using talk: what kind of questions are being asked, how is he or she responding to the children's ideas?

A child has chosen a pot plant from a collection of objects as representing an example of something that is 'living' and the class is discussing it. The teacher is interested in their ideas about living things and about plants in particular, as this is the start of a topic on plants.

Teacher: What is it that makes it living? If you had to explain to someone else what it is about the plant that makes it alive, what would you say?
Matt: It's a plant.
Teacher: It's a plant.
Matt: It has either a seed or a bulb to make it grow... and it needs water and light.
Teacher: So it needs water and light, it might have a bulb to make it grow. Lots of ideas there. Anyone else? Toby?

Toby:	It moves.
Teacher:	It moves, in what way might it move?
Toby:	Side to side, to get the sun... when it...
Teacher:	So it might follow the sun
Max:	If it's living, it has to eat or drink to live. Say like a table, is non-living because it doesn't eat, it doesn't drink!
Teacher:	So what about a plant then?
Max:	Well down in the soil, it's got that and they eat it through the roots.
Teacher:	I see, does anyone want to add anything?
Mike:	You can give them food, if they haven't got enough in the soil you can give them food.
Teacher:	I see, you can buy something called plant food can't you? Paul?
Paul:	Well another thing about how plants live is, when we breathe out oxygen, they get it, when we breathe in, carbon dioxide, they get it.

Tape and transcribe a discussion you have with a group of children to elicit their ideas. What changes could you make to improve your use of talk to ensure that you are gaining valuable formative assessment material rather than answers they think you want to hear?

Restructuring

'Restructuring' pupils' ideas may take many forms (see below), but the use of language is central to each, since it is the means by which children can be helped to reflect critically upon their learning. This is particularly relevant to pupils' understanding of the nature of science as a process through which ideas are modified or changed. This in turn can increase their confidence in behaving like scientists, since it is seen as legitimate to *change* ideas in the light of evidence and discussion.

Watt (1998) identifies five ways of helping children to develop their ideas:

1. through investigation, posing questions based on their own ideas and testing them;
2. testing the 'right' idea alongside the children's ideas, providing opportunities for children to compare their ideas to those of scientists;
3. making imperceptible changes perceptible (eg evaporation, by condensing water on a cold mirror), modelling through drama;
4. helping children to generalize from one context to another;
5. refining children's use of vocabulary.

Once more, skilful questioning plays an important role in each of these strategies.

Restructuring may involve the use of secondary sources of information, for example, books or CD-ROMs, both of which require pupils to use specific literacy skills such as using a contents page, scanning and notetaking.

Discussing the meaning of scientific vocabulary is a key aspect of restructuring. It is important for children to have access to this specialized language, as it provides a means of mentally labelling new concepts and enables the discussion of ideas. However, overuse of scientific terminology can create a barrier to communication, if children do not understand the meaning of the teacher's words or if the teacher does not understand how a child is using a word. Some words that have an everyday meaning and a particular scientific meaning can be confusing, eg we commonly use the word 'animal' to mean mammals other than humans, whereas it has a broader meaning in science (see Chapter 4). The word 'work' has a general meaning, but also a specific definition in the context of physical science. By inviting pupils to explain their use of vocabulary, and introducing scientific terms once the concepts to which they refer have been established, teachers can avoid many of these confusions.

Sutton (1992) discusses the use of *metaphor* in providing explanations and helping children to understand concepts. Using the example 'a blanket of cloud' he describes how the association with a blanket keeping you warm is useful in understanding why cloudy nights can be warmer than clear nights. A more contemporary example is that of a computer 'virus' which brings to mind something small but powerful, that is able to replicate itself, so creating a mental image of an intangible idea. However, Ollerenshaw and Ritchie (1997) and other authors warn that metaphors are only useful if they lie within pupils' experience (eg the metaphor of a central heating system for an electric circuit is meaningless to most children). If taken too literally, metaphors may also reinforce ideas that are scientifically inappropriate (eg the idea of a battery as a 'reservoir' of electricity). Ollerenshaw and Ritchie suggest it may be more helpful to encourage children to create their own metaphors as they struggle to place new ideas within their existing mental frameworks.

Observation Task — Use of metaphors in science lessons

In your observations, make a note of the metaphors used by the teacher and ones used by the pupils. For each set of metaphors consider the following questions:

- Did the metaphor lie within the pupils' own experience?
- Was the metaphor taken up and used by the pupils?
- Did the metaphor provide a suitable vehicle for promoting scientific understanding or did it lead to the reinforcement of ideas that were scientifically inappropriate?

Review

It is vital that a classroom discussion takes place, for instance after an investigation, to help the children to articulate their findings and to interpret them in the context of their previous understanding. Otherwise ideas may become isolated pieces of knowledge that children cannot apply to new contexts. This is important in helping children to generalize, as suggested by Watts above. In the following extract, the teacher introduces the function of the flower and, through discussion, the children make links between the water cycle and what they have learned about flowers, helping them to form the idea of a 'life cycle'. The concept of a cycle is widely used in science.

Teacher:	(*Drawing diagram of flower on the whiteboard*) I'm going to do it as simply as I can. (*Pause*) Flowers, make seeds! (*Pause for dramatic effect*) That's their job!
Max:	Huh?
Sam:	I didn't know that.
Anna:	I did.
Teacher:	Isn't that interesting?
Max:	I thought seeds make flowers.
Kate:	They do!
Jo:	That's what *I* thought.
Kate:	You know the seeds make flowers right, when the. . . flower. . . does that make the seeds?
Teacher:	It's a bit of a cycle really.
Paul:	Like the water cycle.
Teacher:	The seeds grow into the flowers, the flowers produce the seeds and round and round we go! Like a little cycle.

Millar and Osborne (1998) recommend the use of 'explanatory stories' for science to help children to understand how powerful ideas such as particle theory underpin different aspects of what they are studying in science. They suggest that the use of narratives in presenting historical case studies will help children to understand the human context of science and how the processes of science have led to our present day understanding. Together these could help children to build up a coherent set of interrelated ideas and concepts that would form a framework in which details would have more meaning.

Pupils are often asked to write a report on an investigation they have carried out. This is a genre of writing that has a set of rules: it is written in the past tense, it may be chronological, but does not have a narrative voice, it is often structured into sections such as 'method' or 'what we found out'. Within the teaching of English, 'writing frames' are increasingly used to scaffold children's use of particular genres and this has been applied to scientific writing. Feasey (1999) suggests the use of a 'bank' of sentence openers and connectives, eg 'I predict that...'; 'We think... because...'; '... however our evidence shows that...' Examples such as these can be employed to model use of appropriate language. It is important however that writing frames are used as supportive structures and do not become restrictive.

There is evidence (Ofsted, 1998b) that many pupils at upper primary and lower secondary level do not find it easy to distinguish between descriptions and explanations, often offering the former when asked for the latter. It is important that teachers explain the difference: descriptions use *temporal* connectives such as 'then', 'next', 'and', whereas explanations use *causal* connectives such as 'because', 'so', 'this causes'. Here is an example:

Description: When you stand in the sun then you get a shadow.
Explanation: The sun can't get through you so it makes a shadow.

As a new science teacher it is vital that you make clear to your pupils the difference between the terms 'describe' and 'explain'. By scaffolding this process, children's thinking is extended and they are encouraged to make connections between the results of their investigations and their existing ideas. Of course, scientific recording does not have to take the form of a report and could easily be written as a poem, performed as a play or told as a story. An account of the water cycle from the point of view of a molecule of water would make a welcome change from the familiar diagram and could be a better way of assessing children's understanding.

Using numbers to enhance procedural learning in science

Numeracy skills are of vital importance at each stage of a scientific enquiry, yet research indicates that even secondary pupils often prefer to conduct investigations and describe phenomena qualitatively rather than assign numbers to them (Foulds *et al*, 1992). We will take each stage of the investigative process in turn and describe the potential for development in quantitative procedures.

Predicting

Children in Key Stages 2 and 3 will be familiar with the process of predicting qualitative relationships between two variables, eg 'I think that the hotter the water, the less time it will take for the sugar to dissolve.' Yet they are seldom asked to *quantify* rates of change in predictions, eg 'I think the temperature will fall by 2 degrees Celsius in five minutes.' Neither are they asked to specify an algebraic relationship of proportionality or draw the shape of the line graph they think will result from a particular test, eg 'I think the graph will look like this.' (See Figure 13.1.)

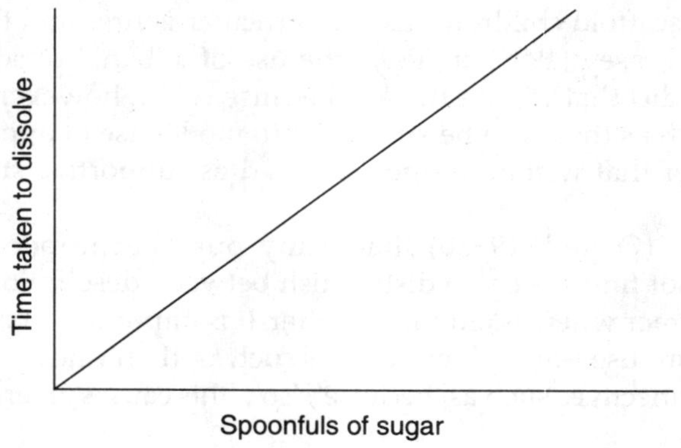

Figure 13.1 Simple graph used to provide a prediction

This is part of the development of a sense of scale – getting the 'feel' for the size of numbers and their algebraic relationship. It is a skill that can be practised, for example by getting children to estimate the number of marbles in a jar or spoonfuls of sugar in a 1 kg bag.

Planning/testing

Planning an investigation involves the identification of key variables – *independent*, *dependent* and *controls*. Helping children to do this through the use of whole class brainstorming onto 'Post-it' notes and transferring these to charts representing the stages of planning is one way of achieving this (see Goldsworthy and Feasey, 1994). Yet in order to make decisions about appropriate measurement equipment pupils need to be able to classify the key variables *mathematically*, as follows:

- *Categoric* – a variable without a numeric value, eg a type of surface.
- *Discrete* or *Ordinal* – a variable which can only take whole number values, eg number of people.
- *Continuous* – a variable which can take any numeric value, eg time.

These categories have implications for graphical representation (see below) and the overall difficulty of an investigation – a general progression would be from categoric to discrete to continuous variables. This provides the teacher with opportunities for differentiating scientific enquiry for pupils of differing mathematical attainment.

Measuring

Almost all measuring equipment commonly used in school science lessons involves the use of a wide range of numeracy skills. For example, using a thermometer generally requires pupils to select a scale (Farenheit or Celsius), interpret the meaning of subdivisions (eg five divisions from 20 to 30 degrees) and round up or down from the actual position of the thread of alcohol. Some equipment has complex conceptual problems associated with it, for example the appearance of gram and Newton scales on a force meter/spring balance gives ample opportunity for confusion between mass and weight. Even digital equipment such as a stop-watch has implications for children's numeracy. It gives times to the nearest millisecond, requiring complex rounding operations. It has two different number systems (hexadecimal for minutes and seconds, decimal for milliseconds) and three 'decimal points' creating scope for errors by factors of 60 or more.

It is clear that use of such equipment needs to be *explicitly taught* both before and during use in an investigation. Children at Key Stage 1 need to have extensive experience of using non-standard units to provide a rationale for standardization and address basic errors such as counting from zero rather than one on a scale. The progressive introduction of more complex and accurate measurement equipment needs to be planned within the school's scheme of work for science (eg strip thermometers with colours/large digits leading to digital probe and large glass versions by upper primary level). Pupils need to have repeated experiences of using equipment, since Summerfield (1996) found that many encounter science kit such as measuring cylinders only once or twice during their primary school years. Teachers can demonstrate correct usage and use 'deliberate errors' to help pupils identify potential mathematical 'pitfalls' such as starting from the wrong end of the scale.

Once we have taught pupils the correct use of equipment, they still need to make a number of mathematical decisions when deciding what, when and how to measure:

- *Frequency* – What is a sensible number of readings to take, how often and over how long a period?
- *Accuracy* – What is realistic? How many decimal points?
- *Repeat measurements* – Why? How many repeats?

Theory Task Use of science apparatus

Look at the following pieces of measuring equipment:

- metre rule;
- thermometer;
- measuring cylinder or beaker;
- forcemeter;
- stop-watch;
- electronic balance.

1. What mathematical skills and understanding do children need in order to use these pieces of equipment accurately?
2. Is there a case for practising these measurement skills separately from practical/investigative work?
3. Select a particular piece of measuring equipment and design a series of simple activities which will teach children how to use it safely and accurately. What key numeracy skills will you need to demonstrate?

Recording

The first step in recording numerical data from an investigation is usually to construct a *table of results*. This again is a procedure that does not come naturally to children. If repeat measurements have been made, children will need to calculate *means*, and the raw data may need to be further processed by identifying the *mode* (most popular value), *median* (mid-point value) or percentages.

We may wish pupils to use databases and spreadsheets to record measurements. The laborious task of loading data into a card-type database program often precludes its use for interrogation, which is why it may be better to use pre-loaded sample files to develop higher order numeracy skills. Spreadsheets can be effectively substituted for tables of results, with the advantage that charts are generated at the click of a button – though this may have its dangers (see below). Spreadsheets can also be used to set up simple mathematical models in which calculations can be pasted from cell to cell, for example to work out a pupil's weight on different planets.

Very few 11–13-year-olds spontaneously produce graphs of data. This may be because choosing the right graph for the data is a complex numeracy skill, which needs to be taught explicitly and progressively. The type of data collected dictates the most appropriate graphical representation, as in the following examples:

- 'Eye colour' is a *categoric* variable, with whole numbers of cases, so can be represented in a *pictogram* or *block graph*. Since every case has an eye colour these are also proportions of the whole, so we could alternatively use a pie chart.
- If we had a *categoric* independent variable and a *continuous* dependent variable (eg height of ball bounce on different floor surfaces) it would be more appropriate to use a bar chart. There should be gaps between the bars because they represent separate categories.
- 'Height' is a *continuous* variable. If we want frequencies of different heights we need to use a *histogram* which divides the variable into 'class intervals' (eg 5 cm). A histogram looks very like a bar chart, but the bars touch (showing that the variable is continuous).
- If we want to plot two *continuous* variables against each other (eg height and weight) the most appropriate chart is a *scattergram* which shows strength of association between variables. If a relationship emerges, a 'best fit' line can be drawn between the points, making it a *line graph.*

Teachers need to help children make appropriate choices initially, then give them increasing responsibility to choose the chart to match their data. Data logging software (eg *RM Investigate*) can graph data in 'real time', enabling children to predict and interpret as the investigation progresses, whilst removing the painstaking procedure of constructing charts manually. However – as with spreadsheets – this can take the decision about the appropriate presentation format from children, leaving them without the necessary numeracy skills.

Observation Task Pupils' measurements

Collect some examples of scientific tables and graphs produced by children in your current class. Analyse them for types of errors:

- Has the table been constructed correctly?
- Has an appropriate form of graphical representation been selected?
- Is the choice of axes and scales sensible?
- Have points been plotted accurately?
- Has the pupil made an attempt to interpret the findings?

Interpreting

Of all scientific process skills, those associated with the analysis and explanation of data are perhaps the most difficult and, from inspection evidence, are performed least well. Pupils have few opportunities in most classrooms to examine data from sources other than their own investigations and draw conclusions from them. This should improve with the implementation of relevant aspects of the National Numeracy Strategy, together with an analysis of past Statutory Attainment Tasks (SATs) which contain numerous examples of tabular and graphical data with questions inviting children to interrogate them in different ways. Teachers need to set time aside for such activities, and also for proper plenary sessions at the end of scientific enquiry in which pupils are directed to examine their data, look for patterns and anomalies, and offer hypotheses to explain them.

Practice Task Interpreting information with pupils

Use examples of graphs (from SATs) with a group of pupils to teach interpretation skills. Ask questions such as:

- **What is happening when the line suddenly goes up?**
- **Why do you think the line levels out here?**

Invite pupils to draw graphs to predict what will happen in everyday circumstances (eg amount of litter collected against number of collectors).

Summary

In this chapter we have investigated the use of literacy and numeracy skills to support pupils' conceptual and procedural learning in science. We have suggested a number of strategies that teachers can use to ensure that pupils are oriented towards a scientific topic through use of contextualizing literature; that their pre-existing ideas are elicited and restructured through use of skilful questioning and discussion; and that they are supported in communicating their understanding using appropriate written genres and vocabulary. We have addressed important mathematical components of scientific process skills, including the use of estimation in predicting; reading of scales in measurement; data tabulation and graphing in recording; and mathematical pattern-seeking to support the interpretation of findings. Throughout the chapter we have stressed the fundamental role of words and numbers in science, and proposed a range of approaches for bringing literacy, numeracy and scientific learning closer together in the school curriculum.

Further reading for this chapter is included at the end of the References section at the back of this book.

14 Science education for citizenship

Gill Nicholls

The context of science

The aim of this chapter is to position the role of citizenship and values within the science curriculum. This is no easy task as the science curriculum itself has been, and still is in a constant state of flux. We only have to look at the numerous changes that the science curriculum has gone through in the last decade to appreciate that science educators and policy makers themselves do not have a cohesive approach to the constitution of a science curriculum. Yet despite this, new and increased demands are made of the science curriculum. Citizenship and values being just one of the components. The growing concern is summed up in the Nuffield Foundation Report, *Beyond 2000: Science education for the future*. Its opening words state:

> This report is the product of a desire to provide a new vision of an education in science for our young people. It is driven by a sense of a growing disparity between the science education provided in our schools and the needs and interests of the young people who will be our future citizens. Education, at the end of the 20th century, no longer prepares individuals for secure, lifelong employment in local industry or services.
>
> (Millar and Osborne, 1998: 1)

This gives an indication that, whatever, the science curriculum's present shortfalls, it is still clearly associated with future citizens. The final quote on the introductory page demonstrates the importance of science to future citizens: 'The ever-growing importance of scientific issues in our daily lives demands a populace who has sufficient knowledge and understanding to follow science and scientific debates' (Millar and Osborne, 1998: 1).

With the above statement in mind it is important to place the significance of science within the whole school curriculum in perspective, before a discussion of citizenship and science education can be addressed. *Beyond 2000* highlights science's role within the curriculum:

> The current significance of science is reflected in the fact that it now occupies the curriculum high table with literacy and numeracy as the essential core of the primary curriculum. In addition, science is also a core subject of the 11–16 curriculum, along with English and Mathematics.
>
> (Millar and Osborne, 1998: 4)

Effectively, science is high in the education stakes, however the changing curricular position of science has not been accompanied by a corresponding change in the content of the science curriculum, in particular at the secondary level. The Report suggests that: 'Contemporary analysis of the labour market would suggest that our future society would need a larger number of individuals with a broader understanding of science both for their work and to enable them to participate as citizens in a democratic society' (Millar and Osborne, 1998: 4).

Why is this so important to science and the role science education can play with regards citizenship and values? Over the last 30 years, the image of science has changed with both negative and positive events. Science is often regarded as absolute truth, yet recent events such as Chernobyl, CFCs, depletion of the ozone layer, genetically modified (GM) foods and cloning have tarnished science's profile; while successes in the medical world continue. How are pupils – our future citizens – to interpret such data and information?

The Crick Report (DfEE/QCA, 1998b: 37) states as one of its primary aims for citizenship: 'for people to think of themselves as active citizens, willing, able and equipped to have an influence in public life and with the critical capacities to weight evidence before speaking and acting'. The Report further enforces this by suggesting that: 'Individuals must be helped and prepared to shape the terms of such engagement by political understanding and action' (DfEE/QCA, 1998b: 10). These statements imply that to sustain a healthy and vibrant democracy, such issues do not require an acquiescent (nor a hostile and suspicious) public, but one with a broad understanding of major scientific ideas who, whilst appreciating the value of science and its contribution to our culture, can engage critically with issues and arguments which involve scientific knowledge (Nuffield Foundation, 1998: 4).

If science educators are to attempt meeting such expectations we need to be able to provide our pupils with teaching and learning opportunities that allow them to actively explore issues and events in science through a variety of contexts. This can include case studies within the local community, which can lead to critical discussion, and debate within the classroom. The main focus of these types of involvement is to challenge and stimulate pupils, to make science relevant to their everyday lives and help them understand their role in society. As Heater (1990) suggests 'a citizen is a person furnished with knowledge of public affairs, instilled with attitudes of civic virtue and equipped with skills to participate in the political arena'.

In an attempt to define the knowledge, attitudes and skills that science education can contribute to citizenship and values, the learning objectives set out in Table 14.1 can help formulate the types of lessons that can be introduced to pupils of all ages.

When using the following table to help develop science lessons with citizenship and values in mind, it must be remembered that the categories suggested are permeable. Knowledge about citizenship and values is only partially useful if it does not lead to the formulation of attitudes and the acquisition of skills. Attitudes are but prejudices unless

Table 14.1 Learning objectives

Knowledge	*Attitudes*	*Skills*
Facts	Self-understanding	Intellect and judgement
Interpretation	Respect for others	Communication
Personal role	Respect for values	Action

grounded in a firm and clear understanding, and action is wanting direction without attitudes and is irresponsible and/or inefficient if born in ignorance. It is important to understand what is meant by each objective.

Knowledge, attitudes and skills

Pupils need to know basic facts surrounding the scientific area for discussion or investigation. They need to understand how the status and role of the citizen has evolved in science, particularly in their own community and the state at large. They need to be informed how citizenship and values are articulated through scientific institutions, and present day laws. Pupils also need to realize that citizenship and values operate in a context, one which deals with practical issues. As such they need to realize that as individuals they will be confronted with problems and issues that affect them both at a local and global level. In this context, scientific knowledge and information is only part of the pupils' requirements. The knowledge that is given to them has to be at an appropriate level and introduced in such a way that pupils can make sense of it and come to understand the implications of their decision making. Science has a key role to play in bringing the young citizen to understand his or her own potential personal role in the community and society in which they live. A clear understanding, for example, of CFCs might make the individuals choose not to purchase goods containing CFC.

Clearly the first task for the science teacher is to motivate and stimulate their pupils' interest in the subject matter, whether this is nuclear fuel, cloning or personal health issues. It is essential that the pupils feel that current issues such as GM foods are of equal interest to the teacher as they are to the pupils themselves. Here the science teacher must play a significant part in clarifying pupils' anxieties and feelings with respect to the issues under discussion. Equally many of the issues that could and will be discussed in science lessons are emotive and sensitive. Teachers must be aware of pupils' feelings, as well as appreciate that a pupil will have his or her own prejudices towards the subject. As such it is the teacher's responsibility to lead the pupil into understanding these prejudices.

Allowing pupils to develop rational and flexible thought is not a simple task, however, science can and ought to play its part. Science is in a strong position to influence the way pupils can become critical, ask questions and seek information from a variety of sources as means to answering the questions posed. The way the science curriculum functions demands that pupils draw conclusions from data collected. It expects pupils to argue their case based on evidence; what the teacher can influence is how pupils can be cultivated to realize that the judgements they make can influence the public arena.

The development of judgement is a vital aspect in citizenship. Beiner (1983: 163) suggests that: 'Judgement is... irreducible to algorithm. What is required is not a "decision procedure", but an education in hermeneutic insight, taste, and understanding.' What does this mean in terms of pedagogy for the science teacher? The science teacher needs to enable the student to understand the values and bias he/she holds, and how they will be used in judgements that are made. The teacher must also allow the pupil room to explore the consequences of the action or inaction that a pupil might wish to take in certain circumstances. Here such issues as apathy and active demonstration may be considered, by allowing the pupil to appreciate other people's point of view. Good examples here are pollution and cloning:

Pollution

- Pupils could consider the issues related to pollution from a variety of angles.
- Why do Greenpeace actively demonstrate and attack the state about pollution when individuals continually pollute their own environment?
- What effects do individuals polluting their environment have on the local community?
- What responsibility does the individual have to global pollution?

Cloning

Pupils should be encouraged to consider issues related to cloning, for example Dolly the sheep. This could take the form of a research and debate exercise.

In the above examples, pupils should be actively encouraged to consider evidence and reflect on the decisions they make, both from an individual point of view and as a collective decision making force as a class. Teachers should adopt a teaching style that facilitates and actively encourages pupils to be critical in their thinking and analytical in their approach to problems. Science and scientific issues as expressed in the media can be used as a vehicle for such activities. For example, genetically modified crops are frequently discussed in the media without a clear explanation of what GM means, there is an implicit assumption that this is not only known but also understood. Yet, many pupils do not know what GM crops or foods are. As a consequence pupils' critical analysis and thinking related to such issues are impeded. Science teachers should think about how the teaching of the scientific information could be integrated into the evaluation of issues related to GM crops and foods.

Science education should play a part in future citizens being critical about the information they are given and the value that can be placed upon that information.

Practice Task GM foods and crops

Pupils in rural and urban areas can be encouraged to conduct a survey related to GM crops, by asking farmers and/or visiting supermarkets to find out which products contain GM ingredients. The results can be brought back to the lesson, analysed, then presented to the class for discussion.

There is an argument that when pupils encounter science in their daily lives, it is rarely in the context of 'doing or engaging in science'. For example, here are two randomly selected headlines from a daily newspaper:

> 'War launched on killer bug'
> 'Use recycled paper blocks as a more environmentally friendly fuel'

Each has something to do with science, and something else. The first example is about immunization against meningitis and the other about fuel and the environment. In other words, science presents itself to the pupil in the context of a problem or an issue, one that needs to be thought about systematically and critically. These types of stimulating activities allow pupils to engage in the arguments that show science is not perfect, nor does it give us all the answers, and indeed, sometimes it gives the wrong answers. Carl Sagan (1996: 30) expresses this notion well:

> Science is far from a perfect instrument of knowledge. It's just the best we have. In this respect, as in many others, it's like democracy. Science by itself cannot advocate human action, but it can certainly illuminate the possible consequences of alternative courses of action.
>
> (Sagan 1996: 30)

What I am suggesting is that science is preoccupied with everyday, serious questions of values and citizenship. Therefore, values and citizenship education need science education in the curriculum, if pupils are to be able to discuss action, and understand the consequences of those actions in a more global world.

The Crick Report (QCA/DfEE 1988b: 37) states that: 'School and its local community provide a perfect context for pupils to examine issues and events and to become involved in activities, participatory activities and experiences where emphasis is on learning through action.' Through this type of involvement, pupils can be helped and guided through the political, civic and social issues related to scientific information and knowledge. Engagement of this nature can lead to balanced decision making, incorporating some of the requirements and expectations of citizenship and values. These include:

- the belief that individuals must be helped and prepared to shape the terms of such engagements by political understanding and action;
- some knowledge of what social problems affect them and even what different pressure groups and parties say about them;

- the knowledge that it will empower them (pupils) to participate in society effectively as active, informed, critical and responsible citizens.

(QCA/DfEE, 1998b)

The above statements from the Crick Report and Nuffield Foundation must and do have implications for the science curriculum and citizenship and values education.

Implications for the science curriculum

Citizenship is fundamentally concerned with social relationships between people and the institutional arrangements of complex industrial societies. Thus exploring citizenship and values within the science curriculum requires an examination and consideration of both pupils and the institution (school and society as a whole). In Mills' (1970) terms, we are concerned with what kinds of persons we are able to be and the kinds of persons we might be. What kinds of opportunities and constraints confront pupils in terms of current institutional arrangements? Understanding the concept of citizenship and values in science requires an understanding of the concept of 'self' and the manner in which institutional arrangements (in this case the school) may provide opportunities for, or place constraints upon, self-development (in this case the pupil).

Why is this important in science education?

We can start from the perspective of the pupil as a human being, one that is influenced both biologically through genetic inheritance, but also socially where they require a social milieu to develop their recognizable human qualities. The nature of human beings is developmental: one would expect pupils to change and develop over a period of time. These changes will be in response to a variety of aspects such as economic, political and social contexts.

Equally as pupils develop and mature, their own actions and beliefs will affect the contexts they find themselves in. For example, exploring cloning of Dolly the sheep in year 3, 4 or 5 can be as exciting and stimulating as it can be in years 9 and 10, but by years 11, 12 and beyond the individuals' overt actions could influence future debates on cloning. Where science education is important to citizenship and values education is in helping future individuals choose the course of action that could or might be taken. The key thing here for the classroom is that choices for action are different and opportunities to take action are also different. However, all are influenced by political, economic and social contexts.

What science education can do is to introduce pupils to such contexts through everyday examples that can be investigated through the community, environment and social/cultural elements of their lives. As Gould (1988: 40) suggests: 'Self-development refers to the freedom to develop oneself through one's own actions… a process of the development of the person over time.' He goes on to say: '… in order to effect such choices concretely a wide range of actual options need to be available to people… It is through making choices in their actions in particular situations over the course of time that people come to know who they are'

(1988: 41–46). If we apply this concept to the science classroom it allows us to conceptualize the notion of citizenship and values in our teaching, that of developing in pupils the capacity to make decisions related to science issues, and what action they may choose to take.

The way the present curriculum is constructed does at times constrain what pupils might engage in. If pupils and teachers feel such constraints, alternatives are needed, alternatives that require forms of reasoning that enable pupils and teachers to make links between personal experience of science and social structures. For many pupils, science is done to them, and they feel they are subject to vast impersonal facts that they cannot understand, let alone control and act upon. What we need our pupils to achieve in science is 'a quality of mind that will help them to use information and to develop reason in order to achieve lucid summations of what is going on in the world and of what may be happening within themselves' (Mills, 1970: 11).

It is this quality of understanding that science education should be aiming for. It provides a framework for pupils to understand themselves and the relationship to the larger world of science in terms of their civil, political and social rights. At present most pupils and young adults do not possess the quality of mind essential to grasp the interplay between man, science and society. For many, the world is experienced as one in which they are constantly subjected to forces and events that they do not understand, such as BSE, GM foods, cloning and nuclear fuel. It is often difficult for pupils and adults to relate their personal and scientific knowledge and expectations to the understanding of such complex issues. It is also difficult for them to appreciate the complexities of opportunities and the constraints that are on them from society in making their own choices and decisions about scientific issues.

Added to this is the dimension of citizenship related to developing attitudes and values, which underpin rights, duties and obligations. These can be considered from two points of view when teaching science: 1) what values and attitudes can or should the science curriculum engender in pupils; or 2) what do we mean by duties and obligations within a science context?

The very nature of science and scientific enquiry encourages discussion and debate. Debate requires skills as well as knowledge. Science is in a key position to allow pupils of all ages to engage in debate related to scientific concepts and issues and contemporary problems. Within this context, debate allows for science literacy to occur in the classroom. We live in a society increasingly dependent on science-based technologies, a society reliant on scientific research for new modes of production and communication, new materials for consumption. An understanding of the scientific ideas associated with such production is essential if pupils are to make decisions for themselves in the future – whether these decision are related to diet or the type of fuel that they will use, or car they will drive.

Debate and discussion surrounding such issues are of key importance to future citizens. The science curriculum can accommodate such issues, which can be planned into normal lesson time. Often researching issues as a precursor for teaching requires pupils to be collaborative and work as teams. These are crucial for citizenship and values education.

Alternative views of citizenship and the role of science education

Alternative views of citizenship and values can be identified; what needs to be explored is the role science education can play within these alternatives. The first consideration is that of the division between the individual and citizenship and values, and the importance of citizenship for society. MacIntyre (1982) refers to the liberal tradition whereby citizenship is largely considered in terms of individual rights. As Mills proposes the individual qua citizen has certain rights to be free of interference from, or oppression by, the state. The essential character of the citizen is consequently vigilance in defence of his or her rights and liberties. Morality consists in the full flowering of the individual person, and citizenship and values provide the necessary freedom for this to occur. The alternative to this is the Greek tradition, which places priority on the positive view of liberty – citizenship provided opportunities to serve the community. Morality consists of the conscientious discharge of one's civic duties and obligations.

The above perspectives can be taken account of within the science curriculum. The role science education can play is to make the individual aware of both their individual rights to knowledge and decision making, as well as the individual's commitment to the community. A good example of this is the case of nuclear fuel and power stations. How do pupils perceive these issues? Is there a difference between pupils who live near a power station and those who do not? Such a discussion can stimulate lively debate within a science classroom, while bringing pupils' attention to their roles as citizens within such issues.

The second related approach towards citizenship and values is that of the private and public citizen. It is a truism that the state impinges on the individual's life with so much greater pressure than at almost any other time in history. The demands and opportunities for the citizen to actively participate in this relationship have similarly never been greater. It can also be argued that the desire to simply switch off is equally powerful. The 'let them (government) get on with it' approach. The demands here are those of the two kinds of freedom: the freedom from civic concerns in order to pursue a private, family life; and the need to participate democratically in order to preserve political freedom. Here too science education has a role to play.

A good case for consideration here is that of the recent controversy surrounding fields of GM crops:

Genetically modified crops

Pupils even as young as years 3 and 4 in the primary school can be introduced to this topic. The questions can be posed in such a way that pupils have to consider the arguments about GM crops from the government's perspective (that is, the need for more food at less cost) and the individual consumer's perspective (the choice of not having food contaminated or experimented with).

As has been indicated earlier, part of educating for citizenship and values is cultivating the art of exchange of views, debate, communication and respect for others' points of view. The science teacher can, with good planning, allow for such activities to happen in a constructive way within the classroom. However, implicit in such planning is the need to understand one's own feelings, prejudices and values.

To meet the learning objectives in science for citizenship and values, the teacher must choose carefully the subject content and the relationships presented within the body of knowledge with which pupils are going to be involved.

Conclusion

This chapter has attempted to draw together current debates about the nature and context of the science curriculum and the part citizenship and values have to play within that context. It has made explicit the view that science is a key function of our present society and as such our pupils need to have a good understanding of the limitations and expectations of science in their everyday life. However, within that understanding is a deeper and more pressing issue of how pupils, as individuals, can influence what may or may not happen as a consequence of science in society. I have argued that science and science education have a key role to play in creating an environment of critical thinking and judgement making for our pupils. Investigating, collecting data and evidence is an intrinsic part of the science curriculum. Such skills can be used to facilitate some of the elements of citizenship and values our pupils need to acquire and understand, in order to play a full and active part as future citizens.

The science teacher's pedagogic practice is key to establishing the types of learning objectives suggested. Incorporating the notion of self-understanding into science lessons is a good way of encouraging citizenship and values, as it facilitates the need for pupils of all ages to confront their values, prejudices and biases, in an environment that has to consider others' views as well as their own.

Further reading

This chapter is taken from the following title, which considers the issues of teaching values and citizenship across the curriculum:

Bailey, R (ed) (2001) *Teaching Values and Citizenship*, Kogan Page, London

Other further reading is:

Cross, R and Fensham, P (2001) *Science and the Citizen: For educators and the public*, Melbourne studies in education, Avena Publishing, Fitzroy, Australia

15 Science technology society

Steve Alsop and Erminia Pedretti

All people need some science education, so that they can think, speak and act on those matters related to science, which may affect their quality of living. (Solomon, 1993: 15)

STS science is also expected to fill a critical void in the traditional curriculum – the social responsibility in collective decision making on issues related to science and technology. (Aikenhead, 1994: 18)

Objectives

The intention of this chapter is to facilitate a critical reflection on issues of science, technology and society education. The chapter explores, in relation to science:

- science, technology and society (STS);
- teaching with STS in mind;
- ways of integrating STS into science teaching.

Introduction

Genetically modified (GM) foods, cloning, nuclear power, ozone depletion, dietary advice, advances in medical science, reproductive technologies, pollution, space exploration – the list goes on: it seems almost impossible to escape advances in science and technology. We live in a time of rapid scientific and technological change and issues and controversies abound both within the scientific community and in the public at large. Knowledge of science and technology, it seems, has become a requirement of everyday life, as Giddens (1994: 7) writes: 'Individuals have to engage with the wider social world if they are to survive in it. Information by specialists (including scientific knowledge) can no longer be wholly confined to specific groups, but becomes routinely interpreted and acted upon by lay individuals in the course of everyday actions.'

This chapter explores science, technology and society (STS) curricular initiatives and the place of these in the curriculum. We start by considering what STS education might be.

Science, technology and society

Science, technology and society programmes and themes interpret science and technology as complex socially embedded enterprises. One representation of the relationship between science, technology and society, after Aikenhead (1994), is provided in Figure 15.1.

In general, STS education seeks to promote the development of a critical, scientifically and technologically literate citizenry; one that is capable of understanding science, technology and society and is empowered to make informed and responsible decisions (and act upon those decisions). In other words, STS is about considering science in a larger social, cultural and political context to make decisions. To give a concrete example, STS education might include discussions about a contemporary scientific issue, such as genetically modified foods, with the explicit aim of promoting informed decision making and action. In this context, discussion could focus on the broader question of whether GM foods should be sold as well as whether pupils would eat GM foods themselves.

The following activity focuses on another STS issue, that of animal experimentation (after Selby, 1995: 262). The activity is designed to provide you with a sense of the range of perspectives at play when considering a controversial issue.

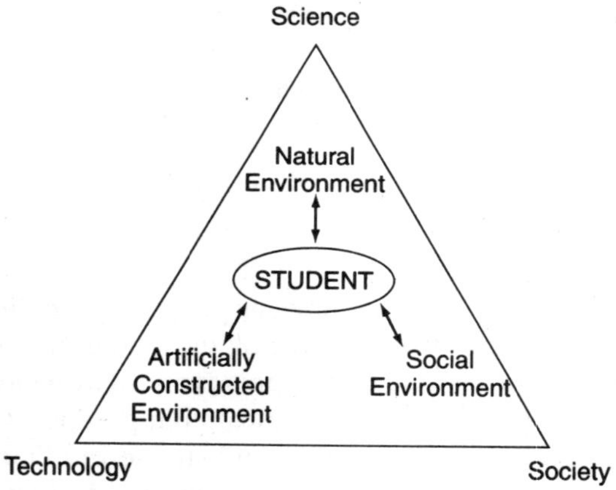

Figure 15.1 A representation of STS education
Source: Aikenhead (1994)

Theory Task An STS issue – where do you stand?

Complete the following tick sheet and discuss your beliefs and opinions with colleagues.

Statement	*Agree*	*Undecided*	*Disagree*
Other animals, like humans, feel pain, fear and distress.			
Preventing human suffering justifies the use of animals in scientific experiments to test new medicines.			
Given the choice, I would buy a 'cruelty-free' shampoo rather than one tested on animals if it was double the cost.			
Testing substances on animals is unreliable because they often respond differently to human beings.			
Animal experimentation to ensure the safety of products that make us look, smell or feel nicer is absolutely unjustified.			
With diseases such as cancer, Aids and multiple sclerosis to conquer, animals will have an important part to play in medical research for the foreseeable future.			
The major killers in wealthy societies (heart disease, cancer and road accidents) can best be prevented by changes in life-style not animal tests.			
Animals should not be subjected to painful and often lethal tests just to satisfy the business world's incessant demand for new products to maintain or improve profit levels.			
We need to conduct experiments on animals to cure diseases in the so-called Third World.			
There are good alternatives (eg computer simulations, tissue culture and testing outside the body) which, with the right financial investment to refine procedures, could replace all animal tests.			
Animal experiments have played an essential part in medical progress.			
Firms advertising 'cruelty-free' cosmetics are deceiving the public in that they are using ingredients previously screened on animals and, hence, not requiring retesting.			

What are your beliefs about animal experimentation? How do these differ from your colleagues? Might we discuss this issue in the classroom? Should we, for instance, try to present material in a 'neutral way', by perhaps spending equal time on different viewpoints – or should we make our own opinions known? Is it ever possible to be neutral?

During the past 20 years or so, science, technology and society education has become a major force in science curriculum development in many countries around the world (Solomon and Aikenhead, 1994). In the UK, STS is often closely associated with particular science curriculum materials: Science in a Social Context (SISCON), Salters Science and the Association for Science Education's Science and Technology in Society (SATIS) 5–19 projects. SISCON is a slightly older resource introduced in 1983, while Salters and SATIS are more recent materials widely available in most schools (details about these resources is provided shortly).

Theory Task Locating and reflecting upon curriculum materials

If possible, take a look at the Salters or SATIS curriculum materials. What are your thoughts about the approach adopted? How does it differ from more traditional teaching? Have you observed lessons with an STS focus? What are your initial thoughts about including an STS focus in your science lessons?

So what is STS science education?

To start with, it would be a mistake to assume that STS is a single, well-articulated approach to science education. Rather, it is a movement with a number of different strands, each with a distinct history, and some tensions as well.

Phrases like 'scientific literacy', 'responsible citizenry' and 'informed decision making' are examples of some of the goals articulated by STS advocates and programmes (Kumar and Chubin, 2000). STS education is rooted in notions of promoting literacy. According to Lewis and Gagel (1992: 135), the literate person is aware of the 'economic, political, moral, ethical, ecological, and even psychic or spiritual aspects' of science. It is clear, from this brief description, that there are diverse views as to what constitutes STS education, and if we are not thoughtful or diligent about STS it may become something of a rallying slogan amongst science educators, with little presence in science classroom practice.

So what are some of the cornerstones of STS education? Generally speaking, STS is a multi-disciplinary subject that includes moral, ethical, political, philosophical, historical and economic perspectives. Such perspectives are an attempt to acknowledge, explore and critique the connections among science, technology and society. Solomon (1993: 18) highlights the following features of STS education:

1. understanding environmental threats, including global ones;
2. understanding economic and industrial aspects of technology;
3. understanding the fallible nature of science;
4. discussion of personal opinion and values, as well as democratic action;
5. understanding the multi-cultural dimensions of science and technology.

An STS framework developed by Pedretti (1996) includes five guiding principles – summarized in Table 15.1.

Theory Task Using Pedretti's framework

Reflect upon each of the five features of STS education described by Pedretti in Table 15.1. Consider the possible meanings and implications of these features for science education. How could you (or should you) include these features in your teaching? Try to provide some concrete examples if possible. Wherever possible discuss you thoughts with colleagues.

STS in the Science National Curriculum

STS features permeate the Science National Curriculum at Key Stages 2, 3 and 4. For instance, the general programmes of study for Key Stage 2 highlight that pupils should: 'Apply their knowledge and understanding of scientific ideas to familiar phenomena,

Table 15.1 Five components of STS education

Component	*Comment*
Sustainable development	STS education involves the study and utilization of resources for human long-term needs in an effort to maintain a life-giving and life-sustaining environment.
Decision-making	In STS education, students should gain a clear understanding of how decisions are made at the local, provincial and national government levels, and within the private and industrial sectors.
Ethics	STS education attempts to combine science and values education. Such a perspective departs from the more traditional presentation of science as a value-free, objective, linear enterprise.
Personal and political	An STS curriculum includes discussion of politics, economics and science. STS education not only addresses the traditional question of whether the science is good, but also who benefits and who loses.
Action	Action ideally empowers people, leading to personal and social change, and prepares citizens to function responsibly and effectively. Not only is it sufficient to develop the potential to act, but the disposition to do so. Those who act are those who have a deep personal understanding of the issues and their human implications and feel some sense of ownership and empowerment.

Source: Pedretti (1996)

everyday things and their personal health. They [should] begin thinking about the positive and negative effects of scientific and technological developments on the environment and other contexts' (DfEE, 1999: 21).

Similar emphasis is found at Key Stage 3 and Key Stage 4; for instance, within the 'Breadth of study section' in KS4 (DfEE, 1999: 57) the orders specify that pupils should be taught the knowledge, skills and understanding through: 'considering and evaluating the benefits and drawbacks of scientific and technological developments, including those related to the environment, personal health and quality of life, and those raising ethical issues'.

This broad statement provides a teaching context to explore specified content and skills. Statements of this nature, however, lend themselves more readily to some content than others. For instance, learning expectations such as:

- pupils should be taught about possible effects of burning fossil fuels on the environment (for example, production of acid rain, carbon dioxide and solid particles) and how these effects can be minimized (KS3, Sc3, 2i);
- pupils should be taught the basics of cloning, selective breeding and genetic engineering (KS4 single, Sc2, 3g);

seem to necessitate STS discussions of the potential benefits and drawbacks of science and technology.

So given that it is in the curriculum, at least in Key Stages 2, 3 and 4, how can we incorporate STS into the classroom?

STS in the classroom

Given its presence in the curriculum, perhaps the most surprising part of STS science education is the lack of it in the classroom. Advocates continue to raise concerns about the shortage of STS type education in our UK schools (see McGrath, 1993). There are likely to be a number of reasons for this, including a shortage of curriculum time and a perceived lack of expertise and confidence. The curriculum is large and contains a raft of demanding concepts that are to be assessed. This can result in potentially time-consuming 'issues', 'debates' and 'discussions' being sidelined in favour of traditional content and teaching approaches – as a recent training teacher, Tina, notes with a sense of frustration:

> There are too many issues within science that don't always get talked about because you just stick to the content.

Considerations of STS can also open up 'messiness' in science. They involve discussions of political, moral and ethical dilemmas and this can leave teachers feeling uncomfortable, in part because of a lack of confidence and experience. Such feelings are evident in the following comments from Steven, a training secondary teacher:

> As a new teacher it is difficult enough to plan and teach content you are familiar with. Discussions of contemporary science issues are a good idea but at this stage I think they might

> be too ambitious. For starters, I am not up to date on some of these issues and don't feel comfortable about have debates and discussions. It is very difficult getting children listening to one another.

Steven's concerns relate to expertise and classroom management and control. Often these issues increase anxiety in new teachers, nevertheless the importance of relevance (and motivation) are also pressing concerns. As Judy, another training teacher, notes:

> For all of us possibly, we need to have some kind of personal connection to what we are learning about or as teachers be able to make some kind of personal connections. And so I think a lot of that can be made through some of the STS stuff by taking science out of the textbook.

You should take comfort by noting that often perceptions of 'lack of expertise' and 'losing control' disappear after teaching an STS-style lesson. So what are we saying? Give it a go – try to incorporate STS activities into your early practice wherever possible. In our experience you will not regret it, nor will your pupils. The other good news is that there are some excellent materials available to support your teaching including:

- SATIS Resources: the SATIS materials are intended to supplement traditional science programmes. They contain a wealth of teaching and learning ideas that can be adapted to meet your particular class needs. This excellent resource is available from the ASE and is designed for a wide age range, from the under 8s to post-16. Different packs are available for different age groups: under-8s, 8–14, 14–16, and 16–19. Further details about SATIS, including sample materials, are available from the ASE Web site (http://www.ase.org.uk/satis/). This Web site also has many other useful STS links, including links to the KS3 'SciShop' database (www.Scishop.org) which also contains some good resources.
- Salters Science materials consist of a series of units matched to the curriculum for Key Stages 3, 4 and A-level. For instance, the KS3 science pack includes units exploring the atmosphere, burning and bonding, construction, electricity in the home, and energy. They are widely available and found in many secondary school science departments.

Teaching with STS in mind

STS advocates often emphasize that conventional science teaching strategies can present a clean and rather sterile view of science. In the following subsections, we offer some teaching activities with an STS focus. The list is certainly not exhaustive or exclusive to STS-style content – it is offered here for you to consider adopting and adapting the activities for use in your classrooms.

Debates and discussions

Debates and discussions are a straightforward way of introducing STS into your teaching. Students might, for instance, research and debate issues such as cloning, reproductive technologies or nuclear power. There are several ways of structuring discussions of this nature, for example small groups of students might be asked to research and represent a particular perspective (or interest group) in order to better understand different sides of an issue. This approach results in pupils researching and presenting opinions that are not necessarily their own. This can 'depersonalize' discussions and resolve potential personal clashes of opinions. Further advice about organizing and running a successful classroom discussion is offered in Chapter 7.

Consequence mapping

Consequence mapping (Lock and Ratcliffe, 1998) provides a means of structuring STS discussions. The technique is suitable for a variety of age groups. It involves developing a flow diagram by repeatedly posing 'what if questions' and considering the consequences. For instance, a consequence map could be used to consider:

1. What if the oil ran out? (See Figure 15.2.)
2. What if the hole in the ozone layer continued to grow?
3. What if genetic fingerprinting was widely used?

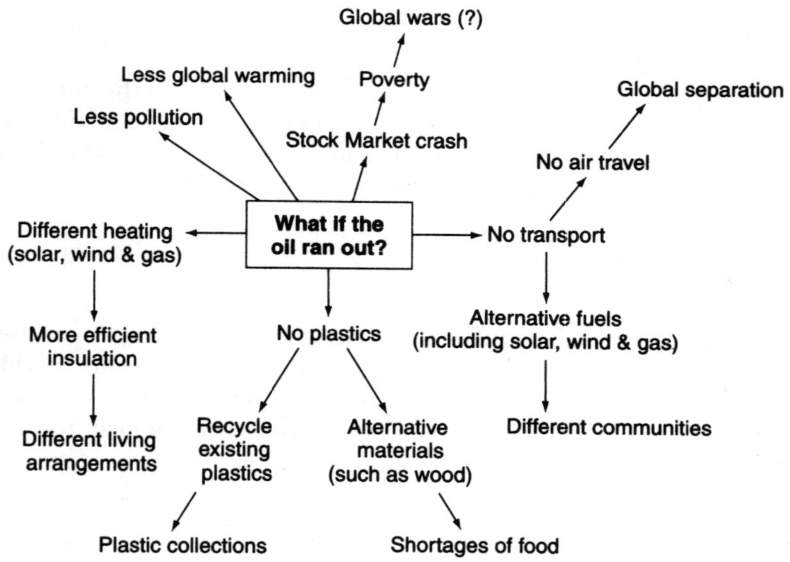

Figure 15.2 A consequence map – what if the oil ran out?

Historical case studies and stories

Exploring the history of science is widely recognized as an interesting and important dimension to teaching science. Ziman (1994) talks of the advantages of including an historical component in science teaching. He writes:

> [The history of science] is an indispensable dimension for any understanding of the nature of science itself. STS education must encompass this dimension. It must show that science and technology grow and change in association with the societies in which they are embedded. It must show the increasingly influential role of science and technology in society, and the increasing demands of society on science and technology. The historical approach, by showing how things got the way they are, is one of the most compelling ways of explaining this present state and also laying out the ground for a discussion of how it might change.
>
> (Ziman, 1994: 26)

To introduce an historical dimension to your teaching, you might get pupils to explore accounts and works of famous scientists (such as Galileo, Einstein, McClintock, Crick and Watson, and Darwin) to better understand how science developed, and to better understand that science is conducted by people who hold particular views, attitudes, passions and prejudices. Historical perspectives also assist in illustrating the role and impact of context, politics and belief systems in the process of science. The Internet is an excellent resource for this type of activity, by entering a scientist's name into a search engine a wealth of interesting, relevant and useful material appears.

You might also focus on a scientific concept and explore the development of this concept. Historical stories concerning the development of science (such as the history of the atom, development of vaccines and heat radiation) provide a fruitful way of helping students to explore and develop their ideas. They also challenge the 'it's obvious' image we often present of science. As one of my previous pupils affectionately noted after we had finished a unit on evolution: 'It's so obvious really isn't it, I can't understand why it took so long to think up a theory that we now learn in Key Stage 3!' Of course evolution is far from obvious (even after my teaching!), Darwin was a genius, and we need to make sure that we represent this in our science teaching. There exist a range of good resources with an historical focus (see Solomon, 1989; ASE 1997; Gribbin and Gribbin, 1997; Hellman, 1998).

A historical approach also provides a much needed way of broadening the western male focus of much of the science we teach. There are some excellent resources available that highlight the contributions of women and different ethic groups to science (see Kass-Simon and Farnes, 1990; Reiss, 1993).

Role play and simulations

Commonly during a role play, students take on and act out particular parts in order to begin to understand reactions of different characters and to emphasize that science is about people. Pupils might explore, for instance, Dr Jenner's vaccination of young James, Darwin's voyage on the *Beagle*, and Galileo's trial (see Solomon, 1993; Nott, 1994 for more details). This strategy requires information briefs, and not entire scripts. For instance, in a role play (after Alsop and Hollins, 1998) the scene is set in the Parliamentary Office of Science and Technology and the debate is whether the government should support genetically modified food (the case of the cuboid tomato – *Solanum Lycopersicum V. Cuboidus*). Groups of pupils are given time to present an argument based on a particular position including:

- farmers concerned about crop yields and sales;
- supermarket buyers concerned about sales, storage and shelf-life of crops;
- consumers concerned about health risks;
- interest groups concerned about health risks;
- agricultural companies manufacturing GM seeds.

In this approach, students enact roles to better understand the mechanics of decision making and accompanying action. Simulations of this type are often used for learning about industrial decision making and public inquiries. Another more historically based role play (after Hollins, 1998) involves students researching and enacting the role of a famous scientist. The scene is then set at a social gathering (a cocktail party) and pupils (scientists) meander around the room talking to others in role. This can lead to fascinating discussions, for instance 'Einstein' can meet 'Newton', 'Franklin' can meet 'Watson and Crick' and 'Voltaire' could meet 'Needham'.

There are many other creative and imaginative role plays and simulations available. You also should try to dream up some of your own.

Community involvement

In this approach, the emphasis is placed on some type of community involvement. For instance, pollution serves as a local concern and pupils might monitor and suggest solutions to a particular environmental issue. In this case, pupils could monitor pollution in a local stream by taking PH samples and invertebrate counts. Data could be amassed from a variety of years to assess sustainability (are pollution levels rising, falling or remaining constant?). Action might involve writing to local government or industries in search of answers.

Using newspapers and other mass media

After pupils leave school, informal sources of scientific information are likely to have a key role in keeping them up to date with science. In this regard, perhaps the most significant informal information resources are likely to be newspaper articles and television programmes. With this in mind (along with a sense of relevance) it is important to use and discuss newspaper articles in our science teaching. Wellington (1994: 289) provides a wide-ranging list of ways of using newspaper clippings in the science classroom. His lists include using papers:

- to introduce a topic;
- as a prompt or stimulus for discussion;

- as directed reading;
- to perform data extraction and analysis;
- to conduct a vocabulary and terminology study;
- to make a poster, collage and display.

Osborne (1998: 104) describes an activity exploring the evidence base of theoretical claims based upon a newspaper clipping. The issue is the risks involved to babies from long-haul air travel. After reading a short newspaper article pupils are encouraged to contemplate and discuss the following questions:

1. What is the evidence that letting babies fly in aeroplanes may cause a problem?
2. What is the evidence that it does not harm them at all?
3. How sure are you about this evidence?
4. What reasons might there be for the difference between the findings of the researcher and the fact that no babies have been known to die whilst flying with the airline company in question?

We encourage you to incorporate newspapers, TV programmes and magazine articles in your science teaching.

Other non-school settings such as museums, art galleries and science centres can often provide wonderful opportunities for making STS connections. These informal learning environments sometimes tackle 'issues' through particular exhibitions, or provide stimulation for discussing representations of science and social, cultural and political contexts.

Each of the above approaches has its own thematic virtues and pedagogic advantages – there is no single road. Some strategies are more appropriate for a particular curriculum unit or topic than others, and so teachers need to exercise judgement and thoughtfulness when planning.

Practice Task Getting started – adopting STS in your science teaching

This activity involves using an STS focus to explore aspects of the curriculum. Listed below are a range of science concepts contained in the curriculum at Key Stages 2, 3 and 4.

Microbes and disease	Sound and hearing
Energy resources	Environmental chemistry
Ecological relationships	Fit and healthy
Radioactivity	Plants and animals in the local environment
Earth and atmosphere	Microbes and disease

Select one of the above topics and explore ways in which you can incorporate an STS focus into this curriculum area. You might develop a lesson plan including objectives, activities, resources and any teacher notes. Then reflect on some of the difficulties associated with this approach. Wherever possible, we encourage you to teach the lesson you have planned.

Issues-based teaching and learning

In the previous activity the emphasis was on incorporating STS into a more traditional course – a 'bolt-on' approach, if you like. There are many other styles of integration, including ones in which STS has a more central place in the curriculum. In issues-based learning (IBL), or event-centred learning (ECL) societal issues (such as waste management, genetic engineering, nuclear power, cloning, endemic disease, poverty, etc) become central organizers for science curriculum and instruction. Instead of the more common way of integrating STS – teach the content then infuse applications or societal aspects – the process is reversed. STS education translates to teaching science in a social context. One way to accomplish this is through an issues-based approach (Pedretti, 1999; Watts *et al*, 1997). It has been argued that an STS issue 'utilised as a context for instruction, offers the greatest potential for capturing the dynamic interplay of science, technology and society' (Ramsey, 1993: 241). Indeed, authors suggest that societal issues used as organizers for science education present many advantages because the issues provide a rationale for the search for information, and more accurately reflect the multi-disciplined nature, discourse and activities of a scientific pursuit.

Issues (particularly controversial ones) challenge our beliefs, values, fears and action. Furthermore, they can act as valuable tools in curriculum planning, and can provide the impetus for designing relevant and meaningful experiences for your students. The issue forms the building block of the curriculum and encourages explorations that are socially relevant and personally compelling. To give some examples, teachers could use recent concerns about over-fishing in the North Sea as a basis from which to explore scientific principles of food chains and webs, the concepts of food pyramids, biomass and carrying capacity. In addition, students are able to explore the social implications and human costs of closing down fish processing plants and the political dimensions of off-shore sovereignty. In another example, rather than just teaching about nuclear reactions, the curriculum could explore nuclear chemistry and physics with an STS perspective. The science class might examine some of the historical background to the discovery of radioactivity and the development of the atomic bomb (see ASE, 1997). Students could then have the opportunity to debate several controversial issues around the themes of nuclear power, nuclear disarmament, peace and justice.

Concluding thoughts

In this chapter we have sought to provide a general picture of citizenship education and STS education, and what they might look like in the classroom. We have suggested that science and science education have a key role to play in creating an environment of critical thinking and judgement making. Considerations of STS in our science classrooms can be used to facilitate some of the elements of citizenship our pupils need to acquire and understand, in order to play a full and active part in society.

However, implementing STS in the science classroom spawns a number of pedagogical questions and challenges. For example, how do we generate and evaluate ideas? Interpret arguments? Handle controversy? Present various viewpoints? Decide on a course of action? Distinguish between opinion and fact? Other challenges, as discussed, include: lack of STS resources, lack of time, need for appropriate assessment strategies, and integrating values and ethics into science (see Solomon (1993) and Trowbridge, Bybee and Powell (2000) for an in-depth look at these questions).

Nevertheless, in spite of these challenges, we cannot lose sight of STS education as a critical part of what we do with our students in science education. We hope to have provided some sound and robust rationales for infusing STS perspectives coupled with some accompanying strategies to bring STS to life in the classroom. After all, if we believe that science education should be about citizenship and literacy, then STS becomes one effective way of achieving these goals.

In summary, perhaps most significantly, STS education provides opportunities to enrich the experiences of students, sponsors creativity and imagination about alternatives, and provides power and freedom to examine and question social issues related to science and technology. To put it another way, 'The fundamental weakness of valid science as it is usually taught is not what it says about the world, but what it leaves unsaid. The task of STS Education is to fill that gap' (Layton, 1994: 22).

Ultimately, it will be you and your students who bring the what and how of STS and the citizenship curriculum to life.

Further reading

Department of Education and Employment (DfEE) (1999) *Science: The National Curriculum for England*, HMSO, London

Kumar, D and Chubin, D (2000) *Science, Technology, and Society: A sourcebook on research and practice*, Kluwer Academic, London

McGrath, C (1993) Science, technology and society, in *ASE Science Teachers' Handbook: Secondary*, ed R Hull, Simon and Schuster, London

Osborne, J (1998) Learning and teaching about the nature of science, in *ASE Guide to Secondary Science Education*, ed M Ratcliffe, Stanley Thornes, Cheltenham

Solomon, J (1993) *Teaching Science, Technology and Society*, Open University Press, Philadelphia

Solomon, J and Aikenhead, G (eds) (1994) *STS Education: International perspectives on reform*, Teachers College Press, New York

Part 5

Looking to the Future

16 From student to professional teacher

Keith Hicks, Larry Bencze and Steve Alsop

When you get your first science teaching post there is a real sense of relief. You feel excited about having your own classroom and enthusiastic about joining the profession... My first year of teaching was exhausting. Looking back on it, it was probably the most challenging year of my teaching career so far!

(Marcus, a primary science teacher)

Objectives

This chapter facilitates critical reflection on:

- seeking your first job;
- the induction year;
- continual professional development;
- the teacher as researcher.

Introduction

Completing a pre-service course is a moment to savour and to indulge in a little self-congratulation: you are now a qualified science teacher and able to go and seek that first appointment as a qualified teacher. However the end of the pre-service course reflects an end to your *initial* teacher education and in many ways may be said to represent just the first part of a working life of continued education and development. As your career progresses the jobs you take on will involve a variety of different skills which will require from you a commitment to ongoing continual professional development (CPD). Even as an 'ordinary' classroom teacher you will continue to learn and train to improve your classroom skills throughout your professional life. In time you can expect to be involved in the training of others entering the profession and to be continually assessed on your professional performance.

In the Teaching and Higher Education Act (DfEE, 1998d), the government has recently reintroduced the probationary year for new entrants to the teaching profession and built in a series of formal assessments of your professional abilities that will be carried out by colleagues in your new school. All newly qualified teachers (NQTs) are now required to undergo an induction programme that lasts three terms from their first appointment. Details of the requirements for this process were laid down in the DfEE Circular 5/99 *The Induction Period for Newly Qualified Teachers* (DfEE, 1999b).

This chapter will explore the implications for the induction period for new teachers as well as issues relating to getting your first job and your future years working as a science teacher in mainstream schools. It will draw on the experiences of other teachers who have gone through this process and who remain committed to the idea of continuing professional development.

Seeking your first appointment

It is never too early on a pre-service course to start to look for your first appointment. The demand for teachers varies considerably across the country and if you wish to work in a specific area with a low staff turnover you may need to apply to all jobs advertised in that part of the country. Other parts of the country with higher teacher turnover rates may well have vacancies right up to the start of the autumn term, but, if there is a specific school you wish to work in you will need to ensure that you watch the press carefully from the Christmas period of the final year of your course. Most teaching appointments are advertised in *The Times Educational Supplement* (TES) published each Friday; the TES also publishes these vacancies on its Web site (www.jobs.tes.co.uk/index.asp); several of the national newspapers also have education sections in which teaching posts are advertised, notably the *Guardian* and the *Independent*. If you are seeking an appointment in a specific school, having a contact in the school or sending a letter direct to the school can sometimes be profitable. A number of Local Education Authorities publish lists of vacancies and it may be necessary to be on their mailing list. Other authorities only advertise in local papers so these too should be considered.

Choosing the right school to work in needs careful thought and a cool head! The selection process is not only about a school selecting a new teacher but also equally importantly it is you selecting the place where you will enjoy working. There is a tendency among NQTs to jump at the first post offered to them but you need to ensure that the school where you work is one where you feel comfortable. To this end before applying for any job it is important you are clear about the type of school, the area and the type of pupils you want to work with. If possible visit the school before the interview; you should also take into account, however, that many schools nowadays will arrange for a school tour and a visit on the morning of the interview. Through this process you will need to determine how well you are in 'tune' with the ethos of the school and department you will be working in. Make your own assessment of the person who will be your line manager and ask about what support and training you will receive as an NQT.

Theory Task Interview questions

Many schools will ask similar questions of applicants applying for their first teaching appointment. If you already have details about a school you would like to work in try and construct six questions you feel you may be asked in your interview. Having constructed these questions draft out some replies to your answers. If you have not yet obtained any details about a school where you are going to apply for a post, construct the questions for the school where you are undertaking your teaching practice.

At the end of an interview it is usual for a candidate to be asked if she/he has any questions for the panel. Make a brief list of the sort of questions you may wish to ask at this point. Most panels will be very aware if you ask questions whose answers you have been given in the information sent to you when you applied for the job. Be warned!

The shortage of certain science teachers (most notably physics) to an advanced level and science specialists in primary schools puts additional pressures on both schools and candidates seeking appointments. Getting a physics teacher is so problematic that a school may offer additional incentives to attract a physics graduate to join their staff. As a candidate seeking an appointment it is important that you are not 'seduced' by financial incentives into a school that does not suit you. Being placed in the wrong school can result in you making a less than positive start to your career that may well be demotivating.

The induction year – an introduction

Your first year as an NQT is governed by the regulations in DfEE Circular 5/99. This circular itemizes the responsibilities of schools towards NQTs. Presently, as an NQT you have an entitlement to a reduced teaching load and additional support and training in your first year of teaching. This support is expected to take the form of an individualized programme involving observation of experienced teachers, education and advice from within the school and possibly outside the school, and participation in working groups. Circular 5/99 explains the responsibilities of the various parties involved in the induction of NQTs and also a timetable of events governing the induction of NQTs. How one school has organized this is shown in Figure 16.1 (see over).

Responsibilities of the NQT

You are expected to take a proactive role in your own induction process which starts before the end of your pre-service course with the completion of your career entry profile. This contains two main sets of statements that will detail your strengths and areas for development. Ensure you fully agree these statements with your institute of higher education tutor as they will be used by your new school to construct your induction programme. Just as important is to ensure that you fully understand what each of the statements in the career entry profile means.

OUTLINE OF INDUCTION SUPPORT 2000-2001

	DATE	ACTIVITY	APPENDIX SHEETS
AUTUMN	SEPTEMBER	NQTs meet with tutors/mentors to discuss career entry profile targets. First lesson observation and feedback by tutor	NQT profile Lesson observation form
	OCTOBER	Ist lesson observation and feedback by mentor	Lesson observaton form Formative assess-record
	NOVEMBER	*HALF TERM*	
	DECEMBER	Observation and summative assessment by tutor	Lesson observation form Summative assess-ment record
SPRING	JANUARY		
	FEBRUARY	2nd observation and formative assessment by mentor	Lesson observation form Formative assess-ment record
		HALF TERM	
	MARCH APRIL	Observation and summative assessment by tutor	Lesson observation form Summative assess-ment record
SUMMER	MAY JUNE	3rd observation and formative assessment by mentor	Lesson observation form Formative assess-ment record
		HALF TERM	
	JULY	Final observation and summative assessment by tutor **Final decision on induction year outcomes**	Lesson observation form Summative assess-ment form

Figure 16.1 Calendar for the induction year for newly qualified teachers

Practice Task The career entry profile

You will probably carry out this task in conjunction with college staff during the final weeks of your pre-service course:

1. Review the written reports on lessons you have taught and profiles written on your performance on teaching practice.
2. Outline four areas of strength in your teaching and the evidence for the identification of those areas. Write a short (40 word or so) statement about each of those areas for your profile.
3. Identify four areas which you feel need to be your priorities for your professional development during your first year of teaching. Write a short (40 word or so) statement about each of those areas for your profile.
4. Discuss these statements with your college tutor.

During the first few weeks in your new post you should discuss your profile with your induction tutor and, with reference to the induction standards, start to construct a programme of objectives for your professional development. This programme should set targets for your professional development together with evidence for success which will then be recorded in your profile. You are expected to help with the identification and review of these targets and take part in the programme of support agreed with your induction tutor. As the period of induction progresses you will be expected to be familiar with the induction standards and compare your own work to them.

During the induction period it is your responsibility to raise any concerns you have with your induction tutor and to ensure that your induction programme addresses these issues.

The headteacher's responsibilities

It is up to your headteacher to ensure that you are provided with an induction programme that meets your needs and also meets the expectations of Circular 5/99. It is ultimately the headteacher's responsibility to make a recommendation to the LEA as to whether you have met the induction standards at the end of the year.

The headteacher will probably designate another teacher to act as an induction tutor to work with you. In secondary schools this is likely to be your head of science or other post holder in the science department. In a primary school it may well be that your induction tutor is your headteacher or deputy headteacher. The headteacher has to ensure that you are provided with a timetable that represents no more than 90 per cent of the usual contact time of a main scale teacher. Schools may achieve this in a number of ways which may, for instance, include releasing you to attend science specialist training sessions organized at the local teachers' centre or institute of higher education. Often schools will also give NQTs a commitment not to expect them to cover for absent colleagues in their first few moths in the school as part of their reduced teaching load. We recommend finding out about these aspects of your first year during your school interview.

The headteacher retains ultimate authority for ensuring the LEA is informed of the progress made by the NQT and for sending the reports from the formal assessment meetings to the LEA. The final assessment report has to be forwarded by the headteacher to the appropriate body within ten working days of the completion of the induction period.

The induction tutor

Your induction tutor will probably be the most important person providing you with professional advice during your first year as a teacher. During the probationary year your induction tutor will be responsible for providing you with support and guidance as well as making judgements about your performance for your assessments in relation to the induction standards. Your induction tutor will work closely with you throughout your probationary year to ensure that you have an individualized programme of support and will help you carry out the action plan in your career entry profile. Most observations of your lessons will be carried out by your induction tutor who together with you will set targets and monitor your progress and keep you informed about the nature and purpose of assessment in the induction period.

Some schools divide the support and assessment functions between two teachers, possibly giving one teacher a supportive mentor role while the other carries out the more formal assessments. Whatever the division of labour in the school the systems are there to support you during what will probably be one of your most challenging years in your chosen profession. In large secondary schools a senior member of staff (often a deputy headteacher) will be given overall responsibility for the induction programme of all NQTs in the school. This senior member of staff will co-ordinate the work of the induction tutors across the school.

Continual professional development

The successful completion of your first year as a teacher marks your transition to a fully qualified teacher; it does not, however, mark the end of your education and professional development. As a science teacher you have a duty, for instance, to keep up to date with both your subject and the teaching of your subject. To assist you in this it is recommended that you join a professional organization. The Association for Science Education (ASE) (www.ase.org.uk) is a professional association of science teachers, renowned for its excellent publications. By joining the ASE you will receive their quarterly publications and details of their extensive training courses for science teachers and technicians. The journals published by the ASE include *Education in Science, School Science Review, Post Sixteen Science Issues, Science Teacher Education* and *Primary Science Review*. For science teachers in the primary schools the *Primary Science Review* is particularly useful for sharing ideas of good practice for teachers who may be isolated from other subject specialists. Other useful professional organizations include the Institute of Physics (www.ioppublishing.com), the Institute of Biology (www.iob.org) and the Royal Society of Chemistry (www.rsc.org.uk), all of whom produce very helpful materials for science teachers.

Each January the ASE holds its Annual General Meeting at a university over three days. This meeting, which attracts upwards of 10,000 teachers, is a major event for science teachers and is packed with INSET events, exhibitions, talks and lectures aimed at science teachers in all sectors of school education. The ASE is also organized on a regional basis with the regions holding local meetings and INSET events. These meetings will give you an opportunity to make contact with other teachers in your area which is very useful, especially if you are a lone subject specialist in a primary school. Financial support is often available from your school or LEA to attend events such as those organized by the ASE.

In March 2001 the government published its new strategy for teachers' continual professional development (CPD) which had been developed with advice from the General Teaching Council, the teacher unions and other organizations. This strategy document, which can be obtained from www.dfee.gov.uk/teachers/cpd, outlines how the government intends to support CPD over the following three years with an extra £92 million. This is likely to impact on new teachers with a new scheme entitled 'Early professional development' which will offer additional CPD to teachers in their second and third years of teaching and will build on the induction year. This scheme will be piloted in a sample of schools in 2001–2.

Further qualifications

As your career progresses you should start to develop a career plan and extend your skills and knowledge base. For many teachers this means seeking out additional qualifications and these could include undertaking studies leading to MA degrees. Institutes of higher education (IHEs) now offer a wide range of modular MA degrees which are directed at science teachers. For those interested in developing their skills and knowledge an MA in Science Education provides an opportunity for professional growth. The timing of any decision to undertake a further degree course of study needs to be given careful thought. Taking on a degree course as a part-time student is a major commitment in addition to your teaching load and the responsibilities to your employer. Such further study needs a commitment from you in terms of your time that is considerable and you need to carefully assess when you want to give this time up. The first two years of your career in teaching are likely to be spent on a steep learning curve as you come to grips with the demands of a full-time teaching timetable. During the third and fourth years you may well be starting to seek promotion to take on further responsibilities in your curriculum area which may involve a change of school. For many teachers the third year of their full-time career is the time to consider taking on a Master's degree. This is the time when you can bring the experience you have gained as a teacher in the classroom into an intensive course of study before you are weighed down with the additional responsibilities a promotion may bring you.

Having committed yourself to undertake a further degree there are a number of decisions for you to consider. First, whether to undertake a full-time course of study or a part-time course of study. Full-time Master's degrees are usually taught over one whole academic year while part-time courses for these degrees often extend over two years. The days of getting a secondment from your school or employer to undertake a Master's degree are now sadly largely gone and any decision to undertake a full-time course is likely to involve you leaving paid employment for the life of a student again. For many young teachers struggling to pay off student loans accumulated through four years of further education the idea of returning as a full-time student to further education is not economically feasible. Adding to the burden of taking such a course of action would be a responsibility of paying the tuition fees that go with the course, which are not insubstantial. Thus for the majority of young teachers a full-time course of study for a Master's degree is not a credible possibility. Most IHEs are fully aware of this problem and many of them offer part-time courses leading to Master's degrees. The amount of time demanded by these part-time courses varies from institution to institution, ranging from two evenings a week for four semesters to one evening a week over five terms. If you are in a position of being able to 'shop around' for a course this may be a factor you will wish to consider. As a general rule those courses with a smaller taught component will have a higher demand for individual study which may suit some people more than others.

For those teachers aspiring to be curriculum leaders in the field of science a Master of Education in Science Education is an obvious choice. Such a course of study is likely to be of immense benefit to you in your day-to-day work in the classroom and will equip you with the knowledge that will help you gain a promotion to a faculty head or head of department. However there are now a wide range of alternative degrees offered aimed specifically at teachers, including degrees in such subjects as Educational Management and Curricular Management. While these alternative degrees may prove useful in seeking senior management posts in schools, it should be noted that the Teacher Training Agency is increasingly producing its own list of recommended qualifications for senior managers in schools. There is, of course, nothing to stop you undertaking more than one Master's degree during your career and what might be the right course for you at one stage of your career will not necessarily be the correct course for a later stage. Although this discussion has focused on Master's courses, it should be borne in mind that a wide range of other professional qualifications for science teachers are on offer.

The teacher as a researcher

There is a strong move to ensure that it is recognized that teaching is a research-based profession. Classroom research is a very valuable and informative tool which is sadly under-utilized by many teachers. The reason for this is mainly the difficulty teachers have in accessing the results of such research, which is often published in academic journals unlikely to be found in most schools. The Association for Science Education does some very good work in keeping science teachers informed of research and initiatives. Perhaps the best way for teachers to become aware of classroom research is for them to become active researchers themselves.

Research opportunities do exist, for instance the Teacher Training Agency has in recent years made grants available to teachers to undertake classroom-based studies aimed at improving the performance of both teachers and pupils. The results of these studies have been circulated to all schools in the country and have been models of good practice for those wishing to undertake classroom-based research. In addition the DfEE will give teachers 'Best Practice Research Scholarships' of up to £3,000 to do sharply focused research into areas of classroom practice. These grants are open to all teachers and about 1,000 scholarships will be available each year (further details are available from www.dfee.gov.uk/bprs). However, as a teacher committed to your own ongoing continual professional development, there is no need to restrict your activities to those that can be supported by elusive grants awarded by external agencies. For a teacher-researcher the most important tool is the classroom and this is something to which we have access every day. The close relationships now established between schools and those higher education institutes offering PGCE courses means that advice is often available from members of these institutes to help to put together research projects to be carried out in your own school. In addition to this help you may well find that you can negotiate access to the institute's library as part of the arrangements made for your school's involvement with PGCE courses.

Another area of support for classroom-based research is also the Local Education Authority with its network of subject inspectors and advisory teachers. Using these sources, it is often quite possible to put together a classroom-based research project that involves colleagues from several schools. Although you may be involved primarily with research into a science-based issue you may easily find that your work has applications into other subject areas as well. A number of teachers undertaking such classroom-based research activities have found that they have put together a sufficient basis for undertaking a PhD or DEd (EdD in some institutions) with the help of their local university. Publishing and disseminating the results of your research is easily done through the LEA and also the Association for Science Education, which is always pleased to receive articles and papers from practising teachers for publications in their periodicals.

Inventive, inquiring science teachers

Action research is usually viewed as a spiralling (hopefully, ever-improving) process, as depicted in Figure 16.2. In it, teachers repeat cycles of: (i) reviewing teaching and learning; (ii) planning and developing (new approaches and data collection); and (iii) teaching and data collection. Because the first and third phases are very similar, however, action research amounts to repetitions of research and action (explaining its name). That is, the teacher conducts research (review) to identify concerns about teaching and learning, then takes action to change conditions to try to improve teaching and learning, and then conducts research again to determine if, indeed, the actions led to improved teaching and learning. Usually these cycles must be repeated, however, because improvements can always be made.

Although action research is practised in a variety of ways, it is common for its research component to document which current learning conditions may be leading to certain student outcomes, as depicted below:

Learning Conditions ——— (that determine) ——— Student Outcomes

For instance, it may be apparent that boys are succeeding in the science programme to a much greater degree than girls. The boys tend to participate more in class discussions and their test scores tend to exceed those of the girls. While the teacher may recognize some

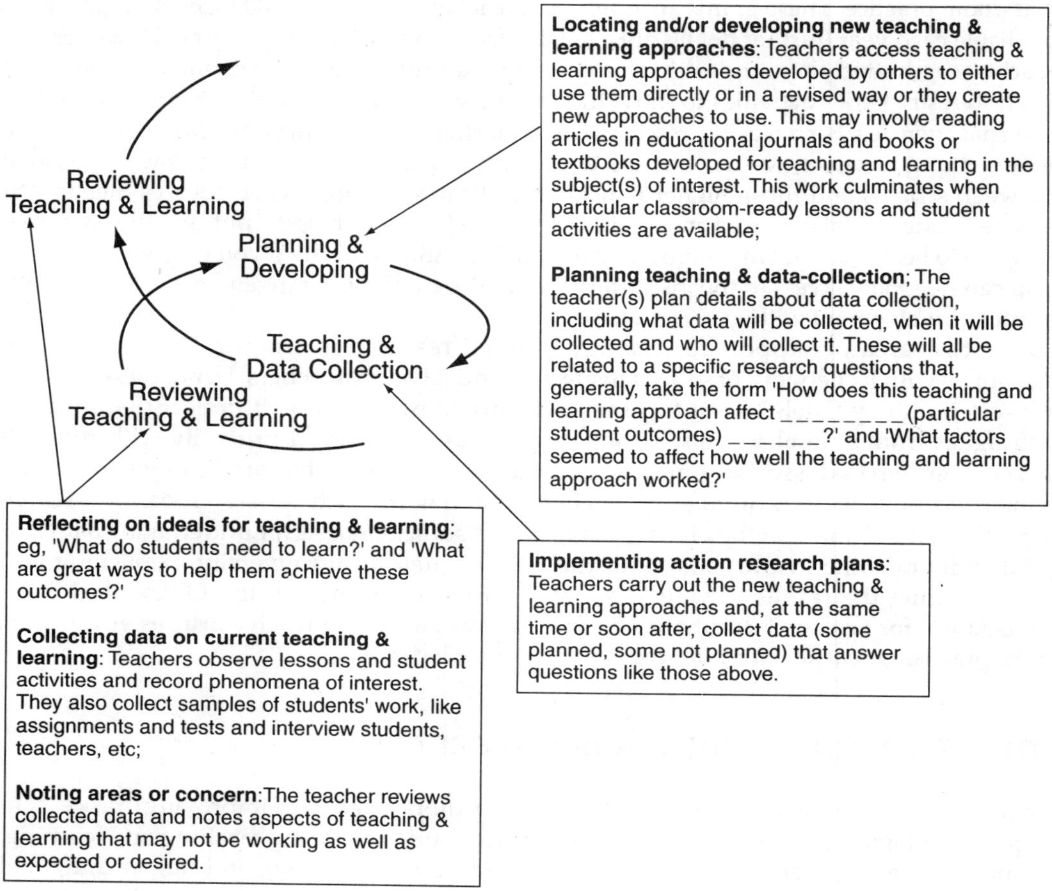

Figure 16.2 The spiral nature of educational action research

other concerns from the initial research – including how over-confident all students seem to be about the certainty of scientific knowledge – the teacher may choose to focus on one concern; in this case, that of girls' relatively poor achievement and negative feelings about careers in science and technology. To overcome the problem of the male bias in the teacher's programme, the (hypothetical) teacher decided to make some changes that may – collectively – improve this situation. A female scientist was invited to talk to students about her work, for example. Also, more co-operative small group learning activities were set up, so that students of both sexes could be equally assigned roles relating to science and technology. Together, these actions appeared to improve student outcomes, including attitudes, by both boys and girls, towards science-related careers.

Action research can be a powerful tool in the hands of teachers. As Carr and Kemmis (1986: 162), who are pioneers in teacher-led action research in school science have said, action research is a: 'form of self-reflective enquiry undertaken by participants in social situations in order to improve the rationality and justice of their own practices, their understanding of these practices, and the situation in which the practices are carried out.'

Indeed there is, apparently, much that teachers of science can investigate and possibly improve. Action researching teachers have, for instance, successfully implemented 'STS' approaches, which place a priority on values and ethics in matters relating to science and technology. Similarly, through action research, secondary school science teachers have demonstrated that they were able, despite pressures, to emphasize products of professional science and technology in their teaching, to help students develop their own conclusions based on scientific investigations and invention projects under pupils' control (Hodson and Bencze, 1998).

Such results are encouraging and make us wonder what else teachers may be able to accomplish through action research.

The teacher as mentor

Although it may seem premature at this stage in your career, becoming a mentor to students undertaking their pre-service courses is a valuable way of continuing your professional development. After a few years working as a science teacher you may wish to take on the role of mentor and guide a new entrant to the profession through their school experience. You know more than most how important this role can be and, as a relatively new entrant to the profession, you are in a better position than most to understand the difficulties and stresses involved in the process of becoming a science teacher. Again there is a need for commitment if you are to undertake this role; initially you may feel that you will gain time from this process as you will have a 'student' undertaking some of your timetable. Do not be deluded by such illusions! Students need a lot of time and support from their mentors and you are unlikely to gain any time by your involvement in being a mentor but you will find it a wonderful opportunity for your own professional development.

Most course providers will offer mentor education for those teachers who supervise students. This includes a description of the mechanics of the courses and also the skills associated with lesson observation and tutoring a student. You will be expected to act as a role model for the student and this will force you to examine your own practice in the classroom and assess your own strengths and weaknesses as a teacher. You will be asked to make judgements on your student's progress against the professional competencies criteria and to set targets and strategies to help your students meet the required standards. Your involvement with PGCE students can act as a catalyst to improving your own practice in the classroom, which will benefit both you and your pupils.

Observation Task Creating an individualized support programme

This activity may be useful for you to carry out in your first few days in your first post, possibly before your first meeting with your induction tutor to discuss your career entry profile and individual induction programme. Remember you are expected to take on a proactive role in the development of your induction programme and this activity gives you the opportunity to take on that role.

Examine your career entry profile and highlight the areas for development. Prioritize those areas for development and identify those for which you feel you will require additional in-service training. Research what INSET is likely to be available to you both within your school and externally to the school. To do this you may find it helpful to talk with colleagues who were probationers last year and examine your school's INSET notice board. Collect details of the INSET provision which most closely matches your development needs. When you meet with your induction tutor give a clear explanation as to how you believe this INSET provision will form part of your induction programme and agree a strategy for taking part in the appropriate INSET events.

Summary

As this chapter has illustrated, undertaking a pre-service course and entering into the profession of being a science teacher is not a matter of following a programme of education that ends when you take up your first post in a school. In order to be an effective science teacher you have to commit yourself to a programme of continual professional development. Through this development you will be able to refine your skills and widen your knowledge to make you a more effective and reflective science teacher.

Further reading

Carr, W and Kemmis, S (1986) *Becoming Critical: Education, knowledge and action research*, Falmer Press, Lewes

Department for Education and Employment (DfEE) (1999) *The Induction Period for Newly Qualified Teachers*, Circular 5/99, DfEE, London

Hodson, D and Bencze, L (1998) Becoming critical about practical work: changing views and changing practice through action research, *International Journal of Science Education*, **20**(6), pp 683–94

References

Adey, P and Shayer, M (1994) *Really Raising Standards: Cognitive intervention and academic achievement*, Routledge, London.

Adey, P, Shayer, M and Yates, C (1989) *Thinking Science*, Nelson, Walton on Thames.

Aikenhead, G (1994) What is STS science teaching? in *STS Education: International perspectives on reform*, ed J Solomon and G Aikenhead, pp 47–59, Teachers College Press, New York.

Alsop, S (1992) Questioning, in *Primary Science and Technology*, D Bentley and M Watts, Open University Press, Buckingham.

Alsop, S and Hollins, M (1998) *The Case of the Square Tomato: Solanum Lycopersicum Cuboidus*, internal mimeograph, University of Surrey at Roehampton.

Alsop, S and Luth, R (1999) Special needs in the mainstream, in *Learning to Teach*, ed G Nicholls, Kogan Page, London.

Alsop, S and Watts, M (2000) Interviews about scenarios: Exploring the affective domain in science education, *Research in Education*, **63**, pp 21–33.

Association for Science Education (ASE) (1997) *One Hundred Years of the Electron*, ASE Publications, Hatfield.

ASE (1997a) *Gender and Science Education: Policy statement*, ASE, Hatfield.

ASE (1997b) *Access to Science Education: Policy statement*, ASE, Hatfield.

ASE and Department for Education and Employment (DfEE) Science Curriculum Support Group (1998) *Teachers Helping Teachers to Teach Science: A response to the TTA ICT consultation process*, ASE and DfEE, London.

ASE (2000a) *School Science Review*, **81**, ASE, Hatfield.

ASE (2000b) *An Evaluation of the 1999 Key Stage 3 Tests in English, Mathematics and Science.* A joint study by the Association of Teachers and Lecturers, Association of Teachers of Mathematics, Association for Science Education and National Association of English Teachers, ASE, Hatfield.

Ausubel, D (1968) *Educational Psychology: A cognitive view*, Holt, Rinehart and Winston, New York.

Barba, R and Cardinale, L (1991) Are females invisible students? An investigation of teacher–student questioning interactions, *School Science and Mathematics*, **91** (7), pp 301–10.

Barnes, D (1976) *From Communication to Curriculum*, Penguin, Harmondsworth.

Beiner, R (1983) *Political Judgement*, Methuen, London.

Bell, B and Cowie, B (1997) *Formative Assessment and Science Education: Summary report of the Learning in Science Project (Assessment),* Hamilton, New Zealand, Centre for Science, Mathematics and Technology Education Research, University of Waikato.

Bell, B and Gilbert, J (1996) *Teacher Development: A model from science education,* Falmer Press, London.

Bentley, D and Watts, M (1992) *Primary Science and Technology,* Open University Press, Buckingham.

Black, P (1993) The purposes of science education, in *Challenges and Opportunities for Science Education,* ed E Whitelegg, J Thomas and S Tresman, Paul Chapman Publishing Ltd, London.

Black, P (1998) *Testing: Friend or Foe? Theory and practice of assessment and testing,* Falmer Press, London.

Black, P and Harrison, C (2000) Formative assessment, in *Good Practice in Science Teaching,* ed M Monk and J Osborne, Open University Press, Buckingham.

Black, P and William, D (1998) Assessment and classroom learning, *Assessment in Education,* **5** (1), pp 7–71.

Bliss, J (1995) Piaget and After: The case of learning science, *Studies in Science Education,* **25**, pp 139–72.

Bloom, B S, Hastings, J T and Madhaus, G F (eds) (1971) *Handbook and the Formative and Summative Evaluation of Student Learning,* McGraw-Hill, New York.

Bloom, J (1998) *Creating a Classroom Community of Young Scientists: A desktop companion,* Irwin Publishing, Toronto.

Blunkett, D (2000) [online] http://www.dfee.gov.uk/speeches/06_01_00/index.sthml.

Brown, G and Wragg, E (1993) *Questioning,* Routledge, London.

Bruner, J (1986) *Actual Minds and Possible Worlds,* Harvard University Press, Cambridge, MA.

Butler Kahle, J (1990) Real students take chemistry and physics: Gender issues, in *Windows into Science Classrooms: Problems associated with higher level cognitive learning,* ed K Tobin, J Butler Kahle and B Fraser, Falmer Press, London.

Carlton, K and Parkinson, E (1994) *Physical Science: A primary teacher's guide,* Cassell, London.

Carr, W and Kemmis, S (1986) *Becoming Critical: Education, knowledge and action research,* Falmer Press, Lewes.

Claxton, G (1989) Cognition doesn't matter if you're scared, depressed and bored, in *Adolescent Development and School Science,* ed P Addey, J Bliss, J Head and M Shayer, Falmer Press, London.

Cox, M (1999) Using information and communication technologies (ICT) for pupils' learning, in *Learning to Teach,* ed G Nicholls, Kogan Page, London.

Daws, N and Singh, B (1996) Formative assessment: To what extent is its potential to enhance pupils' science being realised?, *School Science Review;* **77** (281), pp 261–71.

Department for Education (DFE) (1992) *Education and Training in the 21st Century,* HMSO, London.

Department for Education and Employment (DfEE) (1994) *The Code of Practice for the Identification and Assessment of Pupils with Special Educational Needs,* HMSO, London.

DfEE (1998a) *Requirements for Courses of Initial Teacher Training,* Circular 4/98, DfEE, London. [exemplification materials see http://www teach-tta gov uk/itt/supporting/ict_exemp htm]

DfEE (1998b) *The National Literacy Strategy*, DfEE, London.
DfEE (1998c) *Excellence for All*, Green Paper, HMSO, London.
DfEE (1998d) *Teaching and Higher Education Act*, HMSO, London.
DfEE (1999) *The National Numeracy Strategy*, DfEE, London.
DfEE (1999a) *Science: The National Curriculum for England*, HMSO, London.
DfEE (1999b) *The Induction Period for Newly Qualified Teachers*, Circular 5/99, DfEE, London.
DfEE, (1999c) *The National Curriculum Handbook for Secondary Teachers in England*, HMSO, London.
DfEE (1999d) *Social Inclusion*, Circular 10/99 HMSO, London.
DfEE/Qualifications and Curriculum Authority (QCA) (1998a) *Science: A scheme of work for Key Stages 1 and 2*, DfEE/QCA, London. [see http://www.nc.uk.net]
DfEE/QCA (1998b) [online] http://www.qca.org.uk/pdf.asp?/ca/subjects/citizenship/crick_report_1998.pdf.
DES (1985) *Science 15–16: A statement of policy*, London, HMSO.
Dewey, J (1960) *The Quest For Certainty*, Capricorn, New York.
Docking, J (1990) *Control and Discipline in Schools*, Paul Chapman Publishing, London.
Doherty, A, Dine, D and Gardner, C (1998) Assessment of Sc1 investigations: A pilot study with PGCE students and their mentors, *School Science Review*, **79** (288), pp 75–80.
Donaldson, M (1978) *Children's Minds*, Fontana Press, London.
Driver, R (1989) Changing conceptions, in *Adolescent Development and School Science*, ed P Adey, J Bliss, J Head and M Shayer, Falmer Press, London.
Driver, R, Squires, A, Rushworth, P and Wood-Robinson, V (1994) *Making Sense of Secondary Science: Research into children's ideas*, Routledge, London.
Duschl, R (2000) Making the nature of science explicit, in *Improving Science Education: The contribution of research*, ed R Millar, J Leach and J Osbourne, Open University Press, Buckingham.
Ebenezer, J and Lau, E (1998) *Science on the Internet: A resource for K12 teachers*, Prentice Hall, New Jersey.
Edwards, P, Watts, DM and West, A (1993) *Making the Difference: Environmental problem solving in school science and technology*, World Wide Fund for Nature, Goldalming, Surrey.
Evans, J (1989) *Bias in Human Reasoning: Causes and consequences*, Laurence Erlbaum Associates, New Jersey.
Feasey, R (1999) *Primary Science and Literacy*, ASE, Hatfield.
Flam, F (1991) Still a 'chilly climate' for women? *Science*, **252** (5013), pp 1604–6.
Foulds, K, Gott, R and Feasey, R (1992) *Investigative Work in Science*, University of Durham, Durham.
Gardner, H (1983) *Frames of Mind: The theory of multiple intelligences*, Heinemann, London.
Gardner, H (1999) *Intelligence Reformed: Multiple intelligences for the 21st century*, Basic Books, New York.
Giddens, A (1994) *Beyond Left or Right: The future of radical politics*, Blackwell, Oxford.
Gipps, CV (1994) *Beyond Testing*, Falmer Press, London.
Glaserfeld, E Von (1991) Knowing without metaphysics: Aspects of the radical constructivist position, in *Research and Reflexivity*, ed F Steier, London, Sage.
Goldsworthy, A and Feasey, R (1994) *Making Sense of Primary Science Investigations*, Association for Science Education, Hatfield.

Gould, C (1988) *Rethinking Democracy: Freedom and social co-operation in politics, economy and society*, Cambridge University Press, Cambridge.

Gribbin, J and Gribbin, M (1997) *Einstein in 90 Minutes*, Constable, London.

Harlen, W (1988) *The Teaching of Science in Primary Schools*, 2nd edn, David Fulton Press, London.

Hawking, S (1988) *A Brief History of Time: From the big bang to black holes*, Bantam Press, London.

Head, J (1999) *Understanding the Boys: Issues of behaviour and achievement*, Falmer Press, London.

Head, J and Ramsden, J (1990) Gender, psychology type and science, *International Journal of Science Education*, **12**, pp 115–21.

Heater, D (1990) *Citizenship: The civic ideal in world history, politics and education*, Longman, London.

Hellman, H (1998) *Great Feuds in Science: Ten of the liveliest disputes ever*, John Wiley and Sons, Chichester.

Hodson, D (1998) *Teaching and Learning Science: Towards a personalised approach*, Open University Press, Buckingham.

Hodson, D and Bencze, L (1998) Becoming critical about practical work: Changing views and changing practice through action research, *International Journal of Science Education*, **20** (6), pp 683–94.

Hofstein, A (1988) Practical work in science education II, in *Development and Dilemmas in Science Education*, ed P Fensham, Falmer, London.

Hollins, M (1998) *Meeting Minds: A clash of generations*, internal mimeograph, University of Surrey at Roehampton.

Hoyle, P (1990) *Lesson Strategies for Science*, a survey issued during an in-service course held at the Roehampton Institute, London.

Johnston, K, Needham, R and Brook, A (1990) *Interactive Teaching in Science: Workshops for training courses*, Association for Science Education, Leeds.

Johnstone, A H and Wham, A J B (1982) The demand of practical work, *Education in Chemistry*, **19** (3), pp 71–3.

Kagan, S (1990) The structural approach to co-operative learning, *Education Leadership*, January, 12–18.

Kass-Simon, G and Farnes, P (1990) *Women of Science: Righting the record*, Indiana University Press, Indiana.

Kempa, R (1986) *Assessment in Science*, Cambridge University Press, Cambridge.

Kenway, J and Willis, S (1990) *Hearts and Minds: Self-esteem and the schooling of girls*, Falmer Press, London.

Kumar, D and Chubin, D (2000) *Science, Technology, and Society: A sourcebook on research and practice*, Kluwer Academic, London.

Kyriacou, C (1986) *Effective Teaching in Schools*, Blackwell, London.

Kyriacou, C (1991) *Essential Teaching Skills*, Blackwell, London.

Layton, D (1994) STS in the school curriculum: A movement overtaken by history?, in *STS Education: International perspectives on reform*, ed J Solomon and G Aikenhead, pp 2–23, Teachers College Press, New York.

Lemke, J (1990) *Talking Science*, Ablex Publishing Corporation, New Jersey.

Lewis, T and Gagel, C (1992) Technological literacy: A critical analysis, *Journal of Curriculum Studies*, **24** (2), pp 117–38.
Lock, R and Ratcliffe, M (1998) Learning about social and ethical applications of science, in *ASE Guide to Secondary School Education*, ed M Ratcliffe, ASE, Hatfield.
MacIntyre, A (1982) *After Virtue*, Duckworth, London.
Mathews, M (1994) *Science Teaching: The role of history and philosophy of science*, Routledge, London.
McGrath, C (1993) Science, technology and society, in *ASE Science Teachers' Handbook: Secondary*, ed R Hull, Simon and Schuster, London.
Millar, R (1989) What is scientific method and can it be taught?, in *A Critical Analysis*, ed J Wellington, Routledge, London.
Millar, R and Osborne, J (1998) *Beyond 2000: Science Education for the Future*, King's College London, School of Education, London.
Mills, C W (1970) *The Sociological Imagination*, Penguin, Harmondsworth.
Monk, M (2000) A critique of the QCA specimen scheme of work for key stage 3 science, *School Science Review*, **81** (297).
National Advisory Committee on Creative and Cultural Education (NACCCE) (1999) *All Our Futures: Creativity, culture and education*, DfEE, London.
National Curriculum Council (NCC) *Teaching Science to Pupils with Special Educational Needs*, NCC, York.
Nicholls, G (ed) (1999) *Learning to Teach*, Kogan Page, London.
Nott, M (1994) Practical approaches to teaching and learning about the nature of science, in *Secondary Science: Contemporary issues and practical approaches*, ed J Wellington, Routledge, London.
Novak, J D (1988) Learning science and the science of learning, *Studies in Science Education*, **15**, pp 77–101.
Novak, J D (1993) Learning science and the science of learning, *Studies in Science Education*, **15**, pp 77–101.
Nuffield Foundation (1998) *Education for Citizenship and the Teaching of Democracy in Schools*, QCA, London.
Office for Standards in Education (Ofsted) (1998a) *A Scheme of Work for Key Stages 1 and 2: Science*, HMSO, London.
Ofsted (1998b) *Summary of Inspection Findings for Key Stages 3 and 4*, HMSO, London.
Ofsted (1998c) *The Annual Report of Her Majesty's Inspector of Schools*, HMSO, London.
Ofsted (1999) *A Review of Primary Schools in England, 1994–1998*, The Stationery Office, London.
Ofsted (2000a) *A Scheme of Work for Key Stage 3: Science*, HMSO, London.
Ofsted (2000b) *Progress in Key Stage 3: Science*, Ofsted, London.
Ollerenshaw, C and Ritchie, R (1997) *Primary Science: Making it work*, 2nd edn, David Fulton, London.
Osborne, J (1998) Learning and teaching about the nature of science, in *ASE Guide to Secondary Science Education*, ed M Ratcliffe, Stanley Thornes, Cheltenham.
Osborne, R and Freyberg, P (1985) *Learning in Science: The implications of children's science*, Heinemann, London.
Pedretti, E (1996) Learning about science, technology and society (STS) through an action research project: Co-constructing an issues-based model for STS education, *School Science and Mathematics*, **96** (8), pp 432–40.

Pedretti, E (1999) Decision making and STS education: Exploring scientific knowledge and social responsibility in schools and science centres through an issues-based approach, *School Science and Mathematics*, **99** (4), pp 174–81.

Pfundt, H and Druit, R (1994) *Bibliography: Students' alternative frameworks and science education*, University of Keil Publishing, Keil.

Piaget, J (1960) *The Child's Construction of Reality*, Routledge and Kegan Paul, London.

Piaget, J (1980) *The Equilibrium of Cognitive Structures. The Central Problem of Intellectual Development*, University of Chicago Press, Chicago.

QCA (2000) *Science: A scheme of work for Key Stage 3 – Teacher's guide*, QCA, London.

QCA/DfEE (1998) *Education for Citizenship and the Teaching of Democracy in Schools*, QCA, London.

Qualter, A and Taylor, J (1999) Brilliant, Erin Brilliant! Setting a risk taking climate, *Primary Science Review*, **58**.

Ramsey, J (1993) The science education reform movement: Implications for social responsibility, *Science Education*, **77** (2), pp 235–58.

Reid, D and Hodson, D (1987) *Special Needs in Ordinary Schools: Science for all*, Cassell, London.

Reiss, M (1993) *Science Education for a Pluralist Society*, Open University Press, Buckingham.

Rowe, MB (1974) Relation of wait time and rewards to the development of language, logic and fate control: Part II rewards, *Journal of Research in Science Teaching*, **11** (4), pp 291–301.

Rowntree, D (1977) *Assessing Students: How shall we know them?*, Harper and Row, London.

Russell, T and Watt, D (1990) *Primary Space Project Research Report: Space*, Liverpool University Press, Liverpool.

Sagan, C (1996) *The Demon-hunted World: Science as a candle in the dark*, Headline, London.

Schon, D (1983) *The Reflective Practitioner*, Jossey-Bass, San Francisco.

Scott, P and Leach, J (1998) Learning science concepts in the secondary classroom, in *ASE Guide to Secondary Science Education*, ed M Ratcliffe, Stanley Thornes, Hatfield.

Scott, P, Dyson, T and Gater, S (1987) *Children's Learning in Science Project: A constructivist view of learning and teaching science*, Centre for Studies in Science and Mathematics Education, Leeds.

Selby, D (1995) *Earthkind: A teachers' handbook on humane education*, Trentham Books, Toronto.

Shayer, M and Adey, P (1981) *Towards a Science of Science Teaching*, Heinemann, London.

Shulman, L (1987) Knowledge and teaching: Foundations of the new reform, *Harvard Educational Review*, **7** (1), pp 1–22.

Skinner, B F (1976) *About Behaviourism*, Vintage Books, New York.

Solomon, J (1989) *Discovering the Cure for Scurvy*, ASE, Hatfield.

Solomon, J (1993) *Teaching Science, Technology and Society*, Open University Press, Philadelphia.

Solomon, J and Aikenhead, G (eds) (1994) *STS Education: International perspectives on reform*, Teachers College Press, New York.

Summerfield, J (1996) Resourcing practical science: Some issues for primary school science co-ordinators, *Primary Science Review*, 44.

Sutton, C (1992) *Words, Science and Learning*, Open University Press, Buckingham.

Swain, J (2000) Summative assessment, in *Good Practice in Science Teaching*, ed M Monk and J Osborne, Open University Press, Buckingham.

Thorp, S (ed) (1991) *Race, Equality and Science*, Association for Science Education, Hatfield.

Treagust, D, Harrison, A and Venville, G (1996) Using an analogical teaching approach to engender conceptual change, *International Journal of Science Education*, **18** (2), pp 213–29.
Trowbridge, L W and Bybee, R W (1996) *Teaching Secondary School Science: Strategies for developing scientific literacy*, 6th edn, Prentice Hall, New Jersey.
Trowbridge, L W, Bybee, R W and Powell, J C (2000) *Teaching Secondary School Science: Strategies for developing scientific literacy*, 6th edn, Merrill/Prentice-Hall, Columbus, OH.
Vygotsky, L (1978) *Mind in Society: The development of higher psychological processes*, Harvard University Press, London.
Vygotsky, L (1988) *Thought and Language*, 3rd edn, MIT Press, London.
Watt, D (1998) Children's learning of scientific concepts, in *ASE Guide to Primary Science*, ed R Sherrington, ASE/Stanley Thornes, Hatfield.
Watts, M (1983) Gravity – don't take it for granted, *Physics Education*, **17**, 5.
Watts, M (ed) (2000) *Creative Trespass: Fusing science and poetry in classrooms*, ASE, Hatfield.
Watts, M and Alsop, S (1995) Questioning and conceptual understanding: the quality of pupils' questions in science, *School Science Review*, **76**, pp 91–5.
Watts, M, Alsop, S, Zylbersztajn, A and Maria de Silva, S (1997) Event-centred learning: An approach to teaching science technology and societal issues in two countries, *International Journal of Science Education*, **19** (3) pp 341–51.
Wellington, J (1994) *Contemporary Issues and Practical Approaches*, Routledge, London.
Wellington, J (1998) *Practical Work in School Science*, Routledge, London.
Wellington, J (2000) *Teaching and Learning Secondary Science*, Routledge, London.
White, R (1989) *Learning Science*, Basil Blackwell, Oxford.
Wolpert, L (1992) *The Unnatural Nature of Science*, Faber and Faber, London.
Wood, D, Bruner, J and Ross, G (1976) The role of tutoring in problem solving, *Journal of Child Psychology and Psychiatry*, **17**, pp 89–100.
Wragg, T (1993) *Class Management*, Routledge, London.
Ziman, J (1994) The rationale of STS education is in the approach, in *STS Education: International perspectives on reform*, ed J Solomon and G Aikenhead, Teachers College Press, New York.

Further reading for Chapter 13

Department for Education and Employment (DfEE) (1998) *The National Literacy Strategy*, DfEE, London
DfEE (1999) *The National Numeracy Strategy*, DfEE, London
DfEE/Qualifications and Curriculum Authority (QCA) (1998) *Science: A scheme of work for Key Stages 1 and 2*, DfEE/QCA, London
DfEE/QCA (forthcoming) *Science, Mathematics: A scheme of work for Key Stage 3*, DfEE/QCA, London
Feasey, R (1999) *Primary Science and Literacy*, ASE, Hatfield
Feasey, R and Gallear, R (2000) *Primary Science and Numeracy*, ASE, Hatfield
Goldsworthy, A, Watson, R and Wood-Robinson, A (1999) *Getting to Grips with Graphs*, ASE, Hatfield

REFERENCES

Millar, R and Osborne, J (1998) *Beyond 2000: Science education for the future*, King's College London, School of Education, London

Wellington, J and Osborne, J (2001) *Language and Literacy in Science Education*, Open University Press, Milton Keynes

Index